D1798721

Children's Rights
towards the liberation of the child

Children's Rights

towards the liberation of the child

Paul Adams
Leila Berg
Nan Berger
Michael Duane
A.S. Neill
Robert Ollendorff

Elek Books

© 1971
Moving Towards Self-Government — Leila Berg
The Infant, the Family and Society — Paul Adams
The Rights of Adolescents — Robert Ollendorff
Freedom Works — A.S. Neill
The Child, the Law and the State — Nan Berger
Freedom and the State System of Education — Michael Duane

Conceived and edited by Julian Hall

Indexer, Janet Gregory

First edition May 1971
Second impression October 1971

Published in Great Britain by
ELEK BOOKS LIMITED
54-58 Caledonian Road London N1 9RN

ISBN 0.236.15400.1

The poem 'When wilt thou teach the people?' is quoted
by permission of Laurence Pollinger Ltd., and
the estate of the late Mrs. Frieda Lawrence.

Printed in Great Britain by Weatherby Woolnough Ltd
Wellingborough England NN8 4BX

Contents

WHEN wilt thou teach the people,
God of justice, to save themselves—?
They have been saved so often
and sold.

O God of justice, send no more saviours
of the people!

When a saviour has saved a people
they find he has sold them to his father.
They say: We are saved, but we are starving.
He says: The sooner will you eat imaginary cake in the
    mansions of my father.
They say: Can't we have a loaf of common bread?
He says: No, you must go to heaven, and eat the most
    marvellous cake.—

Or Napoleon says: Since I have saved you from the
    ci-devants,
you are my property, be prepared to die for me, and to
    work for me.—

Or later republicans say: You are saved,
therefore you are our savings, our capital
with which we shall do big business.—

Or Lenin says: You are saved, but you are saved whole-
    sale.
You are no longer men, that is bourgeois;
you are items in the soviet state,
and each item will get its ration,
but it is the soviet state alone which counts
the items are of small importance,
the state having saved them all.—

And so it goes on, with the saving of the people.
God of justice, when wilt thou teach them to save them-
    selves?

D. H. LAWRENCE

The patriarchal, authoritarian era in human history has attempted to keep the secondary antisocial drives in check with the aid of compulsive moral restrictions. Thus, what is called the cultured human came to be a living structure *composed of three layers*. On the surface he carries the artificial mask of self-control, of compulsive, insincere politeness and of artificial sociality. With this layer, he covers up the second one, the Freudian 'unconscious', in which sadism, greediness, lasciviousness, envy, perversions of all kinds, etc., are kept in check, without however, having in the least lost any of their power. This second layer is the artifact of a sex-negating culture; consciously, it is mostly experienced only as a gaping inner emptiness. Behind it, in the depths, live and work *natural* sociality and sexuality, *spontaneous* enjoyment of work, *capacity for love*. This third and deepest layer, representing the *biological nucleus* of the human structure, is unconscious and dreaded. It is at variance with every aspect of authoritarian education and régime. It is, at the same time, man's only real hope of ever mastering social misery.

Wilhelm Reich: *The Function of the Orgasm*

Chapter 1

Moving towards Self-government

by Leila Berg

THIS is a chapter whose ending makes one wonder why one bothered to write it in the first place.

I had started off sceptically enough to celebrate Education Year, not with three cheers, not even with Forster's two, but maybe one. Then as I traced what had in fact been done in this last half-century, my depression lifted and a pride, an exhilaration even, began to grow. It seemed to me that we really had achieved the understanding at last, and the experience, to open the cage of our systems, and to allow the children to revitalize this sick society. Then I got the two items that end this chapter.

But perhaps whoever reads them will be angry, not depressed. And anger, when it goes with understanding, can be constructive, even creative. There is no need to rewrite.

I was eighteen when I read my first book on education. It was *The Road to Life*, Stephen Garry's translation of the first part of Anton Makarenko's *Poem of Education*, the story of how he provided a home and education, 'The Gorki Colony', for the young vagabond gangs who roamed the Soviet Union immediately after the Revolution.

I still remember those first months of the colony, how he worked—and I mean *physically* worked—in exhaustion and desperation in that dark dismal shack, isolated and deep in snow, while his first six colonists (four of them experts in armed robbery, the younger two experts only in thieving) cheerily left the colony every night (he heard shouts for help coming nightly over the snow from the highway) then returned even more cheerily in the morning; how within a week the police arrived and took one of them off for murder and armed robbery; and how one morning when Makarenko asked them to give a hand chopping some wood for the stove, and they amiably as usual said 'Do it yourself', he suddenly went wild and socked one of them on the jaw.

I want to make this very clear. This episode riveted me, precisely because I come from a background of continual sadistic violence which continues to haunt me, and I accept will haunt me all my life; but never until that moment had I experienced even vicariously the honest desperate anger of fellowship.

Makarenko was amazed at himself—not only that he had broken the code of non-violence, but that he had hit someone much larger and stronger than himself who was surrounded by large and strong friends, all of them adept in acquiring and using knives and guns—and that at the end of his fury he had shouted at them either to pick up some axes and saws and get busy cutting some wood, or to clear off out of the colony and to hell with them!—and that instead of falling on him with the axes, they had set to in silence to chop the wood, and had finally—all of them—dissolved into roars of laughter.

I am a strong supporter of the Society of Teachers Opposed to Physical Punishment; corporal punishment—the memory of it and even the idea of it—sickens me. But I recommend every 'progressive' to read this book. Not only because it is inspiring, thrilling, exhilarating and very funny. But because almost every one of our most valuable revolutionary educationists in England has been weakened, or even defeated, by a fear of honest anger against anyone. (This is a national vice which we are cleverly conned by authority into believing is a virtue; and it is based on fear of ourselves.)

Makarenko's colonists recognized his anger. It released the creativity and intelligence of all of them, Makarenko too. He never hit anyone again. They were now welded together in honesty. The 'delinquents' knew he was completely on their side, their angry, honest, commonsense, hard-working champion.

They used to arrive at his colony with official carefully-catalogued files of their past crimes, and he refused to look at them (which of course angered many well-meaning theoretical workers, who argued that the children's past was relevant to his understanding and treatment of them; he agreed this was so, but that their present and future was infinitely more important).

Sometimes they would simply follow their private grapevine and make their way to the colony of their own accord—then perhaps run away to carry out a private exploit—and then come back; this was at the beginning of the colony.

He expelled one boy Simeon, and his friend Mityagin, after a long series of raids which they had carried out on the villagers. A month later Simeon came back with the news that his friend and his brother had both been killed, and made a triumphal tour of the colony recounting his adventures to admiring colonists—finally ending up in Makarenko's room asking to be taken back. 'But I don't suppose you will—you wouldn't trust me now.' Unperturbed, Makarenko said, 'You are exciting yourself for nothing, Simeon. I can trust any man, only some more than others. Some for a few kopeks, some for half a rouble.' A few days later Makarenko called him into the office and said, 'This is how much I trust you. I want you to go to the District Treasurer's Office and fetch 500 roubles.' Simeon was almost speechless. At last he got out 'Can I take one of the horses?' 'Of course,' said Makarenko, 'And you'd better take this gun. It's still loaded'—handing him the revolver he had taken off Mityagin a few months before and left in his drawer ever since. Simeon looked at the gun wildly, took it without a word, and left. In the evening he came galloping into the colony again, put the notes and the revolver on Makarenko's desk. Makarenko merely asked if he had counted the money, put it straight in his desk without checking, thanked him courteously for the trouble he had taken, and sent him off to get some supper. Simeon again was speechless. A few days later Makarenko sent him to get 2,000 roubles! When Simeon came back he was almost hysterical. Makarenko calmed him by pointing out that it was the most natural thing in the world for him to choose Simeon for this job—he was far the best horseman in the colony, he was young and strong and could easily cope with any bandit—and besides he had the revolver. Simeon left the room singing at the top of his voice.

But I think the best bit is where the colonists move a train. Filled with colonists, this train has stopped some distance from the platform where the education committee is lined up to greet them; and no engine is now available. Pestered by shouting colonists—one of whom has already almost wrecked a carriage during the night—the angry stationmaster says they can stick there till tomorrow for all he cares. So they beseech Makarenko, until apprehensively he agrees they can move it themselves. They swarm on to the track, and with complete self-organization, discipline, strength, and competence—and finally exhilaration—they push the train into the station. The waiting education committee is utterly appalled at the danger of the exploit. Makarenko is about to speak very meekly, when one of the education committee rushes to the edge of the platform and shouts to him, 'Everyone keeps gabbling how fond Comrade Makarenko is of his pupils! Everybody ought to be shown how he loves them!' And at that a growl rises in Makarenko's throat, and he replies (he thinks 'extremely quietly and politely'): 'Oh you have been cruelly misinformed. On the contrary I'm so callous I prefer common sense to the most passionate love!' Only the still successfully moving train cuts short this interchange.

Makarenko always maintained that learning and practical purposeful work go together; he never thinks in terms of making education something apart from life and rarified. At the very beginning of the Gorki colony, the local blacksmith joins the staff, and soon the colonists are doing repairs not only for their own colony, but for the village; and as this get under way the local wheelwright joins the colony too. Furthermore—to quote W. L. Goodman—'Makarenko's boys in charge of the piggeries had to mix the feed in the proper proportions, draw graphs of weight, etc., write reports of progress and in addition picked up a good deal of practical biology and hygiene, while the carpenters making wooden beehives would not get far with the roofs without knowing a certain amount of geometry. A student can become acquainted with geometry from textbooks, but the best way to "learn" it is to cut the bevels for the rafters, hips, and purlins in an actual roof, or set out the winders for a staircase.' He handed the running of the colony over to the boys and girls at a very early stage, and the rules they made arose naturally out of the way they were living and working—there was nothing artificial, irrelevant or mystic about them.

From early on, Makarenko paid them for work they did. This was not 'anti-Soviet'; but paying them, as he did, not all the same but according to what they did, was definitely 'anti-

Soviet' at that time. Summoned to account for this before a stormy Ukrainian Ministry of Education meeting, he lost his temper and said: 'I don't understand you at all. According to you, initiative is some kind of inspiration. It comes from nobody knows where, and issues out of inaction and pure idleness. I have told you over and over again that initiative only arises when there is a problem set, when someone is responsible for its solution, when there are demands upon the community. You also are unable to see my point, and go back again to your theory of an abstract idea of pure initiative, entirely divorced from any idea of work. According to you, in order to get initiative all you have to do is contemplate your own navel . . .'

Furthermore Makarenko always saw the individual child in front of him, and spoke directly to him, not to an abstraction—as did all the true educationists I was to discover later on—Lane, Neill, Duane, all of them who make this chapter. But unlike Makarenko, who, however fiercely he fought the new theoreticians, the sentimentalists, the bureaucrats, and numerous important cliché-ridden Party members, was acclaimed the foremost Soviet educationist up till his death in 1939—and as far as I know still is (though this just possibly may be because he is dead), they have not been officially honoured in England. Except for one. And he was torn apart in three inquiries, and he and his wife had severe nervous breakdowns, and very few people have ever heard of him since. I doubt if Education Year will remember his awkward moment of official glory.

Makarenko was the start, for me. I did not then know, although I discovered later on, that even before Makarenko started his colony, from 1914 to 1918 a similar colony had been run in England, a self-governing colony of delinquents, though not such violent ones. This was Homer Lane's Little Commonwealth.

Again this was a work community, of forty to fifty children, from babies to eighteen-year olds, sent by magistrates or by parents who couldn't cope with them, run from the outside by a Committee of adults interested in new ideas in penal reform and education, and run on the inside by the children.

Once a boy joined the Commonwealth who spent most of his time demonstrating that he never refused a dare; the Commonwealth was getting rather battered by his drama. One tea-time, Homer Lane dared him to smash up the tea-things (which the boy had said he would like to do) and pleasantly handed him a poker to do it with. Cheerfully encouraged by Homer Lane (who was, by this, horrifying and angering the other kids) he smashed almost everything in sight. 'Go on,' encouraged Homer Lane. The other children interfered; the family would have to pay for the damage—the Little Commonwealth was divided into two families, and they replaced everything broken; it wasn't fair, they said. So Lane handed the boy his own gold watch. 'I dare you to smash that,' he said happily. The group was speechless—the boy frightened. Then someone laughed. The boy, furious, almost hurled the watch to the floor—then stopped in mid-air. 'Go on,' pleasantly, 'I dare you.' 'No.' 'But you never refuse a dare.' 'I won't do it!' 'Go on.' Finally the boy rushed out of the room. The next day he applied to Lane for work as a bricklayer. Half-teasing, Lane asked why he had suddenly decided to work. He replied, actually smiling, 'I've got to earn some money to pay for the dishes you broke.' He later became a judge of the Commonwealth citizens' court.

Another boy, whose mother had visited the Commonwealth and been approved of by the kids, was constantly up before the court. Every penalty only made him worse. In the language of the outside world, he had become a hardened criminal. One day the current judge—a girl—announced that her decision was that Ted had forgotten his mother, and therefore lost his self-respect; he was to be sent home *for a week's holiday*—not a penalty—at the expense of the tax-payers; and his mother was not to be told it was anything but a well-earned holiday. Ted, who up to this moment had been a defiant hero, burst into tears. He spent his week at home, told his mother himself why he was home, and came back happy and enthusiastic.

(Lane commented that he found girl judges more skilful than boys, because they dealt with the individual offender, often ignoring the law and trusting to instinct, whereas the boys, he said, worked by the law and ignored the individual.)

Lane considered that the job of the parent (by which he meant people like himself too, for he ran the Commonwealth as a family, and the kids called him Daddy) was to encourage a child's experiments so that he could reach conclusions that were entirely his own. 'My function has been to encourage all activity,' he said, 'bad as well as good.'

Like the Gorki Colony, the Little Commonwealth was co-educational; in both, each sex developed a concern for, and an understanding of, the other, just as they learned to understand themselves. And in both, the 'citizens' did the work their own community needed, and were paid for it. (In the Little Commonwealth, each citizen started in debt for his clothes and his food, and paid this off before anything else by his work.) So their self-government and their education was always rooted in real life. It was the children who decided to have two hours' compulsory school at the end of each full day's manual work.

By 1917 plans had been made to introduce more art and music into the Commonwealth—it was slow going, because of the difficulties of the war. But before the plans could be carried out, two girls and two boys robbed the Commonwealth and ran away. The two boys returned to the Commonwealth quite quickly but the girls got to London and told the police who picked them up a week later that they ran away because Lane sexually assaulted them. An inquiry was held, the man put in charge by the Home Office announcing with relish that he had had twenty years' experience of the sordid side of human life, that there was no vice or crime with which he was not intimately familiar, and that he was not a man whom it was worth while to try and bamboozle. Despite this strong hint of pre-judgement, the many young citizens of the Commonwealth gave their evidence over the long weeks of inquiry, with dignity, intelligence, courage and good sense. Nevertheless, the Little Commonwealth was closed down.

After its closure, Homer Lane continued to work in London, lecturing and psychoanalysing adults ('pupils', he called them). It was he who inspired A. S. Neill. But his basic strength was in working with children. In 1925, perhaps ironically helped by the fact that the Committee had agreed to close the school in 1918, the police seized on Lane's failure to notify them of a change of address to deport him back to his native America as an 'undesirable alien'. He died the same year.

While the Little Commonwealth was still flourishing, so was another school, in another part of England, in a sense even more revolutionary, for it was a school for 'normal' children—and their parents: Prestolee, a Lancashire State elementary school for 3–15-year-olds.

Teddy O'Neill, the head, had run a previous school at Knuzden, where the children, half a century after the Act we celebrated in 1970, still worked half-time at the mill. He scrapped the orthodox education of the time and, with his wife who was 'untrained', taught the children to make things they needed. They broke up the ugly school desks—and made new ones they liked better. They made beds and cots and bookcases. He would play the piano and sing while the children worked, and they would join in. He bought material in the neighbourhood instead of requisitioning it, so that the neighbourhood and the school became familiar to each other and involved with each other (an educational, human and inexpensive method that even today, more than fifty years later, is dared only by revolutionaries). Learning to live creatively with neighbours, he stated, is more important than passing examinations.

Knuzden was backed by an H. M. I. Bloom, who introduced O'Neill to Edward Holmes, Chief Inspector and author of *What Is and What Might Be*; and with this support he got Prestolee. Here again, the parents were used to the children working with them in the mill, part-time, something O'Neill openly condemned. He had to win them over, and also fight the school board (containing at least two mill managers), the infants' headmistress (who disapproved of his ideas), and his chief assistant (who, while away at the war, had expected the headship to be kept for him). And when he abolished set lessons and set playtimes—which led at first to chaos—he faced the opposition of all the staff, even when soon the chaos changed to deep absorption.

The chief assistant got a question asked in Parliament about the 'go-as-you-please' school where the children were encouraged to be 'illiterate' and 'license' reigned. An inquiry was demanded, and held—and upheld O'Neill.

O'Neill kept the school open after school hours. Elder brothers and sisters came. Parents came—and began to bake cakes and run a refreshment bar for dancing and singing. They made fantastic rose gardens at his home, to be used communally.

They came in charabancs, and the piano would be dragged to the open door so that the singing echoed down the lane. So many people came that separate latrines for the children were built at the school, brought up the lane in wheelbarrows, and erected in the field next to his home. (He bought it for a sports-field.)

A second inquiry was demanded, by the school managers, the chief assistant, and the infants' head. 'The head was working overtime, without pay' . . . 'undermining the standards of the profession' . . . 'all evening and out-of-school activity must stop immediately.' The inquiry was held. Parents were speci-fically excluded—in fact the police stood guard over the place to keep parents out—but they got in at the back, with the school key which they held for the evening activities. Once in, they refused to be thrown out, and insisted they were all wit-nesses. Again the inquiry backed O'Neill.

The infants' department now discovered one of the wheel-barrows that had been used to cart the latrines had broken and been left in the lane; they demanded a third inquiry because O'Neill was 'a thief'—and engaged counsel. The inquiry was held—this time a local one, and it demanded that O'Neill resign or be dismissed. But the report had to be sent to the County Council—who again backed O'Neill.

Teddy O'Neill collapsed, and was ill for a year. When he came back, without asking any permission, he set to again, to build magnificent gardens at the school. They took six years to finish, and when they opened with beautiful 'illuminations', his wife collapsed and was rushed to hospital. (Their children too suffered badly because of the attacks on their parents.)

When later on with the Second World War, the school's evening activities were closed down, the children blacked out *the whole school*, and re-opened it for even more evening activities than before. They made a 'Palace of Youth', then a 'Moonlight Balcony'. The authorities put air raid shelters in the school yard—and parents and children planted them over with masses of flowers, making new gardens. The authorities took away the railings between the boys and girls to use for arma-ments—'at last!' said Prestolee. A tank for static water was needed, so, inspired, the children built a swimming pool and fountains.

O'Neill believed that adults and children should work, learn, and enjoy, side by side; that lessons by the clock were ludicrous and stupid; that 'mistakes' were explorations and should be encouraged; that 'education should deal in realities'.

To everyone's amazement, he was in the 1951 New Year's Honours List. Gerard Holmes, his biographer and warm supporter, suggests that only in Lancashire could he have survived.

But during this period, the influence of Dr Truby King seized England—or rather the influence of a Truby King strangely transformed by the English Establishment into a big stick to keep babies in order.

Dr King, a New Zealander, was a warm supporter of Froebel; he believed that, working with children, one must slowly bring out in their due order and proportion all a child's latent powers and faculties; 'no system which sacrifices energy for information is good'. He publicly stated, when already a famous figure in New Zealand, that 'the compulsion which we exercise with regard to schoolchildren is just as absolute as the compulsion which we exercise in regard to the prisoners in gaol', and said that if Froebel's ideas were put into practice instead of the current educational ones, so many young people wouldn't end up in his Insane Asylum. He completely transformed the Seacliff Asylum, altering the diet, encouraging patients to take long walks ('encouraging them to escape', said his opponents darkly), warning the staff that the first sign of violence would be instantly followed by dismissal and putting this into effect, working with the patients running the farm and turning the asylum grounds into beautiful gardens, woodlands and sportsfields, with cottages tucked out of sight of the hospital for 'border-line' cases who lived there ('at his own expense' his daughter says) and who spent weekends at his holiday house.

'When he found a patient who had absolutely no wish to do anything, he would concentrate on the body with the hope that the mind would eventually respond. After many months, one such patient ventured that what he really would like to do was to build a stone fountain. So, with as much haste as possible, the materials were provided and for a whole year the patient carved his figures and bowls from Oamaru stone. The patient himself supervised the erection of the fountain from the top of its scaffolding, but, alas, when everything was completed but the final stone, a rope which two attendants were holding broke, and the stone crashed to the ground, breaking off a portion of one bowl. The patient turned to Dr King and said, "Who should be in this asylum—me or these Attendants?" However, the work was once more completed and stands there to this day.'

At one stage, an inquiry was demanded into his 'wildness' and 'recklessness'; it was held—and upheld him.

Though physically he had numerous things wrong with him, he had amazing energy. As a JP, he was outraged at the condition in homes for unwanted babies, and transferred thirteen children to his own holiday house and proved that their wretchedness was due not to congenital causes as the homes claimed, but to the way they had been treated. He imported tons of sugar-of-milk for babies who had to be bottle-fed, and wholesaled it to grocers on condition that they sold it at a shilling a pound instead of the usual 5/- to 6/6, which he reckoned still gave a reasonable profit. He covered New Zealand, even the most outlying parts, with a network of nurses who gave their services free to bring down the death-rate from infantile diarrhoea (from which he had almost died as a baby) and to show mothers how to avoid infection. These are merely a few of the things he did. When he died he was the first citizen to be given a State funeral in New Zealand.

Yet when this man came to work in England in 1917, he became the figurehead of a puritanical authoritarian cult that gripped maternity hospitals, welfare clinics and homes in England for fifty years, a cult that obsessively forbade a spontaneous bond between mother and baby, that puritanically insisted on cleanliness and hygiene as the paramount requirements—and that affected far more English people than Homer Lane or Teddy O'Neill. How did this happen?

There seems to have been many reasons, mostly belonging to England. He was made use of, taken over and distorted, by the rigid upper-class Englishwomen, emotionally deprived and emotionally denying, who ran the voluntary societies here, and by the rigid English hospitals. He himself was very depressed by the English class system as soon as he arrived, and wrote to his wife, 'I've got a bad scunner of the British aristocracy. Of course there are exceptions, but my feeling is that nothing corresponding to our New Zealand work can be carried out in England. The woman with the hat won't go to the same place as the woman with the shawl . . .' He was horrified at the way expenses were run up by these societies, 'patronized, rather than run or supported, by society women', compared with the way they had run things in New Zealand where, he said, they had 'real workers', and wrote that he didn't wonder that people in England subjected to this cried out for a central bureaucracy instead.

Secondly he had been concerned in New Zealand to put his ideas into the simplest form, with a simple set of rules, so that a mass movement could grow even in the most uneducated parts. (But together with this had gone his own personal warmth and willing accessibility—'Call me whenever you need me even if it's half-past two in the morning', he used to say.)

Thirdly, women who have just had babies are in a particularly anxious state, and in this anxiety turn to authority for support. And fourthly, he arrived in England during a time of national stress, and his cult reached its height here during the even greater stress of the Second World War when danger, isolation, separation, loneliness, constant anxiety, the continual imminence of death, made most young mothers—and particularly those who had been 'educated'—willing to be loyal to an authority.

They were conditioned to feel it was treacherous and immoral to disobey Truby King; but on a deeper human level they also felt it was treacherous and immoral to obey; many mothers were in a state of private conflict. But, apart from the secret revolt fascinatingly described by John and Elizabeth Newson in *Infant Care in an Urban Community*, there was no escape from the conflict, for the cult had been planted everywhere.

Babies were put on deliberately cold pots practically from birth to make them have a bowel movement, were fed every four hours, not a minute sooner however much they cried, not a minute later however much they slept, were bound up tightly in towels so that they could not touch the breast or the bottle, had their hands gloved and fastened so that they couldn't suck their fingers, were changed on table-tops, preferably cold white enamel ones, so that they might not enjoy the changing nor experience cuddling nor feel the warmth and comfort of a mother's lap (all of which led to 'bad habits'), were given daily cold baths from the age of about twelve months, and kept outside in the bleak English weather in a pram with the hood up, virtually imprisoned. Everything was done to subdue the child, to turn the mother into a prison warder expecting a break-out, and to destroy their confidence in themselves and each other. I cannot believe that Truby King who did the things I mentioned earlier and many more, and who said he wanted to bring back to mothers 'faith in themselves', intended this. The woman with the hat had taken over from the start, and all of us from lower ranks of society have had to pay for the English nanny and public school system. I strongly believe that when you consider anxiety and depression and hysteria today, you must include along with the Bomb, and other political and social monstrosities, the effect of Truby King, English version. Not till Susan Isaacs began to write for *Nursery World* in 1929 was anyone publicly challenging, carefully, gently and discreetly but with controlled anger, what she called 'these fantastic demands'. Her part comes later. But the Truby King cult held the bastions, and in many parts still does.

Most people think of progressive education as belonging axiomatically, with fee-paying and generally boarding schools, to the well-to-do. In fact, it was only after the Little Commonwealth and Prestolee, neither of them for well-to-do children, that A. S. Neill started Summerhill.

Neill ran a school in Germany and Austria in the early 1920s, then came back to England and started a school first in Dorset —mostly problem children sent by parents—then in Suffolk. Summerhill is a fee-paying boarding school, and is run by the General Council of all the children and all the staff; lessons are optional. It has led to other fee-paying progressive schools being set up, all possibly more beautiful than Summerhill, but rarely as truthful or as deliberately unmanipulating.

Neill was inspired by Homer Lane—he did indeed mean to teach at the Little Commonwealth but it was closed before he could start; later he went to Lane for analysis—but being Scottish not American he was more dour than Lane. The kids, even the tiniest, all call him 'Neill', which somehow becomes a first name, whereas the kids at the Little Commonwealth called Lane 'Daddy'.

Summerhill is so thoroughly documented by Neill himself, who speaks again in this book, that it is pointless for me to describe it. But Lucy Francis, one of Neill's earliest colleagues, told me shortly before she died, that Neill once gave a public lecture in Leiston, and she went; so did one of the rare day boys, Johnny. At the end of the lecture someone in the audience asked Neill if the children were afraid of him, and Neill said no. Then someone else asked what he did about swearing, and Neill said, 'Oh we just let them get on with it; after a bit they get bored, and stop.' And then Johnny stood up and said oh no, Neill was wrong there; they didn't stop; they got into a habit— like him, Johnny; he couldn't stop. So then Lucy Francis stood up and said that at any rate Johnny had proved that the first thing Neill had said was right—the kids certainly weren't afraid of him.

When I was collecting some reminiscences of Neill, Bob Cuddihy, who proposed Neill for Lord Rector at Edinburgh University, wrote to me: 'It has recently been suggested that Neill is a little outdated; that State schools, particularly primary schools, have taken him to heart and his work is done; so let's forget about Summerhill and relegate the old boy to some place of honour. I remember telling Michael Swann, Principal of Edinburgh University, that Neill was standing as rector. "Bit old hat isn't he?" he said.

'I wonder what would have happened if he had been elected. When Neill wrote his "Unrectorial Address" for *The Times Educational Supplement* after we were soundly defeated, one could hear sounds of relief that the character who was "a bit old hat" didn't make it. In his address he said "ordered freedom does not exist. All or nothing". He would have resigned as rector. Where Muggeridge had resigned because he could not face even the demands of ordered freedom, Neill would have resigned because freedom did not exist when ordered by the Establishment. He stood in support of student revolt and freedom. And Neill's classroom democracy for a university could well have been the millenium. But students are not ready for it yet. *The Guardian* rightly pointed out that he is more revolutionary than most of the students. In fact, he is almost a permanent revolution.'

About the same time that Neill was setting up Summerhill in England, Susan Isaacs started Malting House School—neither for delinquents nor for ordinary State school children but for children (aged 2 to 10) of Cambridge academics. (As with Summerhill, though, many of the children were 'problem children'.) The school was launched, and financed by Geoffrey Pyke, who was strongly against the moulding of children; it was in his words to be 'a piece of scientific work and research'. Susan Isaacs said 'the key to the school is the growth of the children'; children could not be *taught* to grow; all that one could—and should—do was provide a rich soil for exploration and development; the instruction came much later. The usual stories that circulate about any progressive school circulated about Malting House in Cambridge—culminating in the description, savoured by friend and foe alike, 'a pre-genital brothel'. But no one demanded an inquiry.

Susan Isaacs' two books of records of Malting House, *Intellectual Growth in Young Children* and *Social Development in Young Children*, made the second work on education I read, when I was nineteen. And again I vividly remember the impact on me of the paragraph about the two-year old who—when the children who had been carrying cans of water out into the garden had been told 'No more today'—saw the vases of flowers on the tables; and without saying a word reached up to each vase in turn, took out the flowers, poured the water into his can, put the flowers back, put each vase back on the table—and then walked triumphantly out into the garden, announcing 'Timmy has water!' I was very much aware, as I read the brief record, of Timmy's eye-level. I think my own careful observation of small children and my respect and appreciation of them began at that point.

These two books of records (she intended to do a third but never managed to clear the time) constitute the most valuable material of its kind that we have in England—perhaps in the world. Many people wanted her to suppress *Social Development* because it revealed children's sexuality and hostility, but she refused, and says in the preface, 'I myself happen to be interested in *everything* that little children do and feel. I am unable to accept the idea that anything that is true of children can be too shocking for adults to know . . .'; her second reason for not giving way to pressure, she said, was 'the desperate need of children themselves to be *understood*'.

In 1929, when the school closed because of lack of money, Susan Isaacs (under the name of 'Ursula Wise'—she rebelled against being called 'Jane Strong' because it was too authoritarian) became the psychologist on *Nursery World*, and had the job of answering parents' (and nannies') questions. The Anglo-Truby King movement had been going for ten years now, and was deeply entrenched, and she said she received nine times as many 'pot problems' as any other questions. (When Charlotte Buhler took over from her seven years later, she resigned in disgust after a year, saying she was 'sick of the pot problem'.) It was a most valuable thing for her to have done, to have come out of the academic lecture-room and the school (however revolutionary), and right into people's homes, through a magazine where talk had to be lucid, simple, and start from the asker's standpoint. Although on the face of it *Nursery World* seemed to be a paper for well-to-do people, it was in many ways progressive. (In the early forties I bought it regularly, hiding the upper-class cover under my arm in much the same way as years later my news-agent disapprovingly advised me to hide the first *Private Eye*— 'It don't look nice for someone like you to have such things.')

Susan Isaacs' replies were always gentle and reasonable, though far-reaching. 'It is hard for a child to see why grown-ups should call the same sort of behaviour "lying" in little children and "teasing" in themselves' . . . 'It is a cardinal principle that one should be able to respect the natural modes of feeling of other people, even of one's own children' . . . 'I would cease to reproach the children and look upon them as "disgusting" for carrying out their normal functions in the way normal at their age' . . . 'Feel yourself into the situation as it seems to *her*.' Perhaps the nearest she got to allowing herself anger was, 'It is often very striking how little power of self-control we ourselves show in relation to the child's difficulties at the very time we are expecting him to show far more than is normal for his age!'

—and even here it is permitted only in the exclamation mark.

In this work, and in her lucid book *The Nursery Years* (published in 1929), she aimed always at getting the parent to understand what the young child is doing, and to help the child attain the independence he is choosing to reach out for.

She made a dent in the authoritarian baby cult, but her own sensitive knowledge of English puritans (who had stopped her WEA lectureship, and kept the knowledge of her work out of teachers' training colleges for many years—because she was divorced) made her tread delicately, ready to duck (for she never considered giving way); the real trouncing of the cult was to come years later from someone who, not being English, did not have this painful acquaintance and so was blissfully self-confident.

Before he came on the English scene, however, the Peckham Pioneer Health Centre began.

In 1926 a group of young lay people and doctors came together and discussed an idea that was important to them, and the possibility of doing something about it: the idea that people should be healthy when they conceived children, that they should conceive them because they wanted to, and should continue to grow as their children grew. One of the doctors was Innes Pearce who, from her welfare work in the East End of London, had decided that it was the family that should be helped not the individual baby, and that it was health that needed to be studied—what constitutes it, what interferes with it—rather than disease. The group took a smallish house in Peckham to run as a club which only families, not individuals, could join, and in which every member, even though not ill, had periodic medical examinations. But they discovered that in such a small building they could not provide 'the instruments of health'. They closed down the house, and for the next seven years built up a fund to pay for a new building. The building was ready in 1935—with a swimming pool that took up most of two floors, a gym, a theatre, a nursery, dance-halls, a coffee bar, a library, games rooms and record-playing rooms ('instruments of health')—and just enough money to run for a month. This was not bad management, but deliberate; they had declared that the building fund would all be spent on the building, because the building was to be a demonstration, a challenge, and an irresistible inspiration.

It was. As the founders said, its real purpose would probably escape the casual visitor, but in fact the whole unit was a biologists' laboratory for the study of vitality. Gropius said it was the only interesting building in England. Money came in. Dr Scott Williamson, the Director, was a brilliant man who, like Neill, frequently expressed a rooted distaste for 'leadership'; 'I was the only person with any authority,' he said, 'and I used it to stop anyone from exerting any authority!' 'Full function without full freedom,' the Peckham group declared, 'is impossible.'

One of the first things Dr Williamson and Dr Pearce discovered was that 'individuals from infants to old people, resent or fail to show any interest in anything initially presented to them through discipline, regulation or instruction, which is another aspect of authority. (Even the very "Centre idea" has a certain taint of authority and this is contributing to our slow recruitment.)

'We now proceed by merely providing an environment rich in instruments for action—that is giving a chance to do things. Slowly but surely these chances are seized upon and used as opportunity for development of inherent capacity. The instruments of action have one common characteristic—*they must speak for themselves*. The voice of the salesman or the teacher frightens the potential users . . .'

John Comerford, writing about the Peckham experiment, said, 'Studying their members in the free-for-all of the Peckham Centre, the observing scientists saw over and over again how one member instinctively became, and was instinctively but not officially recognized as, the leader to meet the needs of some particular moment. Such leaders appeared and disappeared as the flux of the Centre required. Because they were not consciously appointed, neither (when they had fulfilled their purpose) were they consciously overthrown. . . . A society, therefore, if left to itself in suitable circumstances to express itself spontaneously works out its own salvation and achieves a harmony of action which superimposed leadership cannot emulate . . .' Because of this biological attitude, Scott Williamson was running this huge building, where 850 families made up of 3,000 adults and children were moving about in complete freedom, with simply one curator helped by a student—and these two were concentrating on what was going on, not on being in charge. When they first opened of course there was wild chaos, but this died down, and soon everyone was 'functioning'.

The effective and graceful anarchy which the Peckham group found existed in people if 'leaders' did not distort them showed perhaps at its clearest in those members who had been distorted for the shortest space of time—the nursery group, and the other children. Every part of the Peckham work is of vital relevance to anyone thinking about education today; their biological discovery that people spontaneously move forward by always uniting the *familiar* with the new is very important. But perhaps this curtailed passage from *The Peckham Experiment* is particularly striking: In the gym, a child 'goes in and learns unaided to swing and to climb, to balance, to leap . . . learning by his eyes, muscles, joints and by every sense organ he has, to judge, to estimate, to *know*. The other twenty-nine boys and girls in the gymnasium are all as active as he, some of them in his immediate vicinity. But as he swings he does not *avoid*. He swings *where there is space*—a very important distinction—and in doing so he threads his way among his twenty-nine fellows. Using all his faculties, he is aware of the total situation in that gymnasium—of his own swinging and of his fellows' actions. . . This "education" in the live use of all his senses can only come if his twenty-nine fellows are also free and active. If the room were cleared and twenty-nine boys sat at the side silent while he swung, we should in effect be saying to him—to his legs, body, eyes—"You give all your attention to swinging; we'll keep the rest of the world away"—in fact—"Be as egotistical as you like" . . . By the existing methods of teaching we are in fact inducing the child's *inco-ordination* in society.'

When war broke out in 1939 the Centre was closed, and the building taken over by a munitions factory. After the war it re-opened in 1946, and 500 families rejoined. But the building had been badly damaged and money was short. In 1946 the National Health Service Act was passed, and the directors asked the government to incorporate the Peckham Centre in their plan and so save it. The government refused. The London

County Council refused. So in 1951 the Peckham Pioneer Centre closed down.

But in 1926, a year after Peckham started to view the home not as a place but as a flowering of relationships from which growth and health start, a doctor was working in Newcastle with a similar biological outlook. This was Sir James Spence who in 1927, in his Baby Hospital, set up the first mother-and-baby unit. He believed that separation from the mother had a deep psychological and physical effect on the child. Fifteen to twenty years later, this work was to inspire, directly or indirectly, D. W. Winnicott and James Robertson in England, and H. Bakwin and René Spitz in America, among many others, and thereby eventually to provide the 'expert' fuel for the demolition of the authoritarianism that had utterly distorted Truby King's transplantation into England.

This new vision, as it happened, was preceded by some lively non-authoritarian and quiet work done among children in Lancashire again, though not children in school. In 1941, Olive Kendon arrived in a slum district of Stockport, near Manchester, a place unknown to her. The wartime streets were full of fighting children—two small girls literally pulling each other's hair out and drawing blood, surrounded by an excited crowd of friends and enemies. She was walking past, apprehensive in these unknown violent streets, when a girl rushed up to her and said, 'That's my sister. Get her out!' So she got her out. She pulled the two girls apart, sided with the one the crowd jeered at (whereupon the girl's defiance of the crowd dissolved into tears) and within minutes was making her way towards the Friends Meeting House (her contact in this city) followed like the Pied Piper, by a procession of children and babies. Seeing where she was going, the children demanded to have a Sunday School. Not for one moment did she think they really wanted a Sunday School. It was quite clear to her they simply wanted a place of their own. (Ironically she later discovered that close by there had been for years the biggest Sunday School in the district.) She told the children to meet her next week. ('Why not tomorrow?' 'Because I haven't got time tomorrow. Next week.') and went to the library, and asked if anyone could find her a room the children could use. The librarian knew of a friend who had a room to let. She looked at it, took it, met the children the next week. Fifty turned up, babies and all. Detectives followed her; permission to use the room was apprehensively withdrawn. Then she found a shop with premises above for fifteen shillings a week, which she persuaded the Quakers to guarantee for a year. Again she told the children and met them outside. 'This is your house. It isn't mine. It's yours. I'll open the door. Be careful of the little ones because the stairs are very steep.' Her last words were almost drowned in the hurricane of children who tore past her, up the stairs, all around . . . shouting, exclaiming, and finally down again where she stood waiting. 'Well,' she said, 'it's very dirty . . .' 'We'll clean it!' 'What with? I've got no buckets and brushes.' 'We'll fetch them from home.' 'All right. Mee· me here.'

When she turned up again there was a horde of children outside—and the filthy windows had already been cleaned outside as high as their arms could reach.

She opened the door and they started at the top and scrubbed the floors, one at each corner of the room, moving towards the middle, the boys lugging the buckets of ice-cold water up the stairs. When they had cleaned several layers of dirt off one room, they made it their headquarters and used it for picnics and singing after the day's work was over. They cleaned out the bathroom—a painter and builder came to help because the children had been working for weeks (no need for 'incentives', teachers note), and when they saw it finished, the children were drunk with the glamour and beauty of it, and all had baths, and bathed their small brothers and sisters. 'Because the children were glad the house was theirs they wanted to learn to work together—and with grown-ups whom they found useful. . . . The adults learned too. They learned not to make rules, but to let the children make their own from their own experience.'

Later Olive Kendon started a second Children's House in Manchester. Again a horde of children turned up to inspect the premises, the house filthy, a terrible stench emanating from somewhere, which she traced to a dead and decomposing ca sin the corner of the room. 'Anyone want to earn sixpence?' the said. 'Yes. Me, miss.' 'Get a shovel then and take away this dead cat and bury it.' And the boy matter-of-factly did so. A few days later, the children arrived to start the House, filling the top room to suffocation. 'No babies,' said Olive. 'And no one over nine. Anyone here over nine?' A few boys put up their hands. 'Sorry,' said Olive, 'You can't come.' One hand remained up. 'What's wrong?' said Olive. 'It was me what buried the cat!' So by common consent a rule was made incorporating 'senior helpers'.

Several other Houses have been started since. The movement would have acquired immediate momentum since it was based on *following* the children, but Miss Kendon was unfortunately frequently in hospital. However since the Plowden Report has permitted people to see what for years has been under their noses, the movement has gathered followers, and thirty years after she first spontaneously started it 'because the children asked', has held its first annual conference.

Olive Kendon is sure the Children's Houses must be their own, run by their own committees, that if rooms are let off to the local pre-school play-group or Darby and Joan Club, it will only be because the children have voted to do this in order to collect the rent and use it for enlarging their own facilities and activities—as well as building friendly and competent and equal relationships with the adult community. An education official once said to her with shocked complacency: 'Oh we can't support this! In England education is free.' 'Free—but compulsory,' said Olive tersely—adding, 'How can children learn grace by compulsion!'

She is also sure that the Children's Houses must be completely separate from schools, and from homes. A year ago, on a new housing estate, children and parents together were digging out the foundations for a new Children's House. Today the House is finished, and 'throughout the operations not a single piece of the machinery, equipment or materials has been stolen or damaged, although they have been enclosed only by a light paling fence'.

During the war, American and English pediatricians began to deal almost simultaneous blows to the authoritarian baby cult. Since the beginning of the century, the infant mortality rate in hospitals and institutions had been appallingly high.

(According to René Spitz, during the first two years of life in the first twenty years of the century in American and German hospitals which he listed, it was from 71 per cent to 100 per cent.) In 1941, Dr Bakwin and several others investigated American hospitals, and discovered in effect that babies dying ostensibly of diarrhoea and 'wasting disease' were dying of lack of cuddling. As an experiment, untrained but motherly people were introduced into the hospital for the sole purpose of picking up, at first only for a moment, and gradually (for they were very weak) beginning to cuddle, these dying babies. And the babies stopped dying, and began to take and hold nourishment.

René Spitz, writing a few years afterwards about the earlier death rate, said, 'The worst offenders were the best equipped and most hygienic institutions,' and that on the other hand 'the presence of the mothers could compensate even for numerous other shortcomings'. But he also pointed out that now the hospitalized babies were surviving physically, it was clear how deeply they had been affected psychologically; for all perception and learning occur through the emotions; and emotion comes to the small child through his relations with his mother (or mother substitute).

In England, Dr Winnicott was giving his wartime broadcasts to mothers, denting the authoritarian baby cult a little more, by suggesting that infant feeding was the practice of a love relationship, that it was the basis for every relationship the child makes later in society, and that no feeding rules or clocks or weighing machines should come between these two important people finding each other, the mother and the baby. His broadcasts, though lucid, were delicate and subtle: '. . . You are now at the beginning of a new relationship with the baby, who cannot communicate with you in an ordinary grown-up way, but who has found a way of talking without words. It is as if he said, "I think I am going to want to pass a motion; are you interested?" and you (without exactly saying so) answer "Yes", and you let him know that if you are interested this is not because you are frightened that he will make a mess, and not because you feel you ought to be teaching him how to be clean. If you are interested it is because you love your baby in the way mothers do, so that whatever is important to the baby is also important to you. So you will not mind if you got there too late, because the important thing was not keeping the baby clean, it was the answering of the call of a fellow human being. Later on, your relationship to the infant in these terms will become richer: sometimes a baby will feel frightened of the motion that is coming, and sometimes he will feel that it is something valuable. Because what you do is based on the simple fact of your love you soon become able to distinguish between the times when you are helping your baby to be rid of bad things, and when you are receiving gifts . . .'

Gradually, through thought and poetry and gentleness, the ground was being prepared for a head-on rumbustious on-slaught, which crashed in, in 1946, when an American paper-back arrived in England, Dr Spock's *Pocket Book of Baby and Child Care*. In the original hardback published earlier the same year it was called *The Common Sense Book of Baby and Child Care*; and breezy avuncular common sense was its style. Where Susan Isaacs had said 'Consider' and Dr Winnicott had added 'Imagine', Dr Spock said 'Relax'. And in 1946 English people did indeed want to relax. Benjamin Spock made no demands of parents, but rather took away demands. To quote his own words from the first edition of his book, 'Don't be afraid to trust your own common sense. . . . We know for a fact that the natural loving care that kindly parents give to their children is a hundred times more valuable than . . . making a formula expertly.' The careful thought of Susan Isaacs over many years and the delicacy of Dr Winnicott had passed into a simplified reassurance to millions.

No one who did not personally experience the tension pro-duced by and exacerbated by the authoritarian cult can imagine the relief, and the release, that followed Dr Spock's book. Mothers bought a copy whenever they had money to spare and gave or resold it to a friend. They felt as if they had been given back to themselves and Spock was their deliverer.

(The only trouble with simplification was that middle-class readers—who have generally been trained to follow a system—might, with no added understanding or sensitivity, merely ex-change one system, one father figure, for another; and this would mean that parents' fear of a child's energy, which is fear of themselves, would remain, untackled, and would eventually show as strongly in 'over-permissiveness' as it did before in authoritarianism. This seems in fact to have happened in a large way in America, since in 1957 Dr Spock decided to revise his book because 'whereas ten years previously the commonest psychological problems brought to a pediatrician like myself were those resulting from excessive rigidity in handling, they now were predominantly difficulties that came from too much parental hesitancy'. And he added, 'I have the impression from reading and from talking with many Europeans in the child-care professions that though they have experienced some of this movement toward decreased parental control, it has been nowhere near as strong as in America. Europeans have certainly been much more resistant to new ideas about child psychology than we.')

In the 1960s he was prominent in the American nuclear disarmament movement, leading demonstrations (in England mothers in CND would say fervently and frequently, 'If only we had a Dr Spock in England!') and in 1968 stood public trial with others on a charge of conspiring to encourage men to resist the Vietnam draft. That year he felt it important to put some of this 'world view' as he called it into his latest edition: 'As a parent, you need to know what you are, in the world'.

Two years after Dr Spock's *Pocket Book* sent the old rules flying in the nursery, the Child Development Research Unit was set up in England, and Dr James Robertson, who had earlier been inspired by Sir James Spence's work in Newcastle, and who had worked in Anna Freud's London wartime nurseries for babies separated from their families, began his studies of children in hospitals, and his campaign for mothers to stay with them, or visit frequently. He made two films in Amersham Hospital where Dr Dermod MacCarthy—who maintained that a child's distress at being abandoned can be far greater than his distress at being sick—had started cubicles for staying-in mothers. (Dr MacCarthy pioneered similar work in Stoke Mandeville Hospital, Aylesbury, and this also was filmed, by Harold Lowenstein.) All this drew a tremendous response from mothers. They had already been released from bondage by Dr Spock, and with this new confidence and vitality they eventually formed a most valuable pressure group.

Almost simultaneously with Spock's early work, a State school headmaster in the East End of London took over a derelict school building in a bombed dock area, and turned it into a creative community. The head was Alex Bloom, the school St George in the East, Stepney, which was run by a school council—no exams, no marks, no corporal punishment. The last point is one I have not mentioned hitherto, merely because corporal punishment is obviously incompatible with any view of the child as a fellow human being. But not only were several of his ten teachers outraged by his abolition of the only kind of control they knew; so was the education authority (and, incidentally, so was the local juvenile court). When Roy Nash, then educational correspondent of the *News Chronicle*, phoned County Hall to ask if he could go down to the school (this being, for some reason, an unwritten law in London), the instant reply was, 'Are you interested in corporal punishment?' Somewhat startled, he replied, 'No, not particularly. I have simply heard that the head is doing some *generally* interesting work.' They then said, 'We have no objections to your going to St George in the East. But if we agree that you go, we would want you to go to see another school with very different methods, to redress the balance.' (This extraordinary reply was exactly the reaction of the London County Council nearly twenty years later when I became interested in Risinghill.)

Roy Nash went to St George in the East several times—though he never went to the other school. It was an ancient dreary building, gloomy hall, gloomy classrooms, tall windows set high up, a very depressing place to be in. 'But Bloom didn't bother about this,' said Roy Nash. 'He didn't seem to notice it. I had an impression that the school was going on quite apart from the four walls—that was just something to keep the rain out. Outside, bomb-sites, shattered skeletons of buildings, street markets, numerous languages and dialects—the sort of district most London teachers try to get out of as soon as the bell goes. For Bloom it was a lifelong devoted job; he belonged there. And this epitomized the conflict between him and his staff.'

Many years later Roy Nash, whom I had got to know over the Risinghill affair, told me, 'Bloom didn't talk to me about education. He talked to me about *children*. Then he just turned

34

me loose, and it was the children themselves who instructed
me how the place was run. They all talked of Bloom as though
he was an extraordinary father-figure. I went round the school
with a whole horde of them, stopping every few minutes to look
at things they pulled out to show me. Bloom had seen in these
kids the need for achievement. It was moving the way they
showed me some not very good paintings and some not very
good work books with an enormous personal pride and no
artificial sense of shame. This was Bloom. It was in the way he
spoke to them. He believed in them. You could call it *truthfully*
man to man, a very different thing from what the Public
schools mean by that phrase. I was very aware of the *way* the
kids said "Mr Bloom" . . . how they had discussed so-and-so
with *Mr Bloom* . . . never "The Head"; a special way, a tremendous closeness. There was a great deal of controversy in the
London educational world at that time about this; they called
it a "dependence" on him, an emotional bond. I put this to
him, and he said it was that kind of dependence he was working
to avoid; but in that kind of area many kids were looking for an
open relationship with adults, because their parents were so
busy coping with a low standard of living and bad housing.
The views of the staff were rather reserved. Bloom was working
on a different plane. Braithwaite, who wrote *To Sir, With Love*—
a teacher there—was himself rather reserved about it. We were
talking about freedom, and Braithwaite said the operative word
was "Javvta". I looked blank, and he explained if you asked a
kid to do something, he would say "Javvta sir?" . . .

'I grew up in the East End myself. I know the fear of authority
is incredibly strong. In my own family there was always a fear
that some obscure authority would accuse someone of some
equally obscure breach of a regulation. So a head who set out to
remove a blind fear of authority was embarking on a revolutionary move. He completely upset the educational pundits,
because they talked about riots and smashing up the school;
but he succeeded. It was clear the LCC disliked the whole
situation intensely. I'm convinced that if they could have got
rid of him they would have done so. Despite the outward
declarations of socialism they were a very narrow bureaucracy.
They were outraged because nothing that Alex Bloom did
fitted in with their ideas of the lines heads were supposed to

observe. I'd go so far as to make the firm comment that the LCC was rather relieved when he died. It removed the problem. They did not want him to be publicized. They objected to his abolition of corporal punishment without really looking at the evidence—one of the worst examples I have ever met of bureaucracy deliberately and coldly turning its back on any sympathetic examination of a situation. This attitude must have been known to members of Bloom's staff, and it worried the more timid teachers . . . (a close parallel to Risinghill afterwards).

'What struck me as most dreadful was that there was among certain members of the education service a totally cynical attitude that there was a sad freak called Alex Bloom who was being taken for a ride by a bunch of tough know-all kids. My own impression was that nothing could be further from the truth. I know from my own experience in the East End that kids like that—and I was one—are very quick to take ruthless advantage of someone who is giving them a bit of extra rope. When they don't, it's a sign of very great respect. They *didn't* burn the place down.'

It seems that some of the kids were taken for a short holiday to a place near Chichester. They decided to spend a few days going round the town, finding out about it in the way Alex Bloom had taught them—stopping people in the street, 'What's that clock tower, mister?' Anyone knowing Chichester would have expected a mob of tough kids from the East End stopping people in the streets to have unnerved and outraged the residents. Not a bit of it. Those kids, educated by Bloom, were irresistible. 'They were so *interested*,' somebody said. This was a remarkable achievement, to make kids like this, with their strident cockney accents, their working-class syntax, their loud laughter and their poor clothes—all those attributes that make contact between themselves and upper middle-class adults so tense, and which Bloom had not tried to alter—so unselfconsciously charming and unthreatening. This grace is a quality that grows from self-acceptance and a belief in oneself; I remarked on it later in Risinghill. It had frequently been remarked on in the Little Commonwealth, and in Prestolee. Such grace, of course, because of its content, is scarcely likely to be appreciated by authoritarians; and Bloom himself, according to the magazine *Anarchy*, used to say there were plenty of people in the educational world who would like to see him thrown out of the profession. One of their weapons was drawn from the fact that the LCC sent Bloom children from outside the district who were backward in reading or particularly difficult to them in other ways—either from admiration, or from a cynical decision to make St George's 'a sink school' (a phrase that was to crop up some years later during the Rising-hill crisis), or more likely from the co-operation of people with both attitudes. His opponents frequently claimed these children 'proved' his methods were disgraceful. But he lasted there ten years, until his death. And when he died, the whole East End packed the streets for his funeral. It was so fantastic, such a unique occurrence, that the *Daily Mirror*, a popular paper not academically devoted to education (though it similarly covered Risinghill later) came out with a double-spread of photographs —distorted faces of crying children, the quiet despair of weeping mothers and the frozen faces of fathers—all those hundreds of people lining the pavements for the funeral of a headmaster from an unknown, broken-down school building somewhere down the docks.

Roy Nash said, 'It was an incredible thing to happen, absolutely unique in State education history. In my time I've reported funerals of prominent people but I've never seen such genuine grief as on that day in the East End. It showed the humanity of true education. I talked to a lot of people and they genuinely felt personally deprived . . . that their kids had lost someone who was *necessary* to them. Women were weeping. They lined the drab little streets in their brilliant coloured head scarves. It wasn't a sombre occasion at all—I remember so well that mass of colour . . .'

Alex Bloom died, and East London schooling went back to conformity.

But by now more things were happening outside the schools and outside the homes. The National Playing Fields Association which had been formed in 1927 and had at first concerned itself with formal directed play now became interested in the junk playgrounds of Copenhagen, thought out in 1931—long before the bomb-sites—by the architect Thorenson, playgrounds for

over-nines, stocked with packing cases and planks, broken-
down old cars, half bricks, sour earth, crude and ugly to adults
and probably needing a high fence to preserve the right to
exist, but places in which a city child 'could create and shape'.
Lady Allen of Hurtwood publicized the idea and campaigned
for its adoption in England. In an article in *Picture Post* in 1946,
she said, 'It is a democratic community in which the leader
never organizes groups or play, and where the children's freedom is limited only by their feeling of responsibility, by the
atmosphere of the place, and by the care they take of other
children . . .'

Lady Allen, Drummond Abernethy of the National Playing
Fields Association, and other supporters began to involve
themselves in transplanting the Danish idea to the British cities
where children, who had been for the war years separated or
half-separated from their parents were now playing on bomb-
sites or in derelict houses, and long before dazed and exhausted
adults had ever begun to formulate rebuilding plans, were
themselves building—with half-bricks, old broken slates, rubble,
doors torn from hinges by bomb-blast. . . . These adults,
alerted by the Copenhagen experiments, were able to see what
was happening in front of their eyes, and followed the children
(as indeed we all do, whether we do it gladly and creatively at
once, cynically, patronizingly and exploitingly a little later, or
unwillingly, furious, lashing out on all sides every inch of the
fiercely contested way).

Joe Benjamin, one of the adventure playground pioneers, is
very conscious of this situation.

'The Newsom Report talked of "widening horizons out of
school", but it seems it has been left to the fourteen- and
fifteen-year-old "school refusers" themselves to put it into practice. The Children's Act has raised the age of criminal responsibility from ten to fourteen—probably because the courts could
not cope with the sheer weight of numbers. We need to have
more faith. The kids are miles ahead, pulling legislation behind
them.'

Adventure playgrounds were set up in London, Liverpool,
Bristol, Grimsby. They were places where a child went voluntarily, experimented freely, where no distinction was made
between play and work, where the only surveillance was that of

a friendly non-dominating adult, and where parents, grand-parents, big brothers and sisters and the lonely person who lived down the street could contribute skills, experience, know-ledge and materials, and where the environment was accepted. In his study, *In Search of Adventure*, Joe Benjamin suggests that any plot awaiting development could become a temporary playground and that local industrial firms could supply fencing and tools and even a rota of practical adults so that the kids could clear the site for themselves. Recently he said to me, 'If ever I became a Member of Parliament, which heaven forbid, the first thing I'd try to do would be to get the Shaftesbury Act repealed—the law won't allow the kids to help the milkman on Saturdays because the dairy is worried about insurance!' In his later reports, the community aspect of the adventure play-grounds—and the play centres for younger children which also grew—became stronger. Isolated adults were getting together, parents were meeting informal 'play leaders' and non-authori-tarian social-workers in a setting where everyone was on the same level and problems came up naturally in friendly conver-sation and were dealt with almost on the spot. Again, the chil-dren, unconcerned and unaware, functioning in their freedom, were healing society.

Through the work of 'Pat' Turner, another adventure play-ground pioneer, and the constant organization of Lady Allen and Drummond Abernethy, play parks also began—play-grounds in places of natural but informal beauty, where trees might be hung with swings made from motor tyres, but unaggressively. And from this, for the under-fives, 'one-o'clock clubs' developed. This in itself brought a further development. For in order for the clubs to run in the parks legally, mothers had to come with their children. The one o'clock clubs became therefore not only a place where mothers, many of whom had scarcely stirred out of their flats before, sat talking on the grass with new-made friends—or if they preferred it lay reading by themselves in a private corner—but a place where children grew away from their parents at their own pace of independence. As a baby a child would be kicking on the grass among a group of mothers; as a crawler he would be crawling away to investigate a rolling ball, looking back to see his mother still, and still hearing the familiar chatter; as a toddler he would be lurching off to play with the sand; as a slightly older child, tackling the climbing frame, then dealing with the problems of an equal child who has climbed into the hefty wooden pram the first one is pushing (an assault? . . . a threat? . . . an enrichment of play? . . . a momentary friend? . . . a recurring friend? . . .). Because the parents are talking to friends, and because there are informal play-leaders around, they are not, or learn not to be, concentrated on the children; the children move away from them because they are still there. And all the time the children are demonstrating to their parents how competently children behave when they have a large measure of freedom—an aspect of under-five care that had not been seen since the Peckham Centre closed down; from this angle, it was an advance both on nursery schools where mothers and children are arbitrarily separated, and on pre-school playgroups where mothers are only there when it is their turn to help with all the children *en bloc*.

In 1956, Paul Goodman's *Growing Up Absurd* was published in America, and a few copies and extracts came to England (five years later it was published here). I will quote just one paragraph from it about a head who was to make an appearance some years later in one of John Holt's books. (At least, I assume it's the same man, Robert Heinemann.) 'At an under-privileged school in Harlem, they used to test the intelligence of all the children at two-year intervals. They found that every two years each advancing class came out ten points lower in "native intelligence". That is, the combined efforts of home influencing and school education, a powerful combination, succeeded in making the children significantly stupider year by year; if they had a few more years of compulsory home ties and compulsory education, all would end up as gibbering idiots. In this same school a new principal, with a better staff, more personal attention to the kids, and more progressive methods—and also willing to give his own time for social work among the parents—has reversed the trend. One method to remedy stupidity that he swears by is to invite the free expression of criticism and hostility, e.g., "Write a composition telling why you hate your father—why you hate school—why you hate me." '

In 1957, another advance was made on the State school front, this time in Scotland, when Bob Mackenzie became head of Braehead School, in a dying mining village in Fyfe, and made it clear he believed traditional imposed schooling was a tragic and farcical prison and that the focus of his work in Braehead was to get his kids into the countryside where they would interact with the natural order of things. He spent seven years trying to get the education authority to *allow* the pupils to use a hunting lodge in the mountains that was *given* them by British Aluminium; the authority said it was in grave disrepair—Bob Mackenzie said that was the point; the kids and the staff working together would rebuilt it; the authority said ah, that was child labour; Bob Mackenzie said if you won't let us do it, then you do it; the authority said ah, that will cost thousands of pounds which comes out of the ratepayers' pockets. . . . Bob Mackenzie said, in effect, I will go on and on pressing courteously for the children's right to live in their mountain lodge, as distinct from the brief expeditions we already run to the mountains. ('Much of the trouble in the classrooms, to cope with which the teachers insist on the retention of corporal punishment, is due to the curriculum' . . . 'Away up there, unhurried and untroubled, our lives take on, although temporarily, a largeness and a generosity and a confidence and a feeling that there is no human problem that we couldn't cope with' . . . 'The mountain expeditions and the opposition to the use of the belt are integral parts of the same policy, based on a different attitude to children . . .') The education authority decided to close the school ('reorganize' was the word).

Braehead was the only school I ever visited where the kids' paintings—many magnificent—were glazed, framed and hung, as if in a gallery (he had two very fine art teachers), on the battered walls of that architecturally dismal building; I was convinced on sight of them that one of the reasons the education authority was so hostile was that they couldn't tell the kids' paintings from 'real' paintings, and felt their status tottering.

In 1960, Risinghill School opened in a grim part of London, under the headship of Michael Duane. (I have written its story in detail elsewhere, and in this present book, Duane, like Neill, speaks for himself.) Here, too, children warped by being frustrated at every move they made, dehumanized by being treated as objects to be parcelled out at the decision of bureau-crats, each natural step in their growth being classed as delinquent, began to grow again into their natural grace and serenity, even in those drab and violent surroundings; and the school began to grow spontaneously into a community centre for all ages, all nationalities, a whole district. But the authorities were only concerned that their 'control' was loosening, and their political image slipping (for Michael Duane said openly that his children were not middle-class children with middle-class values). Risinghill and Braehead were informed of their closure at almost the same time, Braehead after nine years of existence, Risinghill after five.

The same month that Risinghill closed, a lively magazine called *Anarchy* printed an article by Colin Ward suggesting a repeal of the Education Act—no more compulsory school, no more obstacle races beginning at five (or earlier) and leaving victims all along the route, no more talk about increasing the term of imprisonment by raising the school leaving age; instead a concentration on making schools (or education) so good it doesn't need to be compulsory. This article had already appeared in a college of education magazine. As far as I know it was the first time anyone in England had dared to formulate out loud, even to a possibly friendly audience, what many of us had begun to hear as a question in our heads. This question is dealt with more fully in Nan Berger's chapter in this volume.

Paul Goodman, and later John Holt, writing from America (their books were published in England) were saying the same thing, pointing out that real education was taking place outside the school building and that what the orthodox school was teaching was failure. In *How Children Fail*, John Holt recorded detailed and perceptive examples of what many of us had for years observed in children about us, or remembered from our own childhoods, that very many children are so paralysed by the fear of failure and therefore of humiliation, accusation or reproach, or so obsessed by the emotional need to please, that they only try to *guess* what the teacher considers the right answer—and sometimes even give up trying to guess. (I have thought for years that the main reason why there are two sides in education is not that there are two theories, but that some people follow theories and other people follow children.) 'Schools,' he says, 'should be a place where children learn what they most want to know, instead of what we think they ought to know.'

In 1967, an article appeared in *Anarchy* describing First Street School, New York, a school conceived at the start as 'an antidote to the dehumanization' of the State school system, but in a poor, not a well-to-do area. The writer was George Dennison. He stressed several times that a child needs 'reality of encounter', and that his inborn desire to learn is simply an attraction to the real world which he wants to be *in* (and that therefore the best teachers are adults who are clearly *in* the real world.) There were no grades in First Street School, no report cards, no examinations; but there was a school council ('a parliament in which some very fine distinctions have been drawn by tots of six'). No child was compelled to study, to answer questions, to stay in the room, to stay in the building. Two years later we were to hear more about this school, by which time it would be dead, as a punishment for having existed and succeeded instead of being a theory; that this was the reason for its death will be bizarrely shown later.

In the same year, Mary Stapleton and other teachers involved in the English New Education Fellowship, had got together, as far as they knew to discuss school buildings and their dissatisfaction with them. Frank Rutter, the architect, said to them, 'Tell me the function and the shape will follow.' They suggested 'functions', he rapidly sketched shapes; and out of this stimulus came the finally formulated question, did education need a school building at all? Perhaps it simply needed the environment, the local community that was already there offering 'learning resources' of all kinds.

It was becoming clear that architects, artists, scientists, actors, were all prepared to work with children, and had of their own accord begun to do so. Two young architects had made plans for converting double-decker buses into mobile classrooms. (Later, in 1970, someone was to turn a Liverpool Corporation bus into a mobile play centre.) Three other young architects were opposing the London education authority's decision to demolish a large GPO garage in order to build a primary school costing £56,000, and instead were proposing a plan to use the garage as a place where children, craftsmen, artists and artisans and all the adults around worked together. Two artists were running two Junior Arts and Science Centres where, out of school hours, children made life-size sculpture, glass-fibre monsters, photo-electric robots. A sculptor was running Action Space, a group that took 'playful art'—inflatables of all kinds, kites, coloured smoke—into slum areas (their funny and accurate diary of the three weeks they worked—and lived—in Wapping is full of passages like 'We all went together to find somewhere to fly the kites. We tried Waterside Gardens, but the park keepers would not allow the children on the grass and finally said that we could not fly the kites from any GLC property because it was not on our "list of permissions". Finally, after much discussion and despair on the part of the children, we went on local advice to a derelict site on Hermitage Wall.... Soon the largest kite was high over the London Docks like a giant sun in the sky. The children were very impressed and gazed at it in silence from time to time. Not only was it very beautiful—it was a symbol of our triumph over prohibition. Later they flew smaller kites themselves, made a bonfire and played all the usual games of exploring and fighting. One child said very seriously she wished she was a kite . . .' and 'That evening we decided to try and make them see we are tired at 5.30 and it batters us to have to rough around at that time. We won't lecture them but make our point in some dramatic way. We bandage ourselves, wear slings, limp and walk very slowly into the Youth Club. Real concern all round. We say we have been battered, the boys indignant, they want to know who has done it to us. All go upstairs with us and talk. . . . Still believe someone has hurt us and won't accept *they* have done it in some way. They say they only have fun and would never hurt us.')

Since the new art diploma courses had come into force, art had become more and more tied up not only with science but with industry and with new man-made materials, and industrial firms—eager to find out how materials and their by-products could be used, and this use demonstrated—were happy, for a while at any rate, to give such artists surplus material to play with, and the artists took it to the children. As long as the artists were not trying to take play out of the child's hands, this could be invaluable. (Two bizarre examples of this latter: a devoted head who has spent years teaching thousands of children street games, and an article in a Sunday colour magazine giving children designs for sand castles.)

While the New Education Fellowship—which had changed its conference slogan from 'Buildings Matter' (1967 conference) to 'People Matter' (1968)—was concentrating in 1969 on how to use buildings other than school and people other than trained teachers to educate children, a few copies of an American book by George Dennison called *The Lives of Children* filtered into London. First Street School was dead. Here was its story.

First Street had been a school of twenty-three Negro, 'white', and Puerto Rican children, accurately reflecting the make-up of the neighbourhood, and ranging from slow-normal to bright, about half of them on 'welfare', about half with severe learning and behaviour problems, with three full-time teachers and one part-time teacher, and others who came in for singing, dancing, music, and costing only the same as the State schools—because they had no administrators, no central bureaucracy, and they used the neighbourhood. Where Joe Benjamin in 1961 had daringly suggested taking over empty sites for playgrounds, George Dennison (following Paul Goodman's and Elliott Shapiro's ideas) was now suggesting taking over empty buildings for schools.

George Dennison, who had built a great deal on the work of Tolstoy, Neill and Dewey, suggested 'we might cease thinking of school as a place, and learn to believe that it is basically relationships: between children and adults, adults and adults, children and other children. The four walls and the principal's office would cease to loom so hugely as the essential ingredients. . . . The proper concern of a school is not education in a narrow sense, and still less preparation for later life, but the present lives of the children—a point made repeatedly by John Dewey. . . . Our school professionals, taken as a class, an institutionalized centre of power, are fundamentally incompetent and must be displaced. . . . There is no such thing as competence without love'. After the First Street School had run with very moving and competent success, as the book shows, George Dennison and his fellow teachers compiled a brochure, setting out how the children, and their parents, had changed, and how cheaply such a school could be run, and sent it with an appeal for financial help to every Foundation and Agency throughout the country—two pramloads of brochures. The response was zero.

Months later he met a Foundation man at a party—the kind, George Dennison said, who gets out glossy magazines full of artistic photographs of Negro children and are forever and permanently launching 'basic research'—who told him that the reason for rejection was that the format was out of date, the paper not glossy enough, he had listed no research personnel, and that if he had drawn up 'a legitimate project for studying the feasibility' instead of actually running the school, he would have been much more likely to gain interest—for, he concluded, having spoken with apparently great sincerity all the way through, 'there is a great need in this city for schools like yours'. So First Street closed down.

Soon after this, John Holt's third book, *The Underachieving School*, reached England, a book which he prefaces by saying that the future task of educators is 'to let every child be the planner, director and assessor of his own education, to allow and encourage him, with the inspiration and guidance of more experienced and expert people, and as much help as he asked for, to decide what he is to learn, when he is to learn it, how he is to learn it, and how well he is learning it. It would be to make our schools, instead of what they are, which is jails for children, into a resource for free and independent learning, which everyone in the community, of whatever age, could use as much or as little as he wanted'.

Now in this year, which officially is Education Year, and officially a year to be celebrated, I celebrate these unofficial people. These people and others like David Wills, George Lyward, Otto Shaw in England, Bruno Bettelheim, Jonathan Kozol, James Herndon, Herbert Kohl in America, and many rebelling students, and the Society of Teachers Opposed to Physical Punishment, and all those many more who know that education is not the bureaucrats' curriculum, nor the missionaries' fantasy, nor the disciplinarians' prison, but a natural creative instinctive process of growth helped along by adults who trust it and find delight in its movement.

I celebrate too, Solomon, whom Neill always calls 'that old fool', but who, if he ever existed, and if he ever really wrote all those folk sayings, and if you ignore his authoritarian translators and get back to the Hebrew, said, 'Educate a child *in the way that is his own*'. Let the bible-punching educators cope with that one, in Education Year.

I was by now becoming rather drunk on all this companionship. A note I received from John Holt however—July 1970—brought me considerably out of my euphoria (particularly since John Holt always maintains that what happens in America happens in England, seven or eight years later. Joe Benjamin agrees, but makes the time-lag shorter). He enclosed some startling American news reports, and certain scathing letters he had written following them. It seems, according to the *Washington Post* of 29 June 1970, which carries a very long report, that the city of Omaha—which, presumably not fortuitously, contains two large medical education centres strongly subsidized by drug companies (a school official said, 'Look, if I bucked the medical profession in this town, I'd be dead, useless. They are pretty powerful here')—is dosing 5 to 10 per cent of its school-children (that is, three to six thousand) with amphetamine-type drugs specifically to make them amenable to school discipline. These children are almost all in the first six grades, many of them but not all are poor and many of them are black. They are classified by their teachers as 'hyperactive' and suffering from a complex and little-understood learning and behaviour disorder sometimes called 'minimal brain disfunction' which causes them to jump up and down . . . easily, and as needing 'behaviour modification drugs', and are handed over to the enthusiastic doctors of the city who give them—to be taken during school hours so that the children become 'more successful'—Ritalin mainly, and also Dexedrine, Deaner, Aventyl, and Tofranil. (Sweden has banned the sale of Ritalin, and the US Food and Drug Administration has urged extreme care in its use because of the danger of addiction, and because of the side effects of 'marked anxiety, tension and agitation'. But the Omaha enthusiasts say that though they have no idea how it happens it seems to calm children.) By November 1969, according to the *Washington Post*, thousands of Omaha elemen-

47

tary school-children were swopping pills of different colours in the school playgrounds, obtained through the urging of teachers and the prescriptions of doctors.

John Holt's letters were withering:

'We take lively, curious, energetic children, eager to make contact with the world and to learn about it, stick them in barren classrooms with teachers who on the whole neither like nor respect nor understand nor trust them, restrict their freedom of speech and movement to a degree that would be judged excessive and inhuman even in a maximum security prison, and that their teachers themselves could not and would not tolerate. Then, when the children resist this brutalizing and stupefying treatment and retreat from it in anger, bewilderment and terror, we say that they are sick with "complex and little-understood disorders" and proceed to dose them with powerful drugs that are indeed complex and of whose long-run effects we know little or nothing, so that they may be more ready to do the asinine things the schools ask them to do . . .

'. . . Suppose I were to order Dr Satterfield under the threat of heavy penalties to sit absolutely still, without even changing his position, and neither speaking nor making any sound without my permission, for many hours of the day, not just one day but about 180 days out of the year. How would he react to this demand? He would surely resist in any way he could. Suppose I then announced that his reluctance or refusal to obey my orders showed that he was suffering from a malady called "hyperkinesis", and that for his own good, and whether he liked it or not, I was going to dose him with some powerful drug to make him more compliant. What then? As soon as he could, he would probably have me arrested and locked up as some kind of dangerous and criminal lunatic. And most reasonable men would think him quite right to do so.

'There is worse yet. The story tells us of a school nurse who said to a National Education Conference in San Francisco, "I was talking with two fifth-grade pupils, and I could tell that this was their problem. I told these kids that I knew they couldn't be still or sit through class, and that they weren't trying to be bad. They broke down and cried. It is really tragic." Grotesque would be a better word. Consider what we do. We say to children that it is a crime to speak or move, or even to want to. Then we say that in telling them this we are acting only for their own good, that we really care about them, love them; and we are so good at fooling them (and even ourselves) about this that they weep tears of sorrow, shame, and remorse. If only they could be worthy of our great love! And we, to console them, tell them that their badness—nothing more serious in fact than not wanting to sit still—is not really their own fault. It is almost as if a man being flogged should beg pardon of the man flogging him for bothering him with his screams . . .'

I then received another communication that sobered me cold.

It seems that Michael Huberman, a Harvard PhD, who has served in the UNESCO Secretariat since 1967 in the Department of School and Higher Education, was asked by UNESCO to write Paper No. 4, in the series of twelve which they were getting out to celebrate International Education Year.

I have read this document. It is very important. But other people in education have made important statements. If I quote from this one, it is because of what has happened to it.

Michael Huberman says: 'Under the existing system, lower income groups are paying a disproportionate share of the cost of higher education. The poor man seems to be helping to subsidize the higher education of the children of the affluent. Is it legitimate to demand that the government also subsidize those young people who neither desire nor are eligible to take advantage of public education? Why should the State subsidize four years at the University for students, while neglecting apprenticeships, independent study programmes, small community trade schools, or even the purchase of small businesses by non-students? The idea that the only way people get educated is by being enrolled in institutions is long obsolete. We tend to forget that employed adults, when they seek out facilities for further education, neither want nor need anything that resembles the formal school system. The closing down of schools, while retaining teachers in service, can result in imaginative uses of learning resources in the community (public meetings, mass media, mathematics lessons in the markets, museums, visits to civic offices and officials, etc. We seem to have forgotten that, at the base, schooling is simply a set of planned experiences that have been institutionalized . . .'

Michael Huberman not only refers to Paul Goodman, and Kropotkin, but he criticizes UNESCO's previous papers on 'qualitative breakdown in education', by drawing UNESCO's attention to the fact that in the USA 'the percentage of secondary school-leavers in New York City from the most favoured backgrounds and showing the highest IQ results has been increasing each year. This seems to indicate that the brightest students are convinced that they can get a brighter education out of school than inside, that it is more educationally efficient for them to drop out than to stay'.

UNESCO has ordered all copies of this paper—whose cover says REPRODUCTION AUTHORIZED—to be destroyed. Not merely destroyed in any old way, but *burnt*. An unfortunately evocative decision. Well, at least he has not been sent to one of those camps.

Chapter 2

The Infant, The Family and Society

by Paul Adams, M.D.

1. *Family and Society*

'It is our Parents, that first cure us of natural Wildness, and break in us the Spirit of Independency we are all born with: It is to them that we owe the first Rudiments of our Submission; and to the Honour and Deference which Children pay to Parents, all societies are obliged for the Principle of Human Obedience.'

> *Bernard Mandeville*, The Fable of the Bees.

IN this quotation from Mandeville we see stated clearly the place of the family in the socialization, or taming, or domestication, of children. Mandeville praised the authoritarian family, but do we?

Is it desirable that people learn as children to submit, to eschew independence and wildness, and to adopt attitudes of honour-deference-obedience to authority?

Or is it desirable that parents function primarily as *sources* (Latin, *parere*), from which we are 'begotten' and from which we receive nourishing security when we are children, but who do not squelch our spiritedness, crush our wills, and instill a mess of anxiety-shame-guilt-inferiority-conformity-reward-and-punishment during our childhood? What are parents good for?

At times an honest conservative is easier to deal with, easier to co-exist with, than is a wishy-washy liberal. The conservative is more definite, less given to sophistry and casuistry, and more prone to value honest commitment to real values. For, all too often, 'liberal' people are at heart illiberal; or, worse, they are deeply nihilistic in the sense in which Ignazio Silone* used the term 'nihilism'—namely, they believe that all values are fake, and are but masks for selfish interests. Mandeville gave us the classic conservative statement of what family life is all about.

* Ignazio Silone, 'The Choice of Comrades' Dissent 2 (1955): 7–19.

Mandeville stated it clearly: the breaking of children's wills, the 'training' and indoctrination of children within a family is the *modus operandi* of an authoritarian society. For the clarity of the statement we can be grateful; but as Mandeville stated it, in the tenor and phraseology of the eighteenth century, the family's vital role in authoritarianism is entirely repugnant to the free soul in our age. Our very own society does work, nevertheless, through parents, to produce in their children two kinds of gruesome behaviour: both (1) conformity to social convention and (2) neurosis.* Neuroses and conformity are the joint products of authoritarian parents and an authoritarian society.

Later in the chapter there will be a discussion of neurosis. For now, let us look at the defectiveness of conformity. It is not a question here of the economic and political system. Instead, it is a question of a family system, an institution of mature people who copulate, reproduce and bring up children. So it is a matter of family relations, family style, and family values. Here moral rights are more basic than legal rights. It is a familiar matter of earthiness, and of instincts and a claiming of one's humanity through claiming one's animal nature. It is a matter of preserving that 'natural Wildness' and 'Spirit of Independency' with which we appear to be endowed.

A friend of the author, a free soul from Germany, was astounded, upon visiting the United States, at the quality of family life there. The German woman commented, 'If we had built up an equalitarian family in Germany as it exists here (United States) we could not have had a Hitler!' If children know the love of parents who can accept the impulses of children and who do not try to bludgeon their children into subordination, will we have a freer society therefrom?

We can defer looking at her praise for North American families. But now we can ask, was the German visitor correct in saying that family relations and politics are interrelated? When I physically beat up my son am I preparing him to be a young storm trooper? When I use moral or emotional blackmail in order to subdue my son am I training him to submit to some future breed of storm troopers and to revere conformity to the

* See Erich Fromm, 'Individual and Social Origins of Neurosis'. *American Journal of Sociology* 9 (1944): 330–384.

pack? Is the family a microcosm of society? Is family life an important focus for the rebuilding of society as well as for conserving present society?

The family is often neglected in the thinking of revolutionists. Even experts on children, at least in the United States, when they are revolutionaries, often tend to think exclusively in terms of revolution by means of school reform. The revolution is pedagogical, for them. The authors of this book do not hang quite so many hopes on the school by itself, because they know that the formative influences of one's family outweigh those of one's school.

The foremost leftist apostles of violence, such as Ernesto Guevara, Régis Debray, Frantz Fanon, and Jean-Paul Sartre, although they have said much about men*, have said almost nothing about *men in families*. Moreover, they have said almost nothing of women and children. When they do make occasional, brief excursions into the field, what they say is political propaganda, or patriarchal pap, that, for its progressiveness, rivals the assertions of a Saint Paul, a John Calvin, or a Sigmund Freud. When the Guevaras call upon us to murder for their Christ or for their Revolution—'The first duty of a revolutionary is to make violent revolution'—they could not conceivably have any preoccupation with real, living and breathing, young children. Theirs is a patriarchal and masculine rhetoric that sways only the adult, the male, or the authoritarian (female as well as male) who holds to patriarchal values. A youth who has been allowed freedom in childhood has had, on the other hand, experience of 'that light and that spirit that taketh away the occasion of all war'. He is less prone to be violent or authoritarian. Such a childhood of freedom prepares a young man and young woman to decline military service and to work for peace, to oppose violence with revolutionary nonviolence, and ultimately as an adult to proclaim that *the first duty of a revolutionary is to build a society geared to children*. Family living *is* societal life.

In western societies we have, to our own detriment, dwelt too much, when formulating revolutions, upon the economic and

---

* Especially young adult men who are easily converted into militarists in all societies and who, in turn, are always revered by militarists and by civilians of a bent to value military virtues. Of military virtues, youthfulness and physical prowess have always been among the most highly prized.

political matters that are so dear to males. Assuredly, this has something to do with the failure of revolutions to augment freedom. We have given all too little attention to sexual freedom, to family living, to children and to women, even in our utopias. Revolutionaries as well as reactionaries often have viewed women and children as mere chattels, to be used and disposed of at the discretion of men. Revolutionary ideologies as a result have been too authoritarian, too austere, too patriarchal, too abstract, and too artificial to materialize successfully in the concrete and natural cosmos where 'personal' (i.e. interpersonal) relations have a paramount importance. In families people give security to others in a give and take which requires that people are not so highly cerebral.

Feminists in the US who began with great benevolence toward Fidel Castro properly became embittered and antagonistic when Fidel told them later on that women's rights are now of secondary importance. Now that the revolution has been instituted and is *in a consolidation phase*, patriotic men cut sugar cane and 'good' women merely obey the men and care for the children.

Alas, character is not moulded exclusively in the marketplace, nor in the palace, where authority reigns. Still, only rarely have revolutionaries undertaken to think about a world fit for children. A world unfit for women and children is unfit for whole men as well; and by concentrating on political and economic matters we will never bring about a fit society for human persons. Character is moulded in the home, where sexiness and interpersonal values prevail. The home is more than a simple reflection of marketplace, parliament and school. The school, where required, can be important—but only secondarily so— as we shall demonstrate later.

Families assuredly can crush wills, and not only the wild wills of children but also the tamer wills of adults. The human expense of family living among Jews and Christians has been especially taxing for women and children, and but a little less so for men. Women and children are defined by the patriarch's laws as merely chattels, and in their public roles they function as ancillary to the patriarch. Within the household, of course, genuine loving relations based upon mutual respect and reciprocal longings may occur between the patriarch and his wife, or between the patriarch and his children; but in patriarchal society it is the socially inferior women and children who have fallen heir to the 'gutsiest' and most erotic dealings with each other. What men neglect, women and children embrace and enjoy. It is in this way that children and women perpetuate even in our civilization a trend that sticks close to Eros and keeps pockets of freedom viable even in mass, capitalist society. As mass society compounds our sense of idleness, impotency and alienation, the sphere of love or of, generically, intimate interpersonal relations probably will assume greater importance, even for males. Hence, by default, the mother becomes possessed of the hands that rock the cradle, and teaches about love. By being squeezed off the marketplace she enriches the hearth. If mothers rule the world they do so through character formation during infancy, not through control of the economic and political institutions of society, and not because they make international wars and violent revolutions, and not because they can afford to ship off their children to progressive boarding schools.

Mothers can, and do when they have been corrupted themselves, mould their young charges so as to have them 'adjust' to the established institutions, including war, violence, greedy capitalism, and patriotism. Such mothers inculcate a respectful fear for 'irrational authority' and in that inculcation they breed 'good citizens' of coercive and insane States. Many mothers, and for that matter many psychotherapists, go no further than to espouse *adjustment to*, or making do with, established institutions. Most parents transmit conservative values at every turn, and in current society that means that they pass along *defective values*. There is no need for totalitarianism to batter people into conforming as long as a so-called democracy can work, through families, to achieve all of the automatic conformity that any State would desire. As we shall see more fully, our German friend was both right and wrong when she related family to Nazism in Germany, and family to so-called *totalitarian democracy* in the USA.

'Fascism became unnecessary when populations began to behave in a politically apathetic and disciplined fashion under regimes which remained democratic in form.'*

* H. Stuart Hughes, 'Mussolini'. *The New York Review of Books*, II: 11 (July 9, 1964), 9.

Even in a libertarian and pluralistic society, however, it is parents, or their substitutes, who love and care for children, and who have strong influences on their children. To be a parent and yet to have no influence on one's offspring is either (1) to abdicate parenthood by neglecting or overlooking one's children, something often done in the name of Freedom, or (2) to have nothing that one values, believes in, and can offer to children. Simple assertiveness by mothers and fathers in no way negates a child's freedom. For, once the preachment has been offered, the child may reject the advice, of course, as well as adopt it. Free parents can assert themselves without uttering obsessively tentative mouthwash.

Truly free parents can let their children choose from among alternatives. That is the atmosphere of freedom: ever-enlarging, ever searching to expand choices. Many is the politically radical parent known to the author who confuses the simple assertion of one's identity with the desire to subjugate one's children.* Equals are not always ciphers. Parents should not mean to be nonentities. Good parents even, occasionally, have something to teach to their children. Freedom is not a vacuum, or a morass of alienation and indecision; freedom is the existence of alternatives among which one may choose. The alternatives may be clear, and they may be real. They may be chosen with some conviction by the child—and therein lies freedom, not in the child's parents' hiding *their* values from the child, and giving nothing to the child. If they withhold values from the child, parents are promoting nihilism in the blasphemous name of freedom.

2. *Parenthood as a Turning Point*

In order to deepen our perspective on the rights of infants in the modern age, it would be well to look at what parenthood means to the responsible and freely involved young man and young woman. If we are to assume, in deference to realism, that they are not 'chaste' at the time of marriage, indeed we could suppose that they have come to have a loving and intimate adjustment to each other prior to marriage and/or pregnancy. Increasingly, we are able to observe that pregnancy need not

---

* Paul L. Adams, et al., 'Authoritarian Parents and Disturbed Children'. *American Journal of Psychiatry*, 121 (1965): 1162–1167.

have the temporal relation to marriage that Victorians might have pretended to be necessary. There are quite good enough reasons to lead one to advocate premarital intercourse and possibly premarital pregnancy in our day and age, as a step towards freedom of choice. In any event, those whose values will preclude premarital intercourse must assume a larger risk (and take bigger leaps on faith) than most young people would wish to take. Even though psychiatrists tend to think that almost anyone can be married happily to almost anyone, young people want to find out ahead of time about the partner.

Irrespective of their marriage, there are two useful criteria of wholesome adjustment between a young man and young woman. One is that *each has no desire to change the other*, and a second is that *each sees something of himself in the other*. Now, this latter criterion has bisexual overtones which are disconcerting to both the adolescent and the childish but which in no wise trouble a mature couple in love. Exaggerated maleness and femaleness are appropriate for earlier childhood but they are compulsions that healthy adults do not harbour. What of the first criterion, i.e. neither one has any desire to change the other? This is a precondition of the acceptance that love is. It is lacking in many neurotic young men or women. It obviates any need for control, possession, domination, and the like. Moreover, if neither desires to convert or remake the other, each can celebrate his own humanity in the other without that romantic fervour which so often culminates in jealousy, projection and paranoia, and the killing of love.

With the best of planning and precautions there will be accidents resulting in pregnancies that must be decided upon after the fact. Few young couples plan, and those who do are not always able to carry out their intentions. Whether sexual life requires to be as routinized and rational as the economy or the State might well depend upon personal taste. Some radicals are supremely rationalistic in their sexology (and, one suspects, in their sexuality). Anyway, what is crucial is whether there is a willingness on the part of the young woman and young man to shoulder the responsibilities that go with untrammeled sexual pleasures. If they are willing to 'pay for their mishaps' nothing is lost and it is soon converted into no mishap at all!

The pregnancy itself constitutes a kind of turning point in

the relationship of the man and woman. Wonderment, joy, anger and irritation may all appear, presenting new opportunities for dialogue, for compromise and for self-assertion by both partners. A cosmic concern appears fleetingly even to the most blasé of young couples. They begin taking cognizance of their own origin, their place in their original families, and they begin showing a pre-occupation with their own parents. Such attentiveness to *their* parents makes them better prepared for parenthood. It is as if they desired to set aright the relations with those generations which preceded them just at that moment when their own generativity comes to the forefront. For some, this is a time to marry.

3. *Parenthood as Redemption*

THE family itself is a school for parenthood. Our fundamental concepts and attitudes about good or bad mothers and fathers are learned in our earliest childhood. One of the characteristic phenomena of everyday life is the repetition by parents of their own infantile conflicts as they live with their children developing through life's stages. This is interesting to observe, given detachment; but from a stance of commitment and concern for human welfare the phenomenon oftentimes is pathetic. Parenthood can be a time of fruition, of meeting challenges, and of carrying on the work of life. It is probably not dreary ordinarily, and it is not destructive for either parents or children. However, for our present purposes we will discuss principally the snags, pitfalls and encumbrances that beset parenthood.

Re-enactment and transposition are the two major processes that appear during parenthood as it has been depicted by psycho-analysts. The technical term for the human tendency to repeat earlier behaviour compulsively (i.e. neurotically) is 'repetition compulsion'. The technical term for the human proclivity for transposing old patterns, even inappropriately, to new situations is 'transference'. Both of these are processes with a very human face; but both are neurotic when overdone by patients! They are also maladaptive and unhealthy when they are overdone by parents who may or may not be analysands. Neurosis is altogether so natural, so easy, and so beguiling, that it becomes all the more difficult to eradicate.

What are some of the consequences when a parent displays

repetition compulsion? He engages himself and his spouse in continual work with his individual core neurosis, repetitively enacting unresolved conflicts that derive from his earlier life. A person who experiences anxiety when a compeer is praised is such a person, perhaps. If he is repeating an old pattern that reconstitutes the *dramatis personae* of his childhood, he will see to it that his wife, for example, will be forcefully cast into villainous roles in order to assist his own compulsive need to set up conflicts in such a fashion that he can achieve at least fake-triumphs, illusory victories. The wife will feel puzzled to be seen as a rival at odd times and places. The wife will remain primarily the wife, of course, unless the husband is rather seriously ill; but she will be rushed into roles as a competitor from time to time in order to expedite the replay of old themes; old stylized morbid dramas which the spouse seems desperately to require of his wife. Or, to take another example, the husband who was made anxious by competition with brothers and sisters as a child would in his work go to great lengths to set up rivalries in such a way that he could achieve some sense of winning, or, if desperate, at least a sense of having survived the threat of extermination. He will envy colleagues, imagine that colleagues are extremely envious of him, and will convert a working team into a war among prima donnas. At home, with his sons and daughters, life will be played out as an unending contest for mastery, for hegemony, for endurance and for making a 'good show'. It is small wonder that children learn to harbour hatred for their neurotic parents: hatred, then contempt, and finally perhaps the feeling that they are beneath contempt.

A mother driven by repetition compulsion will keep alive, for reasons that she cannot fathom, the kind of uproar that she learned in her own family of origin. Accordingly she will keep the whole household loud and animated. If her own parents were quietly tyrannical, however, she will be driven wild by a noisy husband and children. She will expend large quanta of energy in order to calm things down—not that calmness has realistic merits but only that a family style must be repeated if she is to be comfortable. If she grew up as the darling of the father, and if her narcissistic supplies were copious during courtship and early marriage, she will not be able to switch gears when there are diapers to be changed. As a consequence, her requirement, from deep in her being, for romance—for being idolized—will meet frustration and *she will feel thwarted with marriage and motherhood* when in reality her problem is one of her unadaptability to the requirements of her own growth as a person. Or, she will as a reflex perpetuate the 'do's and don'ts' of her own childhood. Truly, as the psychoanalysts term it, she is fixated and coming out into life with outworn patterns.

What, then, occurs when transference, the second neurotic distortion, afflicts the here and now of parenthood? Stated briefly, it is a question of the parent transposing his or her own childhood neurosis into the current epoch of parenthood. The parent who hoarded as a child will become anxious at every occasion of the child's 'wilful waste'; the parent who was deprived as a child will promulgate an atmosphere of scarcity when in reality the family is sufficiently affluent. The parent who suffered from great Oedipal guilt as a child will foster passionate attachments between mother and son when his wife bears a son and rears him. The bedwetter will produce bed-wetters; the soiler will harvest encopretics; the hysteric will reincarnate himself. What went during the parent's childhood will be made to go in the parent's parenthood.

When a parent's own childhood neurotic patterns have been laid to rest the parent is better equipped to proceed realistically with the work of parenthood, and with feeling comfortable in being a parent. If, from childhood, acceptable self-esteem and satisfactory interpersonal relations have been established, the parent *can move* into parenthood with less fog and distortion, with a lighter pre-existent burden. He (or she) can pick up the actual work of the developmental phase which parenthood is. When, however, parents bring to their parental role a reservoir of emotions, character armour* and attitudes that are not wholesome, both parents and child become enmeshed in neurotic interaction. Particularly for the neurotic parent the human

* Character armour is a Reichian term connoting the accretion of all those attitudes—both normal and pathologic—that defend against anxiety with a character rigidity, a poverty of openness and spontaneity. Outright neurotic symptoms are not present but the character itself precludes the naturalness epitomized by orgasm. This form of defence is expressed in chronic rigidities of the body musculature. See Wilhelm Reich, *The Function of the Orgasm* and *Character Analysis*.

loss is a great one: not having the privilege of experiencing parenthood as a direct, clear, and realistic role that contributes positively to adult living.

Parents often tell themselves quite honestly that they seek to spare their children some of the troubles which they, the parents, experienced when growing up. However noble these protective intentions of parents may be, their parental behaviour serves to sensitize their child to second-hand conflicts. This sensitivity is not necessarily helpful to the child. In its essence, this parental attitude is like having a chip on one's shoulder; it entails a neurotic interference with the child's experience and it rarely accomplishes victory for the parents in the old lingering battles to which parents address themselves.

Looking at some examples of this parental distortion may enable us to arrive at a better understanding of what could possibly be done to bring relief to 'suffering parenthood'. Obviously, whatever is said on this subject, including the most generalized commentary, is far from culture-free. Hence, one should spell out the kind of subculture from which the following examples are drawn.

They are usually (in the USA) parents between the ages of thirty and fifty, whose origins—thanks to Depression and subsequent War—were lower middle-class and working-class, but who in 1970 are middle-class or lower middle-class in position. That is, they became upwardly mobile. Such parents are literate and have some college training. They are eager to learn of parenthood. They manifest a keen fascination for psychological notions. They read considerably in the popular literature for parents, especially cookbooks on child rearing such as those by Benjamin Spock and Arnold Gesell or the manuals on how to outsmart children such as those by Haim Ginott. They show a surprising attentiveness to the numerous experts who flog parents for misbehaving, overprotecting, or being unloving, being overly lenient, and even for being anxious, etc., etc. They are thinking persons who have respect for ideas, and they are prone to be vocal, if not ruminative, about some of the contradictions and conflicts that characterize the culture. They are sometimes the *petit bourgeois* revolutionaries that intellectuals become.

1. *Racial attitudes* in this group of parents are likely to be

non-racist, or at least less racist than the views of their parents. They might bend over backwards, so to speak, in advocating racial justice. They advocate Black Power and 'rap' against *white* racism. Included here are some parents who train their children to be minority group members (white Negroes) in order to let the children 'realize the full tragedy of discrimination'. The children, on their side, often discern that their parents do not treat them as lovable persons but only as pawns in a tactical struggle that holds little meaning for the children. The children perceive more readily than do their parents that inflicting suffering on one's children has rather punitive overtones. It is throwing naturalness quite far, failing to give cognizance to the fact that young children do not vote and hence are irrelevant in electoral politics and that as children they will never be the vanguard in any form of social revolution.

2.   *Materialism, scarcity and abundance* are themes that persistently recur in the moral evaluations of such parents. They are often preoccupied with whether their children are overly pampered materially, whether they should impose more austere ascetic values upon their children, whether the children embody the vulgarities of our mass culture, and so on. Ferreting out the origins of such worries will require help from social scientists other than psychiatrists, but we can see that this thematic preoccupation is emotionally distressing to parents, who are busily comparing their own recollection of childhood with what they can observe of this phase for their children. One has to conclude that children will grow up to see the 'hollowness of affluence' as the poet Archibald Macleish has called our condition. We might do better to let them learn than to inflict needless deprivation upon them. For material abundance can have great humane value for young children. Let us simply recall that the most peace-loving generation, at least in North America, within our historic recall, is the present generation below the age of twenty-five—young people who have known only abundance. It is the richness, naturally, of a warfare state. Nevertheless, it is material abundance, and it has great 'spiritual' meaning.

3.   *Sexual freedom and restriction* is another issue in parenting that consumes time and energy, and deprives parents of naturalness and joy. They want to be one-up by comparison to their

own parents, and this often produces an unnatural and compulsive indulgence (and promotion) of the childhood sexuality of their offspring. They urge their children to masturbate, to seek intercourse, and to succumb to parental dictates that the children be 'free' sexually. Such parents are aware that something is amiss in their own development in sexuality, and they will frequently benefit greatly from the successfully psychosexual development of their own children, if the children can escape parental interference. But how much leniency, how much intrusion, how much snooping, how much encouragement to license—these are the questions held by these parents labouring under the yoke of their own childhood. Implicit in all such questions are the notions that parents can command their children to be uninhibited, that values are transmitted consciously and deliberately, and that children have no right to a lust that escapes parental dictation and control. The old liberal and libertarian notion of leaving the child to find his own genitalia—to his own lusts and his own outlets—does not come easily to such parents. 'Self-regulation' for such parents is a mask for parental control: my children *are told* to have all the freedom they want in sexual matters. Their stance is a far cry from true freedom, and from true self-regulation, of children. In genuine freedom the master is not an intrusive, if benign, despot telling the erstwhile slaves how to live and enjoy sexuality in their 'freedom' which Master has granted, by fiat.

4. *Expression of anger and cruelty* by children is another zone of moral uncertainty for parents of young children. Such parents, recalling, for example, the intense sibling hatred that they experienced, might let one of their children become abusive physically toward a sibling, being reluctant to move in with a prohibition on the cruel behaviour. Or again, such parents might become worried that their pre-school children seem to be obsessed with violent play, warlike toys, and violent television shows. Again, they do not see that it is properly in their adult domain to work for a warless world and to come to grips with their own hatred; they do not see that neither war nor peace between nations will be effected by young children, however necessary pacifism may be for adults. The evidence that war toys make or encourage haters is not firm by any means. We might do better to let children play at violence

than to require grown men to work at it, in deadly earnest.

5. *Obedience to authority* is a ghost haunting many of these parents. The brutally irrational authority of their own parents; the breaking of wills; the battling for autonomy—ah, parental memories are made of these, for 'such, such were the joys', and the parents wish passionately not to perpetrate these inhumanities anew in their own parenting of *their* offspring. Such parents might be prone to water down all of their values, and to propound even their absolutes in a highly tentative fashion, and to wind up wishing that they could find something that would be worth demanding their child's submission! From such moral ambiguity and indecisiveness some of these parents take flight into an authoritarian, insensitive, and nonempathic parenting to which their own forebears could not have held a candle. The end result of both extreme paths is an abdication of humanized parenting.

6. *Religious dogmatism* is what grandparents are accused of regularly, by parents in the groups here discussed. In our multi-group society there is wide choice among religious groups with which to affiliate. Moreover, there is also the option of pronouncing a plague upon all their houses of worship. These parents, even so, tend to vacillate and flounder with respect to choosing. They pronounce nondoctrinaire religions such as Unitarian-Quaker-ethical culture to be 'gutless and sexless', and they by-pass these in a search for doctrines, but of a more innocuous stripe than those held by their forebears. Searching for an appropriate god for their children is not uncommon among such parents. A suitable household god can be worthwhile, they seem to believe. Nor is it rare to find the parents becoming distressed when a childlike religion appeals to their children. They overlook the fact that even religious indoctrination is something that a child will often rebel against in time. If he thinks about religion at all, he will come to make modifications that are more relevant to his own experience. If the parents themselves have modified gravely the theological stands of *their own mothers*, why can the parents not face the fact that members of the next generation are capable of doing the same thing?

There are other dilemmas encountered when parents live out their parental lives so strongly influenced by their own parents, that is, so riddled by transference. And yet it cannot be otherwise, to some extent. For the baby family (family of origin) is our most thorough-going training school for parenthood. It is the most complete school that is available in our society.

How else save from our own parents, in our own childhood, can we learn to let parental behaviour unfold when we become adults? The various modes of counselling and psychotherapy of adults are of limited use when they are compared to the bountiful harvest from living in a family when we were young. So it is logical to expect that every young child is influenced heavily by both paternal and maternal grandparents since the grandparents' ideologies, feelings, and practices are exerted upon the images that the child's immediate parents carry around in their heads. Added to this is the deliberate, conscious effort of parents to outdo their own parents, to avoid (and compensate for) the blunders which they think their own parents made, and we can readily see that even in the conjugal family there are lines of influence, of enculturation, that reach across borders between the generations and give continuity as well as change to both healthy and pathological family patterns. Grim as it is, the children's children pay—very soon!

The following is a brief and sketchy description of some of the general attributes of healthy parents.

1. The wholesome parent identifies with the child positively. He has a deep-seated conviction that the child is basically a 'good egg' as is the parent, and that the child will grow up to be a wholesome human specimen as is the parent. This is more than a feeling of compassion that parent has for child. It is a feeling of acknowledging oneself and one's innermost nature in one's child.

2. The parent, with deliberate grace, sees himself or herself as comfortably in the role of educator, disciplinarian, or even of imposer of the grown-up's rational will and values. This security-giving role is not renounced, but it is claimed whenever good intuition dictates. In the author's clinical practice of child psychiatry there has been a succession of mothers who fear that they will murder their children. This is not a dispassionate or fleeting obsession. One of these mothers might complain, later rather than sooner, that her three- or four-year-old son is not only 'unmanageable' but also 'in danger of being killed'. With some encouragement the mother reveals her

secret, that she vacillates between phobic overconcern for her child and the wish to murder him. She recognizes that her overconcern is only a more respectable form of her wish to kill him. One might think that such a woman is a wretched bitch who requires to have her child snatched away from her. Not at all. Such a mother improves symptomatically, and her son loses incorrigibility apace, if the mother is encouraged to vent some spleen, to tell the child how to behave at times, and in short to get close enough to assert herself. Only when she learns that she has something which she may attempt to teach him can she cease in her desire to kill him. The fear of asserting rational authority can indeed paralyse a parent.

3. The parent is content to watch and wait concerning many things. He is not alarmed to find that his interests are antagonistic at times to those of his children, and he is pleased to settle for a less-than-ideal 'peaceful co-existence' on some issues. He shows a continuing faith in the raw human potential that will unfold, and for that reason he is satisfied to leave the child to an unbuffered experiencing of himself and of others.

4. Finally, he shows the capacity as a parent to stop and take the trouble to see things, at least occasionally, from the child's standpoint. The height of human imaginativeness resides in our empathy, in our capability for standing in another's shoes and seeing the world as if through another's eyes. Parents looking through children's eyes have no doubt about their love for their children.

These four parental characteristics, just alluded to in the foregoing, far from being lofty ideals, are descriptive of parental reality as it quite often exists: many productive and generative persons do not experience parenthood as arduous and highly troublesome, but as a time of fulfilment and of continuing growth.

As the children are being provided with security they are learning how to be both children and parents. And, as the parents are learning how to provide security to others rather than to consume it they are simultaneously re-experiencing their own childhood. It could be said that parents 'become as little children' during parenthood. In some happy instances, parents have an opportunity to redeem their own childhood as well as to replay it. In all of these ways, parenthood brings a new structuring of the psychic life of the parent. One's parenthood is a thoroughgoing turning point that shifts and restructures one's way of life. It is a new structuring but not all of its ingredients are newly encountered. Parenthood builds upon childhood antecedents.*

Let us look at the broad aspects of a mother in her relatedness to her infant. By empathy and identification the mother imagines herself into the baby's skin. The mother is herself developing in parallel with her baby's development.† When her suckling baby is at her breast the mother is engrossed in orality: she makes sucking motions and both her nipples and her lips become engorged and turgid. Who could doubt her involvement in the orality of her suckling infant? Likewise, her thoughts and symbols are altered in collaboration with her developing child. Her self-picture is changed. This is the most pervasive modification that occurs in human beings; for *with a change in self-image, we can add a cubit to our stature.*

During the child's learning to walk and to talk, to say 'No' to the mother, to join with the mother to form *a potting couple*, not only is the child swept up in the great rush of humanization that goes far beyond the pot, but the mother as well is given an opportunity to replay some of her own feelings associated with learning autonomy and individuation, and indeed with enjoyment of defecation and of ownership of one's own bowels. She knows (as baby knows) the shame, the rages, and the feelings of exultation upon discovering one's separate identity and unique will. Her joining lovingly with her baby in his acquisition of bowel patterns is not a harsh authoritarian and coercive stand. These patterns are not imposed upon the child, but they develop spontaneously within child and mother. Such toilet patterning is desired by the child, and is not inflicted upon him. It is, instead, a love-play, a love-feast, but in all respects it is a two-person transaction—a social behaviour. Indeed, the mother discerns that in her parenting she is unfolding herself.

Again, when the child is in nursery school—the pre-school era, as the educators call it in the United States—the parents re-

* For a synopsis of what follows see Paul L. Adams, 'Children of Change', *Young Children XX* (1965): 203–208.
† Therese Benedek, 'Parenthood as a Developmental Phase: a Contribution to the Libido Theory'. *Journal of the American Psychoanalytic Association 7* (1959): 389–417.

experience their own incestuous longings and have an opportunity to accomplish resolutions or acceptances that have never been possible theretofore. Parents flirt with their children in such a sexy way that parents appear to be striving to fulfil the Freudian prophecy that the Oedipus complex is a universal phenomenon. Even if children did not invent it, their parents would, when the children are so young, lustful, appealing and downright enticing. Many parents achieve some release from their own lifelong sexual inhibitions only upon parenting young children through the ages of four and five. Sexual freedom for children at this age accomplishes, as a worthwhile by-product, the sexual liberation of the mother and father.

One can ask if sexual freedom means license to be promiscuous throughout life. One might ask also if sexual free love precludes monogamy or even if it precludes the family as we know it. The answer is that freedom does not rule out prolonged commitment. It doesn't rule out a long-term relationship. One should add, however, that freedom is not consistent with maintaining relationships that have worn themselves out and become depleted of all real love and interest. The serial polygamy of frequently divorced movie stars has a much better standing among many psychiatrists and radicals than the old-fashioned monogamy of the more convention-ridden bourgeoisie. Time will tell which (if either) has the greater viability. The likelihood seems to be that neither will endure.

4. *Rights Concerning Maternity Hospital and Delivery*

An infant has a right to be born amidst surroundings where he and his parents are respected. These rights apply to what happens in the maternity hospital. Hospitals are often among the least functional of agencies in our mass society: they give out the message unmistakably that patients exist for hospitals, not that hospitals are made for patients. In other words dysfunctional bureaucracy has waxed, and any who complain are regarded as ill tempered—never as having justified complaints.* The institution that grew up to give service has determined not to be a service institution. Maternity hospitals do not escape from this development even though they are usually less dreary

---

* Erving Goffman, 'Cooling the Mark Out: Some Aspects of Adaptation to Failure'. *Psychiatry*, 15 (1952): 451–463.

and less lethal than other hospitals, at least in the United States.

When a young infant is about to be born he has the right to free hospitalization and delivery for the mother, and to have had the mother receive free prenatal care. In short, the community must show some signs of caring about the babies that are being born. Such a newborn has a right to home delivery if the mother wishes that, or to hospital delivery if the mother wishes that. The baby has a right to be born without the high risk, the 'higher reproductive casualty'* that befalls the poor infant in a class society. Poor babies run a higher risk of abortion, still-birth, prematurity and congenital defects. For a baby at least, it is clear that he does not have to be poor in order to be happy. Poverty enters the life cycle at every stage, and impresses its scourge. The neonatal period is accursed mostly for the poor.

If the baby is born in a hospital the right must be guaranteed for the father to be freely and fully in attendance during the labour and delivery. If he wants to be present he should be; and similarly he should be free, if he wishes, not to be present. Some 'emancipated' young wives have wanted the husband to see the 'suffering' and to be present for the second baby—and not for the first, because the mother herself was unable to imagine her first delivery. She wanted her husband there only as a device for rubbing it in that the delivery and labour were to be seen as agonizing and brutal experiences. Not for love is such a man invited in, and if he is wise he will decline that sort of invitation.

If the man wishes to be, and is allowed to be, present it can be a shared experience with the wife, and it can be a token of their relatedness in all things sexual and reproductive. In may be one aspect of that taking of total responsibility for the consequences of one's lust which we have alluded to earlier in this chapter.

The hospital should also protect the rights of the mother to be aware of her parturition. Again, it seems foolish to dogmatize in the matter of anaesthesia, although males have often enjoyed this foolish action. The fact that so many physicians have

---

* Benjamin Pasamanick and Hilda Knobloch, 'Complications of Pregnancy and Neuropsychiatric Disorder', *Journal of Obstetrics and Gynaecology of the British Empire 66* (1959): 753–755.

contradictory and mutually exclusive dogmas in the matter can be taken as suggestive of the impropriety of anything pontifical being uttered *on either side* of the argument. If a woman feels overwhelmed by the pain of childbirth—for whatever reasons— then and there one should provide some analgesia or anaesthesia. Cultism is wholly out of place. Those who withhold any and all anaesthesia flirt with sadism. Those who use it too much flirt with a mechanistic view of parturition. The net effect of the long and difficult history of anaesthesia is too humane for us to throw it out as an adjunct most welcome in certain deliveries. Pity the young woman who is under the care of a cultist when she is being delivered of her baby. Contrariwise, if the mother does not want to be sedated, or does not crave analgesia or anaesthesia, she should have her way. Childbirth is for mothers not doctors. Her way is more relevant than the doctor's ideas on the subject. Only a fanatic would prescribe anaesthesia in every case. On balance, there is something to be said in favour of keeping the anaesthesia mild, for the postpartum estrangement felt by deeply anaesthetized mothers is great. The belly is emptier but she feels no sense of unity with the now delivered baby. Whatever can be done to assist Nature in helping the mother-child bond to preserve its *symbiosis as it existed before delivery* would appear to be all to the good. If the mother is alert and aware enough so that she knows when the baby goes from inside the uterus to the outside, the mother feels less strange towards the little 'package' that the nurse (or sister) presents to her. Then the mother will be able to view her baby as having transferred compartments but she will see her baby as still responsive to any efforts that the mother can make in order to preserve the dependent relationship of the baby when he was inside her womb. If the mother has made preparations for a more 'natural childbirth' during the pregnancy she will, generally speaking, be less fearful. If she has trained for natural childbirth she can have an experience of labour, although wholly new and different, which will not be attended by so much fear, because of all the prior talk and exercises. Advance guidance has a 'desensitizing' effect. Most women come to their parturition with advance ideology anyway. Old wives' tales, old doctors' myths, and so on, constitute an important part of the woman's preparation for childbirth. Somebody has told her of it, and it is better if that informant can be someone with some experience and understanding.

As a part of the theme, that newborn living should approximate intrauterine existence, it is imperative that the hospital accede to the right of the mother and baby to 'rooming in'. If the mother can have the baby with her physically for twenty-four hours a day she will come more easily into self-awareness of herself as a mother.

From the baby's standpoint, wholesome feeding patterns and breathing patterns are established (if the infant is lucky) in the immediate postpartum. The symbiosis with the mother serves the baby more than the mother. Without some approximation to its intrauterine existence, the baby would die. The need for cuddling and closeness to the mother has been demonstrated over and over by the work of René Spitz and others. The baby thrives best when a loving mother enfolds a healthy baby with her warmth and love, and if the baby is lying crying in the new-born nursery there is no possibility of this approximation of foetal existence ever occurring.

While she is in the maternity hospital and as soon as she leaves, it would be helpful if the new mother had her own mother present in the household—merely to provide mothering, in a final grand infusion, to the young woman who has just had her baby. This means that the young man must coexist with his mother-in-law, and that all that he and his mate have done and said in opposition to the mother-in-law must be taken back in the service of a worthwhile cause: the cause of letting a young woman come to decent terms with her own mother. Some such sequence of events must transpire before a young woman will be able to supply mothering to her new baby. It is a truism of child psychiatry that a mother cannot provide the support her children require until she has come to know her positive feelings toward her own mother. Nature is not easily tricked out of such iron-clad patterns.

In the United States where technology is adopted at breath-taking speed, but where moral matters show great inflexibility, it is almost automatic that young boys are circumcised within a few days after birth. This is done as a matter of routine among Jews and non-Jews, all of them justifying the practice 'on hygienic grounds'. The majority of pediatricians known to the author advocate circumcision as a routine practice for 'health reasons'. A dorsal slit of the foreskin, if indicated to prevent phimosis, is less traumatic and less intrusive (if less cosmetic) than a circumcision. The number of circumcisions done is no testimonial to the values doctors place upon preventive medicine. The mother and father have rights here: the right to make the decision without having to knuckle under to the wishes of the physician.

Breast feeding is another area where the young family should have all the rights, and the physician should have very little to say. If a young mother wants to breast feed, she should be encouraged to do so; but nothing is to be gained by advocacy of breast feeding to the point that the woman who does not wish it feels guilty. The bulk of good judgement lies on the side of breast feeding, mainly because that is what the mammary apparatus is for. Ordinarily, a woman who is not a hysterical character will wish to have her baby suckling at her breast. She will enjoy the baby's taking pleasure from her body. If she likes her own body, accepts it, accepts bodily pleasure as a positive value, and wants to promote all the closeness that is possible between herself and her baby, she will probably choose to breast feed. Why not?

The same can be said with respect to supply-and-demand feeding of infants. Authoritarians have never been content to let disciplines wait until the child is ready for some shaping and direction at the hands of parents. Authoritarians have always decried the plenitude of nature itself, and have stressed the scarcity of materials that are needed to support life. Authoritarians know best how to scrimp and save, how to dole out meagre resources, and how to give exaggerated attention to the short supplies in which things that make for happiness are to be found in this world. A timetable is a way to mete out time and milk *even for newborn infants*, and this has been the imperative of the get-tough jocks all over the world in 'good' societies where Judaism and Christianity have flourished; not at all among the Navajo Indians of the South-west USA, however. The idea of feeding a hungry baby according to a schedule that is superimposed is a horrible notion that has great affinity for an economy of scarcity (not abundance) and for an economic system motivated by greed (not welfare). The values in which children are enveloped from their earliest moments are not foreign but are intimate, swaddling the child round with a world view that gets implanted with a fixity that resembles an organ transplant. Needless to say, the author of this chapter adheres to the idea of self-demand breast feeding initiated solely by the infant's own inner cravings and tensions. Early infancy is fortunate if it provides a happy time, taking nourishment and consolation from the mother's breast.

But breast feeding is also a matter of styles and fads, and some wholesome women will opt for bottle feeding. They have the right to do so. The evidence for the superiority of breasts over bottles is shaky and flimsy, and it is always men who are the most ardent advocates of breast feeding of babies! The very man who advocates a woman's freedom to have an abortion is occasionally in the ludicrous spot of *enforcing* breast feeding. Let freedom be, and let the woman be free. Some women have the notion that it will make their breasts sag; at least they can be assured that the most erect, and least pendulous, breasts are the breasts of older women who have suckled their babies at the breast. But a mother's love does not flow out exclusively with her milk supply, and the basic lessons of trusting dependency can be learned along with bottle feeding—not just with breast feeding.

This might be a good point to come in with the idea that the learning of trusting dependency is both a simple lesson *and* a more complex one than many parents who use mechanistic psychologies like to recognize. I do believe that parents use 'mechanistic psychologies' without even knowing them, at times. An indication of such mechanism is to be seen in the view that some parents have that the most important thing about infant feeding is to supply the caloric needs for the baby's maintenance and growth as an organism (or a machine). With such a view they can excuse inhumane treatment that a cow or dog would never inflict upon her offspring. This view would make it all right for the mother to schedule the feeding of the infant during its first year of life, to let a hungry or wet baby 'cry it out'—good for its lungs, you know—and to prop up a bottle for the baby to draw in its calories from—hence obviating all cuddling and undoing the feeding as an interpersonal transaction. A baby left to cry or viewed in machine-like terms will be the least likely baby to learn the trustworthiness of parents, that parents can be depended upon to provide security and pleasure.

A most important and instructive symbiosis is established between mother and infant in the early postpartum. That symbiosis teaches us that we are made to depend on one another, and best of all that we *can* depend on another with confidence, and that we can get pleasure out of the body of another. To facilitate the learning of such essentials a society should direct all of its prime resources.

5. *Rights of Infants in Society*

AN infant has a right to maternal care, but our society under-writes maternal deprivation. Our society does not provide the services and security that young infants deserve. If we had a decent society the first year of life would be an extremely different epoch for most infants.

An attempt will be made to sketch out some of the features of a society that is detrimental to young children, and to show the necessity for revolutionary and radical change in the goals and means of current society. Such social programmes are usually discussed by psychiatrists in Britain and the United States as if they were 'social psychiatry' or 'preventive psychiatry'. Psychiatrists are reluctant revolutionaries. Under the protective covering of preventive or social psychiatry a little reform or revolution can be advocated. Nonetheless, the present writer is of the opinion that one's social responsibility as a human being, as a member of mankind, provides sufficient protection and justification.

Since 1909, in the United States, there have been White House Conferences, held once in each decade, for consideration of the rights of infants and children. These have given a forum for some expression of what kind of society is required for securing certain children's rights. However, the findings and conclusions of these conferences have typically been watered down in all of their social criticism—they are Presidential conferences, after all. The net effect has been to give us six decades of very little movement. Some of the same commentary could be made concerning the royal and governmental commissions that the British indulge in, for they aim not to unseat established power relations in Britain. During 1969 the US Joint Commission on the Mental Health of Children took steps towards an incisive appraisal of how North American society is, by and large, *a society against children*. As goes the US, so goes the western world. The Joint Commission report proposed as a corrective step that local groups be set up throughout the United States that will serve in each geographic area as Children's Advocate. This orientation towards child welfare, participated in by local people across the continent, could have some remarkable influences on North American life. The fate of the Joint Commission's report is undetermined, and how much of it will get implemented through the US Congress is uncertain. The prognosis is gloomy, to say the least, for either legislative reform or non-electoral change in the USA.

As people we in Britain and in the United States are reluctant to rebuild societies for children. We are only an uncertain distance away from our German friends who, especially doctors in pediatrics and psychiatry having adopted the viewpoint of Nazi 'law and order', wanted to protect their society from undesirable children. In protecting society they subjected German and other children to 'euthanasia' and having decided to protect society permanently they 'studied' the children whom they killed. They performed torture experiments under the most carefully controlled conditions. A sadism that is scientific and antiseptic can efficiently protect rotten régimes from wild and terrifying youth—we all know that. We are not too far away from the Nazis when we club the youths of Chicago and Paris, and erect iron gates at the London School of Economics. Do we want it? It is on our values that we must decide. Which side are we on? What are the impulses within us that we are to honour and cultivate? Shall it be the impulse to preserve established society and bring youths into line? Or, instead, shall it be to side with the youths and bring the society into line? We must choose our comrades, those to whom our affiliation is deep and loving.

If the choice were made to side with infants, and with the people who care for them best, there are some definite steps that could be taken to restructure society so that young infants would benefit. Let us not psychologize here, for that would be to blind our eyes. Instead let us erect our child psychology upon a prior view of society. Paramount among these steps to restructure society for children would be to end war as an institution; then to eliminate poverty; then racism; and finally to put an end to the meaninglessness of living in a bureaucratized society. These are not easy steps at best but not one will be taken *until we wish to take it.*

The militarization and garrisonizing of our everyday lives is pathogenic for young people. When conscription is an established practice, young males—and in a nation such as Israel young females as well—grow up expecting to commit murder at the State's bidding. In the United States the State-supported and privately run schools are infused with cold war ideology, with the nonsensical race to the moon and to bigger, ever more vicious and more interception-proof weapons. What a way for a nation to live! Conscription of sexually active prospective parents is demoralizing by interfering with more positive life-planning. The impersonality of war is debasing to all who partake of it. The exaltation of the national State itself breeds irrationality and idolatry into young people who are at the child-bearing age.

It seems quite modest to propose that the abolition of all military conscription is needed, and that a world police force, if any, should be voluntary entirely. In the United States it is sensible to urge that all industrial plants and companies that benefit financially from any war be nationalized, and that profit-making be outlawed during wartime. Worldwide, there is a need for reduction of armed forces, and of arms; and for abolition of nuclear bombs and of the testing of nuclear devices.

The goal is to demolish the institution of war. To do this, we must first concede: *War can be ended.* Slavery was widely practiced and revered but it has been extirpated almost wholly; therefore, war can be ended. Expansive modern States that allocate ever greater resources toward international conflict will never provide for the health and welfare of their able-bodied citizens, much less their infants and nursing mothers.

After war, poverty must be eradicated in a radical overthrow of the poverty-producing economic system. From a humane standpoint we should be opposed to poverty if only because we see, with George Bernard Shaw, that poverty makes people mean—overly-concerned with material things in such a way that only lifelong affluence can prevent it. Poverty serves too as a constant reminder that one is disvalued, 'played cheap'. This is the breeding ground for violence in contemporary society.

In the United States of America there are 4.5 million people who receive 'public assistance', that is, relief because of their extreme financial deprivation. This group in particular is worthy of radical attention. There are at least another 15 million persons in the US who are below the poverty level. It is so serious that, as has been shown, a separate nation composed of the poor in the USA would rank as fifteenth among the nations of the world in population size! And the poor get babies! As of this writing, little more than public relations, window dressing, and talk have emerged as the 'War Against Poverty'. It sold out to the local power cliques across the United States and the poor were squeezed out. What are needed are neighbourhood-based trials, in great diversity, to alleviate poverty. In these experiments impoverished neighbours should have the major responsibility for bringing help to their impoverished neighbours. We need a serious try at local option in ending poverty. We need to have decentralized authority to care for mothers and infants, not an impersonal bureaucratic superstructure. Some specific things that could be done in the United States to end poverty and to implement a service ethic instead of a private profit ethic include:

1. An inheritance tax that makes it impossible to pass along great fortunes.

2. Higher income tax beginning with family incomes above $5,000 per person per year.

3. Guaranteed annual income set at a level above impoverishment.

4. Direct family subsidies or allowances based on each child born (a giant step in the war against maternal deprivation).

5. Elimination of means tests and of eligibility 'investigation' of people getting public assistance (instead, spot-checks and affidavits as with Internal Revenue Service).

6. Liberalized abortion.

7. Free contraception.

8. Uniform divorce and adoption laws and procedures across the US.

9. Uniform standards for welfare programmes.

10. Uniform neighbourhood health clinics financed by a public health service giving antepartum care, visiting nursing for postpartum care, especially for teenage mothers, and well child care, with counselling casework and educational (re child-rearing) services offered.

11. Free homemaker service for families in crises.

12. Counselling to parents contemplating divorce.

13. Free day care (by women who hold and cuddle the pre-school children of working mothers).

14. Specially programmed social services for families without fathers, or with incompetent fathers: counselling and vocational rehabilitation.

15. A proliferation, for school-aged youths, of after-school day care, special-education facilities and resources, and recreational facilities.

16. The whole educational establishment should be encouraged to engage in wider experimentation (in neighbourhood schools that are run by impoverished adults not by remote, well-to-do Boards of Education).*

17. Expansion of direct subsidies to schools that educate or 'train' aspirants to the helping professions—incentives for poor students will do much to 'recruit manpower' for all professional fields serving the poor: doctors, nurses, social workers, psychologists, teachers. The greatest payoff per dollar invested in training for the group of mental health professionals seems undoubtedly to be the training given to *the social work student*; hence a doubling of high-standard social work schools seems appropriate as a sound investment in a society that truly cares for children. Medical education is sorely in need of an infusion of both money and social responsibility: high-standard health care is a right in a civilized society and doctors must work more arduously amongst the poor or erstwhile poor.

18. Implementation of a war against ignorance, illiteracy and subliteracy through expansions in adult education and in special programmes for youths with academic handicaps.

At the same time that poverty must be eradicated, there must be an end to racism; to the belief that physical and racial features are the basis for legitimate subjugation of one group by

* See George Denison, *The Lives of Children*.

another. New York and London vie for their insults against black people on lavatory walls. In the United States one out of every three young adult Negroes is hopelessly unemployed and thereby the war on poverty is united with the war on racism. In Britain recent evidence shows that Negro school-leavers, the British-born children of immigrants, are being refused jobs commensurate with their capabilities and must either work in menial jobs or else remain unemployed. A society which creates a group of second-class children creates a breeding ground for apathy and withdrawal, delinquency and violence. This has been seen only too clearly in the USA, where the appalling effects of both poverty and racism on children have been vividly described at first hand in Lisa Aversa Richette's book, *The Throwaway Children*.

To borrow still more of the militarist's phraseology, we could refer to a fourth war that must be fought and won if we are to have a world that is suitable for the growth and development of human beings: it is the war against normlessness. How can human beings emerge in a society that has such rampant nihilism as does ours? where all values are discredited and unmasked? where the order of the day is opportunism, expediency, action rooted in no ethical judgement? where people grow up immersed in anomie, aloofness, relativity, absurdity, indefiniteness, alienation and non-participation? What we have in the United States is not merely a cultural pluralism that enlarges the areas of freedom and choice; what we have instead is a rather widespread consensus that it is only proper for all of us to believe in very little and for each to commit himself to almost nothing.

It is difficult to envision a campaign that would successfully implant values in an estranged and relativistic people. But alienation vanishes not by direct programmes against it; it goes away as real values are adopted and enacted, and as economic and social realities change. If we truly want a society fit for children—that fits children, and does not require children to do all the adapting and fitting into society—we will fight against war, poverty, maternal deprivation, ignorance and racism.

A decent society, then, is very different from our society. The society is the context in which children grow, and the place to start out with any consideration of the rights of infants in families. If we start out with maternal deprivation as if it were strictly 'intrapsychic' or 'psychopathology' we would be hard put to deliver ourselves from the personal system to move over into the social system as a frame of reference. To be born into a community that cares is a treat delighting only a small minority of earth's people today; that is what we are set up to change radically.

6. *Rights of Infants in the Family*

IF during infancy there is a plenitude of maternal care—made possible by living in a class or a community where the luxury of loving kindness is permissible—there are some excellent long range effects in individual personality.* The unthwarted infant is an infant, quite simply, who grows up caring for others just because they have love for *him*. He is trusting, confident, and finds pleasure in bodily contacts. These are valuable results of good infant care.

What of the individual who is thwarted in infancy, neglected (literally, not picked up) and deprived of optimal mothering? Such a person is a candidate for misanthropy, for pessimism, and for the sociopathic disturbances that we see in the neurotic delinquents and criminals of the person's later childhood and adulthood.

Children should not be placed in institutions when they are in the first year of life. Wherever possible they should have the warmth of personal attention that is more easily obtainable in a home. That is to say, foster homes are to be desired as superior to orphanages or foundling homes. Today, the mother who works is no longer exclusively a member of the working class or lower class, but may come from higher classes. Whenever a mother does have an option about going back to work following the delivery, she would do best to delay her return to work until the child is almost one year old. From four to 10 months of age the baby undergoes the most crucial period in its development. Those months are nearly what ethologists call a 'critical period' during which deprivation of mothering wrests the greatest toll from the developing personality. Obviously, most

---

* What follows is a very sketchy running over of the varied epochs or eras of psychosocial development in children. For a fuller and better treatment, see Erik Homburger Erikson, 'Growth and Crises of the Healthy Personality'. *Psychological Issues 1* (1969), no. 1. New York, International Universities Press.

women are not free to stay out of work, and they must inflict deprivation upon their infant children. Our society does, as was stated earlier, underwrite and encourage maternal deprivation. This is the exact juncture at which social restructuring becomes an essential feature of childrearing.

By the time the infant reaches the second year of life he is ready to experience a great leap forward in socialization. Socialization in the sense of enculturation, learning the culture patterns, is what rushes ahead in the second year of infant life. This era is the prime one for the crushing of wildness and independency as recommended by that early British expert on childrearing, Bernard Mandeville. Punishment by deprivation of rewards, by restriction of locomotion, by imposing physical pain and shock, and by the moral tyranny of shaming, bullying, withdrawing love—i.e., the whole ghastly repertoire of child subjugation—really 'takes' during this second year of life. In many ways it is the *anal stage*, the stage for efficient learning of the sadism and cruelty which are so much a part of human cultures. Again, we must recall that childhood is an animal or biologic phase but that it is culturally defined.

During his second year some developmental landmarks are walking, talking—especially the capacity to say 'No' to mother —and learning the importance of being on one's own. The delights of autonomy are sweet. Bowel and bladder control are perhaps only limited segments of the overall progression towards independence or autonomy. Indeed, in permissive families the urethral sphincter may not be 'owned' by the child until he is up close to the end of this third year of life. Then, for parents who hesitate to teach anything to their children, or who have strong unconscious wishes to prolong the infantile dependency of their children, there may be a persistent bedwetting beyond four years of age. In these cases, the child psychiatrist finds character problems underlying the behaviour, more of parents than of child.

Especially through speech, the fullness of humanity begins to emerge. It is odd that few Americans are inclined to make an issue out of speech as they eagerly do with toilet disciplines. Since they have tongues and teeth, we freely encourage children to talk; we even help them; and we do not tyrannize over them if they individualize their rate of progress—how lucky infants would be if we had the same benign and encouraging interest in their walking and toileting and all other skills that are being acquired during the second year of life. It may be our attitudes, again, that make this such an *anal* phase. But to turn from irony to some practical consideration of what sensible parents can do with their children in this anal stage: the parents can watch and wait, ready to offer help and to assert their own rational authority only when what is endangered is the child's future, but not the parents' respectability. By careful watchdog activities an alertly anal and obsessive mother can accomplish miracles of toileting efficiency with a child below one year of age, but more easily during the second year of the child's life. She can have a child dry and clean as a testimonial to her own vigilance and to her own anality. A woman who thinks of motherhood as a competition to get her child 'trained' is losing out on many of the delights that would be available otherwise. What should she do? Towards the end of the second year, when some speech has been established and the capacity for bowel and bladder control exists in the neuromuscular apparatus of the child, is early enough to start some facilitation or encouragement of toilet training: buying a potty, etc. If the mother and father can think of it as a time for the child to establish his own inner disciplines, to make growth strides, to come into ownership and control of his own bodily functions, and in short to *train himself* for a new skill, then the proper atmosphere is set up for the child and the parents.

The parental patience of this second year of watchful waiting, but mostly waiting, sometimes requires extension throughout the third year of the child's life; and if bowel and bladder accidents occur the parents do not become vicious and punitive towards the derelict child. By four years old he will come to cleanliness; but, if he does not learn by the age of four, professional help should be sought in the fifth year of the child's life (in the USA the fifth year is the year of nursery school preparatory to kindergarten).

It is useful to think of the second and third years of life as an epoch during which the infant is 'separating and individuating'.* We should not wish to describe the process in overly

* This is a theme that has been discussed at length by Otto Rank, and by Margaret Mahler and others.

technical terms but should make it clear that at this age the infant has a right to individuate, to step out of the symbiotic tie to the mother, to stand on his own two feet, and to know all the delights of being unique and capable of going in his own course. This stage is a very easy sequel to a satisfying oral stage—the first year of life when the joys of dependency and pleasure out of another's body was the lesson to be experienced by the lucky infant.

If the anal stage infant (second year of life) is unlucky and deprived of the ecstasy of the anal stage, of developing his own patterns and his own style, and of the pleasures of separation, he can suffer for an entire lifetime. In a child psychiatry clinic, the major problems that appear are those experienced by children of the poor and of neurotic bourgeois parents. Understandably, the poor mother has a chip on her shoulder and becomes a harsh disciplinarian. Equally understandably, the neurotic middle-class mother does the same. For some mothers it is a trauma to go from giving and suckling into a stage where things are to be explicitly taught and fought out with a child. At this stage of infant development the father too is able to partake of the child's growth in autonomy, and the mother (if she is a sound person) will practically live out a second anal stage. She will re-experience a preoccupation with faeces, with toileting, with rages, with the desire to be left alone, and so on.

This is a time when infants appear to have a well-developed and uninhibited sense of smell. They are at the right height for smelling some of the more odoriferous parts of grown-ups who are not always perfectly douched, cleaned, and deodorized. Later on, however, the children will stop smelling under adult prohibitions but at two years old the olfactory sense has its heyday. This olfaction is one of the joys of the anal stage. The child is not invulnerable at this age, however, for this is the age at which self-esteem can be crushed into a sense of shame, of humiliation. The child has some grandiose strivings and he or she can be ridiculed in a way that mercilessly deflates him. He may break on the rocks of trying, against his parents' wills, to do his own thing, to have his own feelings, and to have his self-worth validated by others in the household. Parents, brothers and sisters and members of the extended family all participate in this growing sense of worth.

The problem of sibling relations is a basic issue deserving some consideration at this point. Alfred Adler had the genius to stress the importance of one's brothers and sisters, in the construction of one's reality world as well as in the formation of one's concept of self. The family is not only our school for parenthood, and for relations between generations, but also a proving ground for peer relations. It is a school for brotherhood, for compeer society, and for whatever we will learn about sharing and communing with age mates.

The infant does not, of course, come into the two-person family as we have been depicting it and create afresh the triad of relatedness that is so often sung about as The Family. There are a lot of second, third, and fourth children being born into the sibling group, if we take families around the world into our purview. If we included working-class or rural families, we know that there are even larger possibilities (as with the writer's own seven older siblings).

This anal stage is not the age of guilt. It is the age for shame. A rather global self-concept is laid down by the end of this era. Assuredly, an awareness of one's gender is laid down, and in such a fashion that it is almost unchangeable subsequently. We know this from study of cases where the gender was misidentified in early infancy. One's love of his own genitalia reaches fruition in the new phase of child development; but some of the new experiences of body pleasure are added, in this stage, to those from the first year of life. A child at this age has a right to be himself, to be a child consuming security from adults but making strides towards autonomous functioning. An impoverished mother who lives without a male and who comes home from work irritable and tired has a tough time providing what the child needs at this age. It is small wonder that adults prefer passive infants. Likewise, it is no wonder that an assertive, aggressive, high-strung infant is nearly always resented. Any parent would like to 'send back' the hyperactive infant. So much more is the poor or working-class mother entitled to her negative sentiments. How much easier her life would be, in essence, if the infant would never grow up, and would always remain passive and symbiotic.

Child psychiatry itself is not free of the 'false consciousness' that accompanies its rootedness not in the lower classes but in the upper middle class. Yet the overall impact of child psychiatry's ideology is to regard children as worthwhile, as having rights, and as deserving of the care of adults in families and in communities. That stand might not originate in the lower classes but it is not uncongenial to lower-class groups, at least in the United States. Increasingly, child psychiatric services have been made available to the poor and to the working class in the United States. And the consumers have been receptive of the help offered them. To the extent that 'permissiveness' in childrearing is part of the unified package, we can probably expect more and not less free choice by children as child psychiatry waxes. Hence, in the eyes of authoritarians, family life and childrearing will get worse, not better. It is an attitude o acceptance of anal-stage and Oedipal-stage children that tears authoritarians to pieces. Mandeville should be spinning in his grave.

Now to some things that are psychiatrically and humanistically sound about children 'on the make'—or, in psychoanalytic terms, Oedipal. The most unhealthy lessons to be learned (and hung up on) in this era—from three to five years—have to do with guilt that comes when one initiates anything. The healthiest lesson is the lesson that one can be on the make, enterprising, trying to stir up things all around one, fully engaging in sexual play, and in full enjoyment of one's sexual prowess, and that there are no disastrous consequences.

For a child to resolve the dilemmas of this age without fears of annihilation (by adults) or mutilation (the Freudian castration complex) is unusual and unusually salutary. He will not do it if the parents want to crush all his sexual and expansive impulses and make the child into a conventional person, a conformist. *When parents are determined to crush the child's will they contribute to the child's formation of neurosis.* That is an assertion to which many threads of investigation give support. Even if the Oedipus complex is not universal, the confrontation of child with a ruthless and inconsiderate authority does seem, universally, to lead to mental illness. If not illness, then to conformity in robot fashion. This has been the lifelong contention of Erich Fromm, and it is with a sound basis. The kernel of neurosis was thought by Freud to be the Oedipal conflict; by Reich to be some kind of disturbance of the libido on a still more physical basis (actually, based in the metaphors of rational mechanics, a branch of physics); by Adler to be more *social* than either Freud or Reich; and finally by Horney and Fromm to be altogether social: a resultant of the child's encounter with 'irrational authority'. Irrational authority is authority that has no genuine human warrant, and no justification based upon either love or reason. A prime example of irrational authority is the parental statement, 'I require you to do it because I am your parent. I say that you must do it. I do not have to give reasons. I can *make* you do it, and I will have you do it. Do it because I say so, etc.' Out of experiences such as these comes neurosis. It is only to the extent that Oedipal conflicts relate to irrational authority that neurosis is born; it is only to the extent that anal stage difficulties relate to irrational authority that neurosis is born. To knuckle under and be subdued by a stronger physical force is what lays the groundwork for neurosis in childhood. Regrettable as it sometimes is, our ways of childrearing have consequences. We have to be accountable for the choices we make in living with our children.

7. *The Rights of School-aged Children*

FOLLOWING his first year of life when he learned to trust, the second and third years when he learned that he can use his own resources, and the fourth to sixth years when he learned that he can elicit responses from others, the child in our society next goes to school. The child mentally or spiritually is ready to learn, to be industrious, to set up projects that are challenging and that he sees through to successful conclusion. We ordinarily think that this bespeaks a 'readiness for going to school', and wherever compulsory education is enforced, going to school is like second nature. But the fact is that school is not the unique setting in which children can be educated. In the United States, where elementary school is a sacred cow of sorts, voices are increasingly raised to proclaim society's job to be one of providing teachers or tuitional resources to young children, *but not requiring that they go to school*. The effect of this is to question the wisdom and benefits of compulsory education.* Books, parks,

* See the chapter by Nan Berger in this book, and the book by George B. Leonard, *Education and Ecstasy.* New York, Delacorte Press, 1968. London, J. Murray 1970.

libraries, teaching machines, and neighbourhood playgrounds in abundance could very easily supplant the routinized and regimented system that presently constitutes elementary school in both Britain and the United States.

Elementary schools were first made compulsory in order to get children off the streets and out of delinquent acts, and they are run all too often in both countries as if they were reformatories. Parents like their children to be in school where they will be policed and disciplined. And indeed they are ruled and regulated until all creativity is wrung out of them. A neglected right of the school-age child, therefore, is to be provided with the tools needed for true learning. Again, his community must care about him. The child has a right to competent teachers. He has a right to schools that are not so formal and detached from the neighbourhood in which he lives. He has a right to more than schooling to choose from—in other words, to attend no school if he has alternative educational modes available for him. He has the right to stay clear of boarding schools and to remain—except in most exceptional situations—at home with his parents during his elementary school years. Affluent but negligent parents often elect to send their children to boarding schools, inasmuch as the free, State-supported school does not take their child away for long enough periods of time. Therefore, they hire a remotely located group of adults to function as round-the-clock baby sitters and policemen or as mercenaries who stand in for parents. Naturally, they get rid of their children with beautiful rationalizations as to how academically superb this or that 'Public school' or boarding school has been found to be. A child has a right to live with his parents until he is old enough to move out to an independent status.

A child of school age (six to twelve years) has the right to learn all secrets, with no holds barred. This includes a right to sexual knowledge and also, in our day and age, a right to knowledge of violence and of the highly important role it plays in human affairs. In her book, *Teacher*, Sylvia Ashton-Warner describes how unintrusive, how natural and genuine, the educative process can be when a teacher has come to grips with her own sexual lust and violence, and when she has accepted the fact that sexual and aggressive topics are also important vehicles for a child's learning and teaching, in many areas, including reading and writing and arithmetic. When teaching and learning are consonant with the child's biologic status and the state of his developing values and interests, there is no problem of 'motivation to learn' because the child has the motivation already. What is lacking is only an accessible teacher who knows more than the child about the things the child wants to know; the child has a right to such a teacher. And, of course, a parent can be such a teacher. The child has a right to learn, without outside pressures, only under pressures from his own encounter with the world. Problem-centred learning is what counts. For, without a problem, without some curiosity, some stimulus, some frustration and puzzlement, the child would neither think nor learn.

School does have much psychic importance to the average child: it is his first opportunity to be away from the nest for rather lengthy periods of time, among people who are not relatives. The child of this age—six to twelve years—has a right to friends, to rich peer interactions, to loving relations with someone highly similar to him or her but not within the family. Such love from a non-relative gives tremendous valida-tion of one's worth as a human being. The child of elementary school age was regarded by early psychoanalysts as in latency. Child psychiatrists are doubtful that even normal children live out a time when sex and aggression are all so subdued and muted. Instead, there is a great amount of humanity transpiring during the so-called latency—erotic and turbulent humanity. Children, we can see, consequently, can enter their puberty and adolescence without sexual *Sturm und Drang*. Sexual activity is not the brand new phenomenon of adolescence that everyone knew about in a more Victorian age. It is only a very unlucky child who enters puberty as ignorant (so-called innocent) and as sexually inept as the prudish ideology would require. If a child has not had a good elementary school epoch, that is, if he has not learned the joys of orderly productive work, and of indus-triousness, then he will be smitten by inferiority feelings, and by the ignorance and fear of learning that makes for actual inferiority.

In summing up, it is obvious that children do have basic rights in their infancy and so-called latency. These rights are rather universally denied them by contemporary society. Fortunate children grow from total dependency into greater autonomy, but always remain dependent because they are human. Then the healthy child learns how to instigate and initiate and to crave body gratifications without the pain of guilt and self-destruction; and he learns how to work with enjoyment and with learning. He is living out a life with fullness, with both sex and anger, love and hate, and with self-acceptance validated by others. He comes to like himself, to love his friends, and be ready for the fuller developments that come with love relations that can be procreative in a life of meaning in which one lives with and for others. In short he grows up—equipped for parenthood.

Every child has a right to a healthy childhood.

The dimensions of healthy childhood are sometimes things that can be seen from the outside, and sometimes they are inward and subjective. Among the more objective dimensions of healthy childhood are these two things which psychiatrists and psychologists can see and measure:

1. True competence becoming established progressively, with validation by adults and compeers. He gets better at many more things, and both he and the others know he is getting more competent.

2. Domestic or custodial stability resting with adults who provide protection and parenting, and toward whom the child can be oriented with trusting love. He has a stable household where trustworthy adults love him.

Not entirely objective, yet not totally subjective, are the following dimensions to which every child is entitled:

1. Growing, learning and incorporation of viable values—developing a conscience in a milieu where nihilism and absurdity are minimal. He lives in a meaningful world. He lives by values. He has a moral sense.

2. Opportunity for unfolding of loving relations with other people ranging from mother to broader kinship to same-sex friends to heterosexual mates, and ultimately, in adulthood, to one's offspring and on to all children and all Mankind. The love objects grow from those whose breasts he suckles to all people, ultimately.

Finally, there are some dimensions of healthy childhood,

dimensions that every child has right to, which are even more subjective and felt from the inside of the growing animal and person:

1.   Favourable picture of self, enjoyment of bodily pleasure (or affects, or id-resources)—that is, an inner awareness of positive self-esteem.

2.   A sense of some unsocialized uniqueness: creativity, autonomy, spontaneity, unprogrammed ecstasy—all free from adult intrusion. Included here is the right to play, to engage in non-instrumental behaviour, to do 'useless' things for the sheer fun of it.

If these are the dimensions of health in childhood, and if these are rights to which all children are entitled, and if our society deprives children of these rights, what then? We live under the necessity to restructure a society *whenever and because* it breeds alienation, inferiority feelings, and true incompetency, according to economic class. A reconstituted society is paramount among the rights of children.

Chapter 3

The Rights of Adolescents

by Robert Ollendorff, M.D.

1. *Some Historical Notes on Adolescents*

To decide what the rights of adolescents are, or what the young person's role in society and in the family should be, and to understand the different forces which combine to act upon the adolescent, some the forces of growth, others more hostile forces, it will be well to start with a review, at least a superficial one, of the history of the adolescent.

To begin writing about a subject by delving into its historical progress may seem trite, and in some ways follows the Marxist cart-horse. Nevertheless, it must be possible to deduce a living principle, a 'truth' underlying the history of human societies, because otherwise the human race would have failed to survive at a very early stage. The violence of recorded history, the destructiveness of the society of our own century—which devotes enormous ingenuity, wealth, manpower and organization to causing and counteracting one great destructive eruption after another, which carries millions of people into sudden death by remote control—must be seen as an indication that the same unrealistic schizophrenic killing, the extermination on a genocidal scale, would have destroyed society in its tender, earliest, prehistoric groupings if this type of aggression had not been curbed.

One must accept that the young human being has always been biologically ready, in fact optimally equipped, to mate between the ages of thirteen and sixteen. And yet an adolescent cannot learn to be a lover in our society. Even today, when it is said that a sexual revolution has happened, and the adolescent is allowed to masturbate, although even that is only just tolerated, she or he must not love.

Sex is a lonely genital kick—a nostalgia. It is there but it is surrounded as ever—as it was especially in the paralysing and choking moralism and respectability of the Victorian age—by a conspiracy of silence. It has never been in the foreground of people's minds to train the child, the youngster, to become a lover, to make this an accepted faculty of learning, to develop and clarify and focus without prudery on this deepest, most natural instrument of happiness.

Generation after generation of this sad society has misread the intrinsic truth of the only way to acquire the discipline of living: by living together with one beloved: that love, in its totality, which includes sexual love, is a great teacher of adjustment on the basis of interaction and co-ordination of two people, thus preparing them to fit, without aggression and destructive urges, into a community as a whole.

From the psychopathology of destruction in the wake of sex repression in our own society, we can deduce that in primitive prehistoric societies sexual freedom must have been present to allow sheer survival. The hazards of finding food, fighting natural catastrophes and overcoming illness were in themselves huge.

Thirty years ago, living most of the time in inaccessible tribal areas of East Africa, I was still able to discern some of these direct earth-bound living patterns.

The most revealing of my observations was the total acceptance and integration of sexuality in the infant, found in what is now called 'the extended family'. This is still a pattern in tribal East Africa and must have been a reality over many thousands of years in the early days of human prehistoric existence.

It is basically a matriarchal structure in which the dominating father is absent. Mother and infant are deeply and sexually conjoined in loving feeding activity—but even this can be, and still is, delegated to the breast of any female willing to suckle, fondle, caress and carry the infant. Usually the most powerful male image in the infant's life is the mother's brother or a male somehow able to adopt the father stance without injury to the often very complicated incest taboos.

The most essential processes by which a child is continuously kept in bondage to his mother and father were absent in the broad upbringing of the matriarchal pattern. Again we have to grope for a very slender historical deduction, but the destruction of surviving examples of such societies, which existed on the South Sea Islands and were described by Malinowski, commenced only with the military occupation of World War II. The Central-Indian society of the Muria, as described by Verier Elwin, became immediately corrupted on contact with aggressive modern western civilizations. Photographs of a Ghotul boy of the Muria—free, easy, graceful—and a State school boy of the same tribe, rigidly holding himself in with a mask-like face with life bleached out by fear, speak volumes and clearly illustrate these processes.

With the dawn of history, several parallel developments more and more disenfranchized the adolescent. Let us reconstruct how it happened.

We shall observe two contrasting forms of social organization, each serving a different style of existence. The first pattern would have been found among the dwellers in fertile valleys, living in closed settlements, in forest clearings or on islands comparatively well protected from wild animals and marauders, and regularly rewarded for communal labour by harvesting some of the natural crops. Under the heading of crops would commonly come fishing, hunting, gathering of fruit and sowing of the forerunner types of edible vegetables, grasses and wheats.

Property would not be a prominent feature of the settlement. Communal activities would be the centre of existence and, in the absence of the nuclear family, the child-bearing woman would be the focal centre of private life.

Sexuality would have been unknown as a preoccupation, but would have been an integrated element of the person from infancy onward. Sexual activity, varying in nature with the child's age, would have been considered normal. There would have been no taboo on sex-play in infancy, pre-adolescence and adolescence. There would presumably be a promiscuous learning stage when, as in young adulthood and later life, sexual activity would have been acceptable as a private matter between two people. After this early phase there would probably be very little promiscuity.

It had to be more or less like this, because the hazards of life and the physical demands—the gathering of food, the protection against the weather, the building of shelter—in all, the sheer strain of survival, must have made sexual intercourse a happy but rare event. Even today the East African tribal farmers who live in fertile valleys must protect their crops day and night between sowing and harvest from deer, buffalo, hippopotami and elephants.

The remnants of this archaic way of life are still discernible. The children's houses in which both girls and boys live together such as the Bukamatula of the Trobriand Islanders, the Ghotul of the Muria, mentioned on page 93, and the Manyatta of the Masai, show that the child at the age of five or six or earlier was moved from even the extended family and sent to live with his peers. This meant that there was total freedom sexually and socially, and that education and the learning of etiquette took place in the interaction of a child with his equals and not, as in other societies, by authoritarian adults enforcing patterns of life on the child and the adolescent by command.

The second pattern of social organization was probably evolved by nomadic herdsmen. Here rigorous aggression, a sense of property and possession, and the ruthless destruction of anything which endangered their herds or their pastures were the basic formulae of survival.

They most likely learned to enlarge their herds by theft or by enslaving other tribal units. They had to be aggressive to defend themselves against others on similar missions and, of course, against wild animals.

In the wanderings of the nomads our two patterns must have clashed and no doubt the matriarchal pattern was the loser. In fact, one would think that slavery was part of the way in which the tribal nomadic people thrived and enforced their rule over rich valley populations.

The sexual pattern of such a society would develop a totally different perspective. The child would be over-protected and over-sheltered by the mother and kept under the mother for a lengthy time. This dependency would suddenly be broken and the male child would then be disciplined as an aggressive soldier and the virtues of aggression and killing would be part of his training. As a male child he would become the herdsman, the hunter, the warrior, and the raider; his role in society would be very much inflated while the role of the female would be deflated until finally we reach the stage where the male child and the male take on a god-like status. Consider the Jewish religion in which every young male is a rabbi, whereas a female has no legal rights at all. In fact, the acceptance of women's rights in all fields of life in any nation or race is a very slow process which has by no means been completed.

This dependence on father and mother, and the dependence on property, have increased the length of time during which the child remains unable to free himself from the tyranny of his elders. The autocratic régime has progressively raised the age of dependency. Puberty, which was and must have been the biological signal for procreative mating, was not at all recognized by patriarchal society as a rightful claim to enter manhood. Thus, a boy of thirteen became a rabbi—at his barmitzvah—but this is merely a token from a matriarchal past and the youngster of thirteen has neither sexual nor social rights, but usually remains dependent and under parental authority for many years to come.

The female child has no status socially, or sexually, at this age according to the Jewish religion. Thus, the great honour bestowed on the boy must be quite a trauma for his sisters. And to top it, the young male is supposed to thank God every day, in his morning prayers, for being a male.

In previous centuries the enormous infant mortality rate and the brevity of life made an early use of the biological coming of age imperative. Even with feudal families, and certainly with the common folk whose sex life in any case was disvalued socially, an early sexual union was usually accepted.

In fact, marriages were arranged very early for the male child with a potentially rich heiress and not until the nineteenth century did the process of prolonged dependency begin. This dependency was a privilege confined to the upper classes and it is a strange fact that upper- and middle-class habits and mores percolate slowly into the broad masses of the population, which has brought the long dependency of the child on his parents up to late puberty—up to the age of sixteen. The university student, of course, may remain dependent on his parents for even longer, for another six to ten years.

The economic dependency of the adolescent is combined with a structured education, a structured life-guidance, relying on the nineteenth-century moralities which presumed that sex and sexuality were non-existent. Theoretically sexuality certainly did not exist in the child, in the adolescent, or in the woman, and it was presumed that whenever such dirty preoccupations had to arise, it could only be in the process of marital procreation.

Thus we find that nowadays the whole civilized world is permeated with moralistic concepts which hold the child, the adolescent, and the woman in bondage. Even though every member of society knows these concepts to be patently false, the official codes—legal, educational and religious—continue to spread the myth.

Historically this is important because the instruments of power, of money, and of manipulative influence are identified with these moralistic and rigid concepts which, of course, makes a modification of the structure very difficult.

We can sum up our historical notes on the adolescent by saying that the remnants of a matriarchal pattern have rapidly disappeared. Even such phenomena as described by anthropologists (the Ghotul, etc.) which remain chiefly in symbolic traditions, such as child marriages in India, are by now on their last legs.

The patriarchal pattern which has found two models in civilization—the Anglo-American-democratic pattern on one side and the totalitarian pattern on the other—has diminished the status of the adolescent to an unheard-of extent. The dependency of the adolescent on structured society, be it his parents, social institutions or educators, is growing more and more intense; and sexual freedom and the right of the adolescent to his or her own life are still considered to be outrageous and unfulfillable demands by both the democratic and totalitarian models of society.

I shall close this historical survey by recalling two attempts made in the last fifty years of pre-adolescents and adolescents to form their own societies although they were under enormous pressure and provocation. There is very little literature on either and some of the things I say here must be open to correction.

One attempt was made by Russian civil-war orphans, the Besprisornji in the early 1920s. Many hundred thousands of children were forced to fight for physical survival after their parents and relations had been killed by the Whites or the

Reds. Although this was not a voluntary or spontaneous opting out of society, but was enforced by practically unthinkable hardship and the will to survive, these children and adolescents did organize themselves in well-functioning gangs. Clearly their way to survive was to prey on society, or rather on those who were comparatively better off then in civil war-ridden Russia. They showed that children, pre-adolescents, and adolescents can organize their own lives and survive. The communist authorities felt them to be a terrifying menace on two counts. First, because they were, of course, anti-social and totally delinquent in their behaviour towards the rest of society; but also because they felt the unstructured anarchic grouping as a threat to the rigid structure of their totalitarian society.

The other spontaneous organization of children, pre-adolescents, and adolescents is described by José Gutiérez in a very interesting unpublished thesis on the *Gamines of Bogota*. Again, the historical background for this was a civil war—in Colombia in the early 1950s. Hundreds of thousands of people fled from the country during the extensive slaughter of people and livestock. They went to the suburbs of the big towns, especially the capital, Bogota. There, on the periphery, shack towns sprang up and, as birth control was practically un-known, these poverty-stricken families had more mouths than they were able to feed. Two kinds of reaction were seen—the *chinos*, beggar children who lived with their parents, were one kind; but a number of children from the age of five onwards organized themselves in gangs and completely broke away from society. The gang was hierarchically structured and organized. Sadism and the rule of the strongest were quite absolute. They usually lived by anti-social activities, but newspaper selling and other casual work was acceptable. Interestingly, the gang split into couples and each couple had their lair where they slept and ate. Lairs were kept absolutely private and hidden even from the gang. One must assume that the relationship in the lair, which sometimes extended up to three, was a very close one.

The Gamines were very strongly against society and mem-bers of the Gamines had virtually broken with society. In fact, the gang would never allow a member to return to society, probably because once he was an initiate of the Gamines he would constitute a great danger to the whole organization if he gave their secrets away. The Gamines, which are estimated to number between five and ten thousand in Bogota, have an age grouping from five to sixteen.

The point here is again that pre-adolescents and adolescents can form their societies. In the matriarchal society, the peer group is the formative element of the person from early years onward. It was usually a gentle and loving pattern, however primitive life was.

The two spontaneous societies of adolescents in a sick and hostile world, which I have just described, show the potential of the pre-adolescent and adolescent for self-regulation. What this can be in favourable conditions is seen in the societies described by Malinowski and Verrier Elwin.

It might be as well here to mention the communities of drop-outs and hippies which are flowering all over Western Europe and the United States of America and which may easily be mis-read as a third group of a spontaneous society of adolescents in a sick and hostile world. This would be a grave error. First, the groups concerned are very much older and consist mostly of young adults; one finds very rarely people who are not already in their late teens—more often, however, in their early twenties. Furthermore, these people have, in no way, produced a com-munity pattern, neither have they groped their way into a new, more spontaneous kind of living and working: they are, in fact, mostly exhausting themselves in gestures of defiance, rebellion and 'square baiting'. They are cult-promoting without genuinely opting out, which means that their indoctrination in a sick society is clearly still in existence.

The mistaken view of their relationship to this society is very nearly related to the very common mistake of calling the United States a matriarchal society. The United States are a pseudo-matriarchal society and the reason for this is that the under-lying patriarchal patterns are, of course, present in the United States, as in any other Western society, with the same sex negation, the same suppression of the rights of children, adolescents and women.

All that happened was that there was originally, in this very wide open and unpopulated continent, a surplus of men—and women were at a premium. This led to a romanticizing, sentimentalizing of women, who were put on a pedestal. Women were quick to use this situation in usurping secret power. They bullied and domineered their males ruthlessly. They ruled through their men, and had a rather doubtful influence on American life, especially as a reactionary force. Through the 'Daughters of the American Revolution' and similar upper middle-class institutions they are still very powerful as lobbies and pressure groups. From there the false idea hails that America is a matriarchal society.

Now we can consider the hippies in a similar light. The hippies and dropouts are not ultimately a revolutionary element but are just another product of the sickness of our society.

Their solutions are primarily selfish and directed to their own salvation. In fact, they demonstrate with their clothes, their language, their behaviour, their drug cults, their mysticism, and use of ancient philosophies which they rarely understand, the attitude 'Fuck you Jack, I am all right, I am saved and the rest of mankind can look after themselves'. They do not get involved in social functioning, they do not get involved in understanding their own sickness and that of others, and although some of their artistic fringe has produced some original work the bulk of their participants are failures who live on the fat of the land in one way or another.

2. Some Psychological Notes on Adolescents

ADOLESCENCE is the most important transitional period in human life. It is a transition from childhood, dependency, immaturity, non-productive and non-responsible sexuality into productive sexuality and adulthood. The psychology of this period has two roots. On the one hand, it goes back to developmental psychology common to virtually all children and infants. On the other hand, the adolescent is groping forward into adult life and trying to tackle the problems, the important factors of life which make adult life adult. Here then are the conditions which are involved in the overall image of adolescence and this is the dichotomy which makes adolescence psychologically a time of great importance and of great brittleness to the person.

If we discuss adolescence, we have to go back to childhood, to the one essential process which drives the impact of society into the infant. This process I call *Induction*. The word is taken from physics and it refers to the generation of energy in an object which is surrounded by a magnetic field; the metaphor stands for the way life modes or attitudes of society are inducted into the infant. I consider our society a hostile, a sick society. Why I call it hostile and sick will be discussed later in much greater detail, but whatever the pattern—whether hostile, disagreeable, good or bad—the social environment is the field from which the infant picks up its living patterns. There are numberless ways in which the infant can and does become alerted to the signals of its surrounding life. The way it is fed, helped, fondled, carressed, the way the mother gives her breast to the infant (or doesn't), how it is toileted, loved, wanted or rejected, the manner in which it is shared by a group—all these are elements to which the infant responds with positive or negative reactions.

Clearly, the infant's reaction-patterns do not come to articulate expression. They are not put into words. They are emotional and all emotions, all feelings, all the living responses in the infant, are amorphous. So, of course, is the infant's sexuality, the amorphous blind force, the motor force, the life force which makes the infant reach out into life to communicate with reality, to grow.

Here is a place to elaborate what must be a new theory of sex. We have stated, and shall repeat, that sex is a blind amorphous force. We have stated that sex is an energy which underlies all living processes and functions. Now let us be more specific.

We accept the ideas of Wilhelm Reich that the sexual energy is much more than the Freudian libido which Freud initially, in the 'Project', visualized as a physical-chemical, rather mechanistic energy in the sense of his teachers Helmholtz and Brücke, and which he later dropped and diminished to a metapsychological abstract. Reich saw it as an all-pervading, all-present energy which charged all processes of growth in the foetus, the infant, with varying foci of concentration, in varying parts of the body, according to functional needs—those of the mouth, the anus, the urethra, the genital and the eyes received more intense charges at certain developmental phases and Reich also showed the regulation of the energy and economy by the four-beat of charge-tension-discharge-relaxation, which, of course, is not necessarily bound up with a mature genital pattern but which has many pregenital forerunners.* These, unfortunately, were defined by Freud as infantile perversions and, in his moralistic Victorian outlook, were supposed to be overcome by sublimation. Reich rightly recognized that this was a socially conditioned, unscientific attitude which he did not share. Reich also knew that social patterns were continuously played on to the infant and that this process doubtlessly channelled the flow of sexuality into manifold ways by holding them in bondage to phases, body parts and persons which one would expect the person to outgrow in time. Of course, the energy, once having made its way like a river flowing into a new bed, is quite apt to stay there for a lifetime, and here I disagree with Reich who continued to have an analytical and medical model in his teaching in that he was overrating the therapeutic potential of the psychotherapist in bringing people back to whatever was considered, by declared fashion, to be sanity, normality and health. Reich had the idea that the function of orgasm is particularly important but he only feels it is important if and when experienced on a heterosexual level, deeply intravaginal and concomitant with momentary loss of consciousness, a somewhat convulsive contraction of the whole body. Nothing else would do and thousands and thousands of women are now going in search of this orgasm which is practically non-existent in our society, and thus a new myth has been created, bringing more unhappiness.

The numerous signals which the infant is given are implanted into him and dictate his responses to his environment. On these dictated responses is built the character structure which the person will show to the outer world and which will be part of him all his life. Freudians try to find some special trauma which introduced anxiety into the life of the infant. They search for catastrophe, they search for special environmental factors to explain why a child may be especially anxious, especially worried, especially rebellious or almost completely withdrawn. This search very often has a background of genuine fact. The research of René Spitz, and work with children who have slowly developed depressive or practically psychotic or autistic

* William Reich, *The Function of the Orgasm.*

patterns, has shown that these are sometimes evoked by traumatic experiences. But not in the majority of children! A more acceptable and therapeutically useful formula is that the continuous frustration, hostility, and relentless impact of society in which repressive mechanisms are used continually and never broken or relaxed, as in the sex-repressive mechanisms of our own civilization, are in fact the character-forming, the structuring, the armour-building events that are inducted into the infant. And this is the fate of everyone in our society. These are processes from which very few, if any of us, can escape at all.

If it is practically inevitable that the processes of induction (unlike the special trauma dear to the Freudians) should happen to every member of our civilization, then it should be obvious that in the matrix of a sick civilization, a sick infant is produced. There are, of course, definite degrees, determined by the individual background and history, and a spectrum from comparative health to complete sickness is clearly evident. But in this broad setting induction imposes the pattern of a sick society upon every child, and we must consider this as happening in the average child. Therefore, in order to comment on the psychology of the adolescent, we must find the psychological mechanisms which promote induction in the infant.

It is here that the understanding and definition of the sexual drive is of prime importance. Sexuality is a bio-energetic, biological phenomenon and, as such, a part of reality. It is not just a conceptual schema like libido or an abstract psychological phenomenon. Sexuality is reality to the infant. His mouth with which he sucks, his urethra through which he feels his warm urine passing, his anus through which his faecal masses move, his skin which glows and reddens in contact with a loving object, his genitals which erect—all are sex organs. The infant's sexuality is experienced as a reality in these zones. The amorphous blind sexuality, which is essential to the infant's growth, survival, and being, has an outward-going direction—towards the mother, the feeder, the partner, who gives love, warmth and affection. Feeding is a sexual process for both mother and child. However, the induction which interferes with the outward driving force of sexuality produces a blocking of the sexual flow, and once it is blocked it will be difficult to regain its primary directness.

This blocking begins very early, at the breast feeding stage. The child's lust in feeding is not tolerated by the mother. Breast feeding should be a great erotic exchange between the mother with her erectile nipples, and the sucking infant which trembles with lust and pleasure; it should give the mother a deep feeling of pleasure. But because of her inhibitions this does not happen; it becomes a mere feeding process; the mother feels no pleasure and so the infant's pleasure is blocked. The inhibited mother's nipple does not erect. The child is given the breast for a short time only, or not often enough, or is fed out of a bottle.

The sexual mechanism, which makes the breast the intermediator between the genital organ of the mouth of the baby boy or girl and the erectile nipple which clearly is a pleasure-giving sex organ of the mother, is still tabooed with ease and this is one of the major catastrophes of our civilization. What is, in fact, the most harmless and most direct and primary source of pleasure and lust has been denied and exposed to shame, fear and modish fashion.

This mouth-breast relationship, which should be the easy fulfilment of both mother and child of either sex, has become the alarming source of the deadliest oral frustrations, which ultimately now lead to the death of people—by lung cancer through smoking and by the destructive pattern of alcoholics the world over, to give but two patterns which follow in the wake of oral frustrations arising from a failed mother-child breast feeding relationship.

One should not make this a fetish, and a bottle, given in love, probably can replace, to a great extent a dry or sterile or painful breast, but unless there is an overriding reason why an infant should not have the mother's breast, even if it is non-functioning in the feeding sense, I would still plead that the breast is much better for the infant than a pacifier.

The blocking of lust in feeding has a physical effect on the infant. Anxiety is produced, which in turn produces greed, compulsive feeding, thumb-sucking, nail-biting, the eating of odd substances, regurgitation or compulsive vomiting. Worst of all an endless war about feeding arises between mother and child—a power conflict between them with the mother forcing food on the child and the child refusing. Any GP will bear witness to the number of mothers who come to their doctor to complain that their child will not eat.

Next in the induction process comes the toilet training stage and our worry about excrement. We must realize that a baby is wrapped up most of the time; even in the most progressive families the infant is only allowed to crawl about naked on newspaper for a small part of the day. A little bit of shit coming out is thought a disaster. Being wrapped up is a castrating process; the child cannot feel itself, play with itself, discover its body. The genital region becomes an anaesthetic area, wrapped in nappies day and night with very few interruptions. In addition the infant is tucked up tightly in its cot so that it has little freedom of movement.

Now, if you cut down the sensorium of any part of the body of an infant, you interfere with that part, more or less, for the rest of his life, because it will never catch up with the loss of the proper developmental stage at the right time. Imagine bandaging the eyes of a child during the first years of infancy; what would happen to the child's visual orientation? The deprivation which the child suffers from non-touch is increased by the non-approval, or active disapproval, he meets when he does get the chance to touch his genital.

Feeding troubles, toilet training, but most of all the power conflict that develops between mother and child, making their relationship a constant battlefield in which the mother is ceaselessly trying to dominate the child, introduce anxiety into the child—and from then on anxiety will always be the most important factor in his life.

Do we exaggerate when we talk of the mother trying to dominate the child? Almost every mother has an image in her mind of the ideal baby. The ideal baby does not cry, sleeps when he should, is laughingly awake when required, eats when he is offered food and eats it all with gusto, and performs cleanly and promptly on the pot. As reality is not like this, the mother becomes extremely anxious. If the divergence between the ideal and the reality is too great the mother's feelings become very ambiguous. She may even grow to hate the baby, especially in a civilization which gives her all sorts of superficial distractions to take her away from mothering. Bingo, the cinema, television compete with the baby's needs and the baby is often the loser in this competition: the mother resents the baby's demands.

The mother forces her ideal image on the child during the formative years between birth and three years old. In these years he is wrongly fed, toilet trained, smacked for touching himself or even for touching objects which arouse his curiosity, and given an endless stream of Don'ts. The chief method of trying to lead the child to conform with the mother's image is by withdrawal of love; the ultimate punishment for showing up the mother's failure to make him the ideal baby. This is a truly horrific punishment which sets up extreme anxiety in the infant. Withdrawal of love is the induction process in the raw.

These then are the mechanisms by which the child's sexual life, as I have explained it, is blocked, the amorphous, blind force of sexuality, once blocked, turning into anxiety.

Anxiety means, and here I follow Freud and Reich, that the infant will become fixated in its developmental phases: in its oral, anal, urethral-phallic and genital phases. It will also become fixated on the person mainly concerned in its care, because the less outward-going expression is permitted, the more the infant will remain dependent and unable to form free relations with new people. It will be frustrated and its primitive emotions will live on in the form of archaic thrusts of an infantile sexuality. The primitive sexuality, the desire for a direct return into the love-object, for total and exclusive possession, imbibing the source of the warmth of the love-object's body, will be the centre of the fixation. To sum up, blocked amorphous sexuality leads to anxiety, which in turn leads to fixation in phase and person; these are the mechanisms with which we 'normally' cope in ourselves. This means that the induction period in infancy leaves the child very exposed and unable to love, live, and feel spontaneously.

Induction leads to other phenomena which are all well-known and well-described. The fixation, for instance, leads to the Oedipal situation as described by Freud, although Freud thinks of it as a universal phenomenon in all societies. I disagree with this and agree instead with Malinowski's thesis that it only really happens in civilized societies. The Oedipal phase then leads to the well-known phenomenon of childhood amnesia, forgetting one's childhood, and to long latency periods in which the child is forbidden to have and so totally suppresses, direct sexual impulses. The child grows up without memories, without really having the wealth of sexual love and experimental affection which it wants. It is usual, if one goes back in a person's history through analysis, that the flow of memory begins with the first sexual experience, be it sex play with other children or with one's self.

We now come to the process which I call *conditioning*. Let me make it clear at once that when I use the word conditioning it is not identical with the term as it is used by the behaviourists. Conditioning, as I see it, is the end-result of the induction period in which suddenly the pre-adolescent, the adolescent comes into puberty. At this time a number of new phenomena occur which create in the child, the adolescent, a totally new world, a battlefield of contradictory feelings.

The first of these new phenomena is that the young girl or the young boy suddenly begins to grow up sexually. Pubic hair appears, and the breasts of the girl begin to develop or she enters the menstrual cycle. The young boy suddenly gets more regular erections and usually, at that time, or somewhat earlier, begins to be interested in sexual matters. Masturbation will become an established habit. Sexuality suddenly reaches a new aspect, a new phase. Sexuality, which so far has been wrapped up in infantile paradigms, suddenly shows an adult direction. There are erection, ejaculation, menstruation. All these are new phenomena with which the unprepared adolescent will have to cope; he will have to learn to come to a compromise between the child's world of fantasy and the new reality. What of this new and secret sexuality can be lived out against a hostile world, which has instilled and engrained anxiety in him since infancy? There is no information, or wrong information, or worst of all there are ponderous moralistic warnings, painting a lurid picture of the evil consequences of a fulfilled sex life.

At the age of puberty, sex and the sexual drive grow into an overwhelming preoccupation, into a force that is not easily repressed. It cannot be repressed in the infantile manner which has been the childhood pattern. The incipient adult drive of sexuality suddenly demands an outlet. It is a situation with which the pre-adolescent and the adolescent have, somehow, to come to grips.

It also means a flooding with emotional feelings which usually cannot be fully understood by the adolescent himself. Not only is he faced with a lack of information, but very often with a hostility, with an open and aggressive negation of sexuality; a negation which is felt and shown to young people in virtually every workshop and factory in the land by most adults, in ridicule and lewd contempt. Not only has he to cope then with his own overwhelming bursting strength of sexuality, with his own insecurity and fear in regard to sexual matters, but he also has to cope with an environment which is jealous of his sexuality, and moreover does not agree or allow him to live out this sexuality in any acceptable pattern.

As if this were not enough, the worst conflict of all is that with the sexual awakening, there comes into the foreground a flow of repressed infantile sexual behaviour patterns which virtually have not been in his behaviour since infancy. Especially the fixation to mother or father reappears with great strength and the resultant confusion leads invariably into depression and withdrawal. The sexual direction is easily deflected into homosexuality in response to the re-occurrence of the 'Oedipal' situation, involving the total rejection of the female because sexual intercourse equals incest. Or else the pubescent may masturbate with fantasies of his mother (or her father) and the concomitant guilt will be great. In either case he is under pressure from official, legal, social and religious sanctions. This becomes a direct challenge to his sexuality.

About this time there usually comes the demand of the official structured institutions on the adolescent to fill certain roles in society. As a workman, he will have to learn a trade, a craft, a job; or as a student he is supposed to reach standards which tax his intellectual potential to the utmost. This is a time where he usually becomes part of a high-powered competitive learning drive, perhaps in schools, in universities, in high schools and special training centers, or perhaps as an apprentice; this is the time when the girl goes into a shop, a factory, a university or a secretarial course. All these are new demands on the adolescent.

Moreover, another aspect of adolescence that plays a role in conditioning comes to the foreground. Young adolescents have to learn to discern what type of ideological stance, what type of political or religious decisions they are going to take. Now there is a stream of ideologies and theologies, trying to lure the youngster and it is up to him to choose which one he thinks will be of some use. This choice, of course, is not a conscious choice. Very often, and this is where the conditioning process comes in, the conflict situation plays a great role. There is a continuous conflict between reality and what one may call the official morality, the official religion, the official legal position on sex, on married morality, the official attitude towards all aspects of freedom which are usually considered to be vicious, vile, and unacceptable. Very often the youngster finds out, however, that these rules of prohibition are adhered to only by word of mouth and not in fact. Thus he learns by bitter experience that one can never live up to the ideals and expectations of others.

All these conflicts—the arrival at the state of adult sexuality; the recurrence of infantile sexual patterns (which have lain dormant from infancy or the 'Oedipal' age); the difficulty of adjustment to adult life; the load of structured learning or structured introduction to adult livelihood which goes with the effort of earning one's own living—these by themselves call for a psychology of the adolescent. The fact that there is a terrific gap between the official moralities, the official religions, the official laws, and the actual way in which the adolescent sees life handled by his elders completes the conditioning process. This, for better or worse, is the 'normal' psychology of the young adolescent. He is not able to overcome the sickness of his society, and he does not grow into a healthy adult. In fact, the years of pre-adolescence and adolescence are usually years of great hardship and misery. The psychological basis of adolescent conditioning is the double standards which lead either to a very perturbing non-acceptance of one's self, or else to disturbances of important functions such as work and sex. All of which is ultimately very destructive to the self, to others and to society.

3.   Psychopathology of Adolescence

PSYCHOPATHOLOGY begins where conditioning breaks down. By conditioning I mean the final result of all the many conflicting pressures which beset the adolescent from within and without: he becomes adapted to live with the least amount of handicap and friction in a sick society, by becoming part of it.

Conditioning is to the adolescent what induction is to the infant, the penetration and permeation of the sickness of a society into a person.

Sometimes, however, the spectrum of conflicts produces a degree of sickness in which even conditioning breaks down and psychopathology arises overtly. We are dealing with a great variety of traumata, especially at the vulnerable period of adolescence, during which most cases of psychotic and pseudo-psychotic illnesses reveal themselves for the first time. Let us begin with some basic factors.

The first one which we have mentioned and which must be mentioned again, is the recall of incest wishes and incest images of the father or mother in the adolescent which grossly disturbs his or her sexual drive. There is a further consequence to this.

The major sexual activity for the young adolescent in patriarchal civilized society is masturbation. Now, although this is in no way meant as a moralistic exhortation, we must state that masturbation is not a normal sexual outlet. It is usually based on fantasies. These fantasies mean that the sexual love, sexual life, the sexual feeling is not directed towards another person and lived outwardly as a sharing with another love object. It is lifted out of reality into a fantasy world of overwhelming force.

Unfortunately the conjuring up of sexual images, to provide a fantasy goal for one's masturbation, re-evokes the whole pattern of infantile sexuality and its repressions.

I said earlier that the infant gets his sexuality disturbed by interference in the developmental phases and that all interference by society produces fixation in phase and person.

Fixation in phase in the infant means that 'polymorph perverted' practices are adhered to, referring to the mouth, the anus, any other aperture of the body, or the body's skin surface as a whole. The fixation to the person is mainly directed towards a mother or father figure.

The fantasy masturbation image recalls all these mechanisms and this explains how and why these particular events happen just at that moment of sexual maturation.

In the first instance there are subconscious fears about incest fantasies involving the father or mother. There is a whole field of great anxiety and disturbance, and also of very strong new repression, because the combination of masturbation-fantasy with the image of the mother or father figure is totally unbearable. Equally, the Oedipal drive to 'kill' the parent of the identical sex reappears and strong withdrawal or aggression towards parents, delinquency, truancy, unexplained violence against siblings, all result from the re-awakening of the drives in one who is not a helpless infant but a physically and sexually capable person.

A character structure which is often seen to come from the early withdrawal of sexual energy from other people and the reversal of its love potential towards the self is the solipsistic-narcissistic structure. This too gets very strongly reinforced in adolescence.

What happens here is that the young adolescent is taking his own self, his own body-image as a primary love-fantasy object and this quasi-sexual self-love reinforces the narcissistic component to a very great extent and ultimately leads to what must be described as a fixation on one's self. The eternal adolescent, the eternal Peter Pan, and the eternal student are types in which this narcissistic self-fixated image of the adolescent repeats itself endlessly and is carried into adulthood.

Other patterns of psychopathology which are moulded during the phases of adolescence are especially found in the patterns of homosexuality. The strongly incest-bound young adolescent avoids sexual contact with any partner who would remind him of the father or mother image. That means the boy would avoid a girl because every female stands symbolically for the mother and the girl would avoid the boy because symbolically every boy stands for the father.

It is, of course, understood that this is only possible in a society in which both induction and conditioning have fully played their part. The devices the adolescent uses to convince himself of his homosexuality are most interesting. Wherever the mother figure was dominant and the mother fixation was quite obviously the strongest element in the person's life, he will repress his mother figure and the incest wish will be overlaid by a sexual attraction to a father figure, i.e. a male figure of the same sex on a masturbation fantasy basis. The adolescent then would pronounce himself a born homosexual and signal to his environment this fact, however distressing to himself, by effeminate gestures, a mincing gait, fluttering his eye-lids, and using the comments of his school friends on his behaviour-pattern as confirmation of his inborn homosexuality.

Needless to say, I do not believe in labelling and the declaration of clear-cut directions in sexual behaviour as an inborn pattern. In fact, I doubt that any such direction exists anyway. Sex, as stated above, is a blind, amorphous force.

The juvenile pattern of protest in the sexual field at times outrages the conventional and the confusion we find very often leads to tragic complications. They are tragic because they ultimately direct the sexual instinct of the adolescent on a fixated basis, and we have to differentiate here between the sincere depth of the homosexuality of Michelangelo, of Shakespeare, with the meaningless superficiality, the bogus femininization of the 'gay boy'. The depth of a loving and of a feeling desire which may involve a life-long friendship, a life-long relationship of greater depth than most marriages, can give a love-life on a homosexual basis which in no way need be inferior to a heterosexual relationship. However, the public-lavatory-quick-masturbation sexual relationship of the society-induced-guilt-ridden adolescent, the occasional fellatio relationship between two room-mates or the desired non-committed whoring of the young male prostitute are equivalent to the equally infantile, equally woman-denying pattern we find in the Don Juan. Here we can spare ourselves a detailed description of the manifold perversions and methods of sexual performance, as we have mentioned that one has total recall on a subconscious level of the 'polymorph perverted' infantile sexuality when the sexual function of the adolescent matures and shows openly in masturbation, but is blocked by anxiety.

From records of the last century such as Mayhew's *The London Poor* (London, 1866) it is shown that the flight of youth into psychopathology went into delinquency and alcoholism. These were mass phenomena and the figures given by Mayhew are very startling.

We are now again having a wave of delinquency and alcoholism but there are two new aspects exactly 100 years later. One is the desperate wish of young people to opt out of this society, and this is partly done by negating all conventional aspects of living as society as a whole accepts it. This can be roughly characterized as the hippie-drop-out attempt.

This is not totally logical because they will live on the food society produces. They will burn the lights society provides. In fact, their participation is, of course, very much more intimate than they wish to acknowledge. However, it is a tendency to declare their independence and it is a manner of opting out which seems of major importance. Only their derision of the work-function makes them a pathological phenomenon.

The other new aspect is the flight or escape into drugs. This, of course, has been done and experimented with for many centuries. In fact, other societies have used cannabis for virtually thousands of years. Western society, however, has a special taboo against drug-taking and although some of the drugs, such as the cannabis derivatives, are comparatively harmless, certainly more harmless than nicotine or alcohol, the social injunction against drug-taking in any form is very strict.

An ever-growing circle of young people is, however, experimenting with cannabis, amphetamines, lysergic acid, heroin and cocaine. It is only the last three which can be considered to constitute a danger to the user and the last two to constitute a mortal illness.

I cannot discuss the implications of drug-taking by adolescents in detail here, but one must say that as a part of the psychopathology of adolescence, it is a measure of desperation on the one hand and on the other, an anti-sexual resignation as especially the hard drugs (heroin and cocaine) replace the function of orgasm, when addiction is complete. Sexual potency is usually completely inhibited and a 'blood orgasm' centred on the mid-brain takes the place of the genital orgasm.*

Here we can only hint at the depth and number of pathological phenomena. Adolescence, indeed, is the tragic age in which, in a sick society, all mental illness commences.

4. The Concept of a Sick Society
FROM the foregoing notes it has become evident that we con-

---

* See Ollendorff, 'Assessment of the Function of the General [Practitioner'– Proceedings of the Royal Society of Medicine, Vol. 61 No. 2, pp. 181–184, February 1968 (section of GP, pp. 7–10).

sider this society of ours a sick society. This sickness, we feel, has its roots in the patriarchal pattern which evolved approximately 8,000 years ago.

Prior to the known history of mankind and the recorded history of society, we assume a loose organization, which was sex-permissive and fundamentally loving, however primitive. We must accept the evidence that a sex-repressive upbringing in infancy, childhood, and adolescence perpetuates a state of hatred, aggression, destructiveness, cunning manipulation, displacement of primary function, meaning that, on a social level work and the acquisition of knowledge are superseded by the acquisition of power and property and these latter are made the ruling agents.

We are aware that political patterns vary and that the fate of the person varies in each different pattern. We certainly prefer to live in a democratic pattern where the right of the individual and the freedom of the subject is still safeguarded to a certain extent and at certain times. We think that this is a better pattern than totalitarian societies in which regimentation and the total disrespect for the individual are even more pernicious, even if they are flying the flag of revolution and liberation of mankind.

Nevertheless, in all forms of civilized society, whether democratic or totalitarian, whether white, black, brown or yellow, the crucial issue with which we are concerned and which we hold to be responsible for the intrinsic sickness of society is sex-negation and sex-repression.

Whether Fascist, Nationalist, Marxist, Traditional Democrat or Militarist, no difference in the development of their social instruments, their leadership, their developed constitution can alter the sickness of societies. And any political revolution will end in the same sex-repressive misery.

This has to be elaborated here because surely, sooner or later, the reader will point out that there are differences between all these social patterns and ask why we have neglected to discuss them. The importance of the concept of a sick society is that both processes of induction and conditioning cannot be understood nor do they make sense if we do not see society as a continuous poisoning of the personality of each of its members.

To understand exactly how a sick person and a sick society are interrelated, we must first dismiss the false standards current in medical, psychological, and educational literature. These false images are the 'healthy' child, the 'healthy' adolescent, the 'healthy' adult, the 'normal' person, the 'sane' person, and 'normal' sexuality, to enumerate just a few of the falsehoods which everybody reiterates when assessing people or society.

These falsehoods, of course, prevent the doctor, the psychologist, the psychiatrist and the teacher from understanding the interrelation of society and man. Instead they bully other people willy-nilly by moralistic exhortation and admonition. They set themselves up on high and untouchable thrones and pontificate. The further damage these concepts of the 'normal' and the 'healthy' do is that they prevent a really good look at the sickness that exists in society itself, the sickness that is *in everyone*, and ultimately they hinder an answer to the question what can be done, what must be done, to alter both sick society and its sick members. If, in fact, there were such a thing as a normal and healthy child, a normal and healthy adolescent, here would be no need to search for evocative causes of the disorders of individuals in the whole fabric of the sickness of society.

The sickness inducted into the child is that of our society: anti-sex, anti-life, the giving of greater importance to power and money than to love; submission of the individual to blind bureaucratic processes, authoritarian institutions, mass movements and mass media; incapacity for freedom, enforced uniformity, and flowing out of all this, the bogus morality and ethics of our society which are still enforced on individuals. Even the non-conforming are guilty and furtive when they meet with the conforming.

The child is automatically trained to fit into this society. As an adult he will continue to perpetuate the sickness of our time without even being aware of the patterns that were imposed on him in infancy. The importance of the rights of children is that by recognizing them we will break the chain of continuity.

Hence, the importance of the concept of the sick society. It explains that we all live on a scale, a spectrum of sickness, and it is imperative to find out, in the first instance, the major elements of illness in society and pinpoint our own position on the spectrum.

5. *The Mechanisms and Patterns that Perpetuate Sickness in Adolescents*

THE specific mechanisms and patterns which anchor sickness in the adolescent are determined by the necessity to adapt. It becomes more and more urgent to find one's bearings in the adult world. The conflict between, on the one hand, one's attempt to be totally accepted and acceptable to the demands of society, to identify with the stream of prejudicial feelings, beliefs and actions, and, on the other hand, one's strong sexual drives, can be quite overwhelming.

Under totalitarian circumstances, the pressure of prejudice is so colossal that the conforming youth cannot resist total surrender to a sick society. My German experience is the most bitter of my life. Friends of one's own age-group, and I was twenty-one when Hitler came to power, suddenly did not know one any more, denounced one, and girls and boys with whom one shared one's childhood and early adolescence became violently hostile to one and were, in fact, delighted when one went to concentration camp, jail, or as happened to some of my friends, if one were killed.

In fact, the means by which Fascism, red or black, permeates the adolescent with its sickness is by giving him the unquestionable super-security of undoubted authority, whether this is God-Mao, God-Stalin, God-Hitler or God-Mussolini. Juvenile idealism is easily corrupted and used by this force.

A second and perhaps even more potent means by which a sick society infiltrates into the mind of the adolescent especially, is by sexual guilt.

We have said that a quasi-adult path of sexuality takes over in adolescence and the early sexual activity—masturbation with mixed homosexual and heterosexual fantasy—leaves an overwhelming sense of guilt in the wake of the sexual act.

The Freudian concept of the superego, which is a conceptualistic way to describe what I call induction into the sick pathology of anti-sexuality, is but a wriggling forefinger placed in the frontal lobe by a sick society, admonishing the adolescent for his wicked deed.

The sexual drive, on the other hand, is not a mere concept but a reality. It is a compulsive-repetitive force and it is fully conscious. However, the guilt goes on and on because it is based on the incarnate induction of infancy and its continuation in the conditioning of adolescence.

Guilt grows, and this is determined by the fact that the masturbation fantasies grow wilder and wilder; the limitations of fantasy against depressing reality being progressively pushed back and one's realm of fantasy expanding more and more. Thus infantile elements will creep into the masturbatory fantasy activities and the explosive build-up of an unbearable conflict between the drab reality and unacceptable and practically insane and hallucinatory fantasies leads the adolescent very often into gross withdrawal.

Withdrawal is often neither possible nor available, as not everybody is constitutionally disposed to it, and aggression and violence are then the way out of the youngster's confusion.

Violence is a very dangerous gamble. Here it is neither repressed sexuality nor the vegetative nervous system's response to a real fear situation, although it involves the same mechanisms of fright, flight and fight as these two other forms of aggression.

There is probably, in all living units, an endless repetitive destructive drive which hails from one's basic identity with all living things. The raging, killing, destructive function was once necessary to produce one's food—this is certainly true for the carnivore—and it is also essential as a protective mechanism for survival. It is not Freud's 'Death instinct'.

The human brain is probably, in the main, an organ of inhibition and here I do not mean the inhibition of sex or the inhibition of the aggressive sex-play which can be integrated safely into one's choreography of love-making. This inhibition refers to the very deep-seated and always present and very sick destructive rages which only break through in the defective, the brain-damaged, and the insane, such as the sexual murderer.

Unfortunately, the mechanism remains the same and violence is one of the major elements of modern living. It is propagated ceaselessly in the cinema, television, books and newspapers. Violence is an accepted less-guilt-making outlet for the adolescent than overt and loving sexuality.

Violence is, of course, a built-in part of our society. It is not only the sadism of the school machineries, the examination tortures and military training; its most glaring expression is in the little civil servant's power to torture other little men. The hatred in the police, in the prison warder, in the minor civil servant who sits behind grilles, is the quintessence of the delegation of violence in a sick society. The adolescent learns it in his contact in schools, in universities, on the street and in offices when he meets the little tyrants.

Although this sounds like a sweeping generalization and everywhere there are well-meaning, kind-hearted people who devote themselves totally and unselfishly to their work, my contact with many hundreds of illegitimate children brought up in homes without love, being forced into psychopathy and destructive hatred through their contact with all the above authoritarian figures, gives my statements a firm basis in experience.

Another fate of the adolescent is to fall victim to what is perhaps the most dangerous weapon of a sick society: the elevation of the youngster by absorption to its higher echelons. Society has developed seats of power which can be described as The Administration or The Establishment, which offer glittering prizes to the conforming youngster. There are scholarships, there are seats on boards, there are clever marriages which can be arranged, there are fraternity or old-school-tie connections and the cunning youngster who plays his role right, who becomes a cynic and can play it both ways, can certainly 'run with the hare and hunt with the hounds'. The cynicism which must be the end result of such corruption no doubt leads to physical illness of some severity because the intrigues and power struggles such a person will have to suffer in his battles for survival will give him duodenal ulcers and coronaries galore.

6. The Breakdown of Structured Institutions Including the Family

WHEN we talked of The Administration, or The Establishment, we were in fact only giving symbolic expression to the make-up of all authoritarian disciplinarian hierarchical forces.

The prototype of this is the Army, the Navy, or similar armed forces. Here, seniority, rigid discipline, implicit obedience, unquestioned structuring where everything is in its place and everyone has his role to play in a well-nigh ritualized function, find a quintessential pinnacle in the God-given tradition. In this Establishment, tradition, that hoary mixture of sentimentality and time-honoured taboo, runs riot and personal initiative, imagination, creativity, in fact anything living and loving, is OUT.

This pattern of the authoritarian and disciplinarian structured institution has conquered western civilized living. Our schools are modelled in this way, our universities are shaped on this matrix, our big businesses built up along similar lines.

The family is a strange social creation. We cannot here go into great sociological lyrics about the herd, about the mother and child, about the 'natural family' consisting of father, mother and child. Our interest here is the family as we meet it today.

Today the patriarchal family is but a remnant of its archetype. The power of the father has declined. He is not the sole owner of property, the sole sexual big-spender, he has no absolute rights about the life and death of his children. In fact, even the way he punishes his children can be questioned in court.

Women, who were rightless and sexless chattels, have taken their revenge with a vengeance and never before has their imitation of the male been so powerful as it is today. Although they have not gained freedom, they certainly got their emancipation and, in the vicious battle for survival in the market place and in the ulcer-making in-fight we talked about above, the woman now has found her own place too, as doctor, as lawyer, as business executive, and she has outbitched the sons-of-the-bitches.

However, even her emancipation is only partial. The wage differential is still very strong and the role of the man in the family is still officially that of the pater-familias which leaves the woman as the secret power, the secret domineering drive who wields her well-disguised battle axe more by manipulation than by overt aggression.

However much the role of man and woman in the battle of the sexes has altered, the role of the child remained unchanged; and it is only in the last few years that a few ideas of self-regulation of the infant, free choice of play instruction and leisure time organization have penetrated into the child's life as a reality.

However, the traditional institutions like schools and univer-sities and the official framework of the family as seen by Church, State, and the law remain rigidly unaltered. This is why there is, at this moment, a complete breakdown of any communica-tion between the generations.

It took two world wars and an affluent society to make adolescents distrust the authorities and leaders of all institutions to such an extent that now seems the time when they demand for once a say in their own affairs. They demand a say in their own love life, which, of course, breaks up the rigid family. All in all, the rule of the old, the patriarchal pattern, is breaking not only in institutions, but most of all in the family. This, to some extent, leads to new confusions and we have not yet found all the answers to replace the old values by new ones that are real values which have real validity for the young.

7. *The Rights of Adolescents*

WE do not want to give here a declaration of impossibilities, nor do we want to give a list of unachievable goals. We may come back later at a point where we discuss how the adolescent would be integrated in an ideal society. But here we wish to state what one may call a minimal programme of the rights of the adolescent.

From our notes on the historical role and the psychological make-up of the adolescent, we can already deduce what the basic rights of the adolescent must be NOW in our society, to establish a bridge between those two entities, the world of the old, and the world of the young.

I often see us, the old and the young, as an island which has broken apart, yet both parts are unable to live without the other. Both are floating away from each other and the ways and means found on both sides to re-unite the pieces are so hairbrained, reactionary and unimaginative that I often despair and do not think that a workable solution will ever be found.

Some of the rights of adolescents are already being demanded by them in a very vociferous and direct way. Some of them are silently and deviously practiced by young people in ever-increasing numbers and some of them are not even yet formu-lated or recognized. Let us then begin with a scale of rights which are demanded loudly. Here we find, in the schools and universities especially, three demands which are made and levelled over and over again against the Administration, the Establishment, the ruling bureaucracy, the old disciplinarian authoritarian pattern: the first is self-determination. The adolescent, the young adult, has a right to find his own way and determine on his own how he is going to learn, what he wants, what he rejects, what kind of art he likes, what kind of art he dislikes, what books he wants to read, in which way, if any, he wants to worship. In fact, the first basic right of the adolescent is SELF-DETERMINATION.

Out of this come bridging and constructive rights. Thus, participation in determining the way one learns, the way one lives, the way one runs one's schools or universities, can make one announce the second of the rights, PARTICIPATION.

Again, partly based on self-determination, wherever the young person lives he will want to meet people of his own choice. This is very often reduced by taboos of social, religious, racial or national issues and snob or class values. The family very often interferes with the third right of the adolescent which we will call here the right of ASSOCIATION.

We are now coming to the rights which are more hypothetical because the adolescents are not overtly demanding them, but really practicing in a more concealed way what in fact they are not clearly articulating as a basic right. We are talking here, of course, of SEXUAL FREEDOM. I will not here go into the necessity for an integrated sex-life for infants, children, and pre-adolescents, but will simply state that sex, in the life of the adolescent, must be understood to exist and recognized as a right.

We must give unanxious, unblushing sex education from childhood onwards. We must discuss sexual patterns and sexual activities with the adolescent and we must, of course, accept sex between adolescents from the age of fourteen or fifteen onwards as a reality.

Whatever one's moralistic concepts, reality now makes it clear that, especially in working-class families, juvenile sexuality is accepted and practiced, and it is now making its way upwards in the class structure. From my observation of American high school children and London working-class boys and girls of 14–15, they have sexual intercourse at least sometimes.

This may be experimental and promiscuous, but it would

also be tragic if it lead to pregnancy. Thus, parallel to the teaching of sex education must go the teaching of methods of contraception until they become second nature to civilized people—like eating with a knife and fork.

Again, the right to acquire knowledge is a basic right of the child, the pre-adolescent and the adolescent.

However, our authoritarian and disciplinarian ways of enforcing education have soured the process to such an extent that the acquisition of knowledge has not only become an uphill struggle, but a battle against schooling, against learning as such. Rebellion very often takes the form of truancy.

That must not deceive us, however. It remains a basic right of all, and especially the adolescent, to acquire knowledge. EDUCATION is thus a right which has to be fought for, but of course, education has to be a spontaneous choice.

In the acquisition of knowledge more than in any other field, the innate gifts of the youngster have to find full play and the creativity which is in the person must find an unhampered outlet. Any attempt to enforce a curriculum, to put a strait jacket of a syllabus over the pre-adolescent, the adolescent and the child is ultimately the death knell of education. This subject is given more detailed consideration in the chapters written by A. S. Neill and Michael Duane.

The last of the rights of the adolescent is one which is bedevilled by the way society has undermined its primary role, but which nevertheless remains a major living function: WORK.

Exploitation of children and adolescents, which has only stopped in recent years, the economic importance of the adolescent as a breadwinner irrespective of the wishes and wants of the person regarding what kind of work he or she wanted to do, have marred the work-aspect out of all proportion.

Delinquency and truancy, shying away from work, doing the clever thing by avoiding work wherever one can pretend to work when one is not, a thousand devious ways have been found to run away from work. Nevertheless, work is a basic life function, as Reich rightly points out over and over again, and it is not only a life function, it is also a right. By that, of course, we mean that the pre-adolescent, the adolescent who is interested in particular work processes or who enters work is entitled to 'do his own thing' in the workshop, in classes, or wherever he is.

Of all the rights, the right to work will probably be the one of most economic importance to the individual, because it is a direct bridge to an adult integration into society. It is also the most difficult one to make people see as a right. It will be described as a necessity. It will be described as an economic function and will be undervalued by the adolescents themselves and under-priced by the employers. But it remains a right.

We have not discussed the right of the adolescent to play, to leisure. This, of course, is a right of every age group from infancy to old age, one which has been discussed by my friends in this book in several chapters. Where work and play are intimately related, this will be the right of the adolescent to Work-Play, often a pointer to a person's creativity—and if he chooses to be an artist, to his life.

8. *The Social Need for Adolescents' Rights*

IN a previous section I used the simile that generations are like an island breaking apart and the two parts floating away from each other. This we are trying to avoid for a few simple reasons. The first one being that we love young people and this love, like any other love, means that we cannot live without them.

The recognition of a total alienation of the young generation is unavoidable and one must not be deceived by the fact that the great majority of young adolescents are, of course, still conniving, conforming, and trying to make their way in this society in a prescribed and formally laid down manner.

The alienation is an emotional one and it is an attitude of deep cynicism, of disbelief, disregard and a secret negation of the values of our society by just this majority group which is the important factor. Historically, in countries where there was more unrest, and where the conflicts came much more directly to the surface, the adolescents went into extreme camps politically, as in Germany and Italy and France. In Germany two generations ago the middle-class youth tried to opt out of the sick society by an idealistic camaraderie and back-to-nature movement, the Wandervögel.

The major difficulty of all movements and the reason for their ultimate failure has always been the impossibility of developing the concept of a sick society and of understanding the reasons for this sickness, especially of its sick sexuality. We have now arrived at a stage where in the most powerful countries in the world, such as the USA, and very probably, as I have been given to understand from well-informed persons, in Russia, the fifteen- to twenty-year-old age group virtually no longer speaks the same language as anybody who is out of this social and chronological stratum. Their contempt for society as a whole is complete. They do not care for their own rights or for the rights of anybody else. Their disrespect for any institution and for the pomp and circumstance which goes with it is absolute. They do not fall for political slogans, they do not fall for theologies, and their cynicism is very frightening because with it goes a contempt for the lives of others and their own life, which to some extent shows in their easy acceptance of violence as a matter of fact. They give and take it without outrage.

What I am trying to say here is that the time has come for a review of our values. It is essential for the survival of our society that we recognize the social need for adolescents' rights and take serious measures to put them into effect.

9. *Establishing the Rights of Adolescents*

AGAIN, one can really continue the previous paragraph and say that a realistic way of doing this is to create an adolescent charter.

There would be a youth group in every village or part of a town which must be run by young people themselves. This group must have NO connection with churches, State organizations, schools, parties, cranks, or power-lusty would-be politicians climbing on a miniature band wagon. These groups should be run and organized like the meetings of a free school where everybody has a right to speak and everybody participates on equal terms. The functionaries of the group are often chosen *ad hoc*, but some of them will be more permanent and no newspaper propaganda should ever be allowed to vitiate their meetings nor should they ever become centres of TV antics These groups can organize in turn all the rights which we have laid out above—the right of association, the right of participation, the right of sexual freedom. They can organize knowledge by founding their own free universities, and, if necessary, find work and play projects in centres of their own. This sounds so far-fetched and outrageous, but the alternative, as I mentioned above, is the breaking up of all our structured institutions, the breaking up of our families and a cynicism which sooner or later will lead to a total destruction of our society to which there will be no resistance.

I am, of course, aware that none of this can be done from one day to another, but that would be my basic plan and any move in the direction of establishing the rights of the adolescent on those lines must be and will be, of course, acceptable.

10. *The Function of the Adolescent in an Ideal Society*

IF we assume that by some miracle the sexual revolution has taken place and two generations of healthy people have grown up without fear, or anxiety, without threat to each other, that there is a society in which love is the prime mover of action, then the fusion of all elements of society into an entity will be in no way impossible. Although it is very upsetting to people to have utopian and idealistic schemata given, I feel I must repeat here my vision of a society in which we can place the adolescent as a valid and maturing member.

From all we have said before, induction would not happen. However, a planned child would have a loving group of people taking care of him and breast feeding would continue up to whatever age mother and child decide they like it and would go on with it. Weaning would be a pleasant and playful process in which exciting substitutes take over if and when the mother runs dry. There would be nothing put into the way of running through the phases of infantile sexuality as there would be nothing to restrict the infant's freedom. The right of the infant and the right of the child would be virtually sacrosanct and the society I dream of has no room for coercion, violence, and disciplining a child.

Children would live with their peers in groups of their own from an early age. That does not imply necessarily, in our complex society, which I dare say we will maintain, that they would give up their natural parents completely, but the fundamental processes of disciplining, which in any case should always be defined and only accepted as a bringing of order into one's experiences, would be done by their equals, their age group comrades. The transition from play to learning would be unstructured and would go on as long as the adolescent wants it. There will never be economic inhibition or a sexual price to pay to end education too early or too late.

On whatever scale the adolescent then decides he wants to function in society, he will; and on whatever scale he wants to function sexually, he will. The sexual responsibility and feeling of responsibility would be practically absolute and adolescence would be a time in which promiscuity and experimentation would be played out and a mature pattern slowly adopted.

Unfortunately, we will have to wait a very long time for this dream to come true.

11. *Therapeutic Considerations*

MEANWHILE, we have to deal with the bitter realities of sick adolescents and my last words are really a plea for the adolescent.

What we see today is quite often a sexually confused delinquent, a truant, a cynic who is torn by powerful influences in numerous directions. This makes adolescence a most preponderant age for mental and emotional illness. On the other hand, the law still considers the adolescent not fully responsible and either treats him as child, totally disregarding the youngster's own wishes, or falls on him with authoritarian and pedagogic discipline.

We need a growing number of doctors, a growing number of psychiatrists who learn to speak the language of the adolescent as he is today. We need psychiatrists specializing in adolescence and its problems. These psychiatrists must face the adolescents without prejudice, without anxiety, without moralistic push. The ideal doctor for the adolescent would be a woman or man who has a great love for this age group and who can feel their needs. This does not exclude him from seeing through their schemes which are often cunning and recognizing when he is being used by the youngsters for devious purposes.

The psychiatrist specializing in adolescence will have part of his work load in courts, with schools, and most of all, with the warring families. One feels that the role of such people would be more and more prominent and they should finally be the accepted ombudsman for the adolescent, whose word should be taken and weighed first, especially if there is a possibility of avoiding a pending punitive action which so often mars the life of the young adolescent.

The whole tragedy of adolescence is really seen in the growing number of adolescent delinquents who are being blunderbussed by this society into jail and there become enemies of society forever.

The rights of the adolescent will slowly be given, as history has shown that no group of society can be robbed forever of their rights. This means, ultimately, the promise of a happier future.

Chapter 4

Freedom Works

by A. S. Neill

To me child-orientated education began with Homer Lane.
There had been progressive schools—the adjective can mean
anything—but they had been schools founded by people who
thought they knew what sort of school children ought to have.
Badley of Bedales, John Russell of King Alfred School and the
rest belonged to the pre-child psychology era, or if you like the
pre-Freud era. The child was conditioned but in a kindly way;
he had pictures of the classics to uplift him; he had moral
lectures on behaviour. A child could call his teacher Bill but he
could not call him a bloody fool. In my teaching days in King
Alfred we were addressed as Sir; in two years there I never
heard a four letter word; everything was so 'nice', so mannerly,
so respectable. The system was seen at its best or worst in
Germany. When we had our international school in Dresden
from 1921 to 1923 our German teachers would not smoke in
front of children; some would not be seen entering a cinema.
The teacher had to be a *Muster*—a model, in short a character
moulder. And our home variety of progressive school was
certainly an indoctrinating school.

Lane arrived among a number of rather dull people with set
ideas, people who knew, or thought they knew what a child
should be, and his message was that we don't know a thing
about children, and that it was wrong to force our personalities
on them. Not until his Little Commonwealth was there any
school that I ever heard of, that said in effect, 'We don't know
what a child should be. We must study the nature of children
and adapt our system to that nature.'

Lane was dealing with delinquents, the vulgar, the slum kids
who knew no superficial manners, no polite language; his was
the raw material of what we call civilization—but what natural
manners the ones I knew had! Lane was the first to say:

'Tommy is cruel, destructive, a bully; my job is to try to find out what is behind his delinquencies.' In fact the Little Commonwealth was the forerunner of the modern group therapy.

It must be acknowledged that being on the side of the child, as Lane phrased it, is very difficult in a civilization that ranks book learning as education, that believes that a child has to be trained. Only a very small minority of parents and teachers believe in freedom for their children. Summerhill has thirty American pupils, two Scandinavians, six Germans, two French and twenty-two English ones. If I suddenly announced that it would be a day school I make the guess that in East Suffolk I wouldn't get three pupils. The sad truth is that only middle-class children can have a free school, for free schools are fee-paying schools. The mass of the proletariat are not educated enough to demand free schools for their children; and the only way they could be educated enough would be by seeing free schools in action. But any attempt to introduce freedom into the State system meets with the utmost resistance from establishment bureaucracy and indeed from the teaching profession. Thus Michael Duane's Risinghill, which successfully made working-class parents see what child-centred education was about, was closed down by the authorities in spite of the protests of both the parents and the children.

The proletariat gets no education, practical or theoretical, in child psychology—neither in school as children, nor later as parents seeing and participating in the education of their own children in child-centred schools. Far from it: the schools are not geared to the children's real needs and the parents are kept at arm's length.

So parents are alienated from their children's development. Sir Alec Clegg's book *Children in Distress* shows the terrible conditions in which poor children live with ignorant or selfish parents. What could a Freud or a Homer Lane mean to them?

We in our middle-class progressive schools are apt to forget about the outside sick world, and here I am not thinking only of the deprived poor children; there is the world of schools with caning and fear, State schools and so-called Public schools Teachers in the main are not interested in the child; as one said to me: 'My job is to teach history, not to bother my arse about whether Tommy is beaten up at home by a drunken father.' And I am afraid that courses in psychology are too often about rats and not about children.

I am stressing the difficulties because I have known them for over fifty years. I saw Lane's great work in the Little Commonwealth and have looked in vain for evidence that the State has learned anything from it. The State has never really altered its borstalization of children,* though a few individuals within the State system have tried to treat children in Homer Lane's way. Howard Case in his State school for difficult little children uses love and not the hate of strict discipline. Michael Duane in Risinghill tried to, as I have mentioned, and got his school closed down. We are up against what Ibsen called the compact majority and it is represented by officials, bureaucrats, themselves products of Public and grammar schools. My school is not 'recognized as efficient' by the Department of Education although it is recognized by thousands of students and teachers and parents in the Western world. If it should be recognized by the Department of Education by the time this book is published I shall be surprised. For to the State, education means exams, 'O' and 'A' levels, book knowledge, not to mention infinite boredom in a plethora of classrooms. That goes for every State in East or West, mass production of heads with the emotions ignored as if they were not there.

The key to all child-centred education is self-government. The Little Commonwealth was as near to a democracy as could be. The children lived in separate houses and they had their own general meetings about each other's behaviour. At King Alfred School, after I had met Homer Lane, I kept agitating for self-government, but the staff opposed it. Finally John Russell announced to the whole school that 'Neill will have self-government in his classes'. The result was that they would come from a rather strict maths teacher into my room for geography, and they would simply go haywire, and make a terrible noise, and all the staff protested. I either resigned or I was chucked out, I forget which. This illustrates the difficulties of all libertarian teachers in more or less authoritarian schools.

But at Summerhill self-government works. Each child has a vote and a voice, irrespective of age. I myself do not take much part in the weekly meetings: sometimes I sit through a meeting

* See Nan Berger's chapter in this book.

without speaking at all, which is something another adult might find it difficult to do. The children are learning to live with others by interaction with their peers, being judged by their equals and not by their fathers and mothers and teachers. One must let them make their own mistakes, having faith that they will correct them in the light of later experience.

I myself never vote at a meeting. If a meeting votes to fine a kid I never vote. I never take any sides against a kid or for a kid because I must remain neutral in case I have to deal with them in private therapy, which is very seldom nowadays.

When I first founded Summerhill I had accepted the idea of psychoanalysis as the right way. For many years I took many problem children expelled from other schools for stealing and so on. I used analysis, basically Freudian analysis, analysing dreams, etc. (Homer Lane had been basically Freudian, or rather he had adapted a lot from Freud for himself). I thought analysis was the answer until I discovered that for two years I had analysed a boy expelled from Eton for stealing, who went out cured, and Jimmie and Lizzie who had also been chucked out of school and hadn't been near me for analysis, went out cured too. So I decided it wasn't analysis but freedom that was doing it. This was a great discovery, and a very important one, because the answer is not analysis: and this is just as well, since we cannot analyse the whole human race.

Lane's use of Freud was less important than his development of the idea that children should be free. Freud and his school, with the exception of Wilhelm Reich, never believed in freedom for children (I have never in my life had a pupil sent to me by a Freudian analyst). Nowadays I am no longer dealing with kids psychologically: I am dealing with them communally, providing a free community in which they are free to be themselves. What does 'being themselves' mean? I can only answer by giving an example: a boy of twelve coming here from an ordinary American or an English school, is a bunch of insincerity, with an insincere voice, smiling when he shouldn't be smiling, pretending to be social when he isn't, and then, in a few weeks, he's bullying other people and breaking things. All his hate is coming out, because he's been conditioned.

I do not take what are usually called 'problem' children any more, having had my day of it, many days and years of it, pulling other people's chestnuts out of the fire; but in our sick society virtually all children are problem children. Thus virtually every child is a problem child when he comes to Summerhill; all have something to let out—except the very few who have been brought up in a very free home. Trying to get away from an artificial personality made by other people, by the parents first and then the schools, trying to get back to themselves, that's where the problem lies. My own theory is that the world is sick because nobody is himself. Everybody is conditioned by somebody else. Artificial products with emotions damped down, and their instincts perverted. On the other hand, if you get a child here of four or five who hasn't been conditioned he doesn't go through this destructive stage. He has no need to. So I think the only answer to the question of children 'being themselves' is that the kid who has been conditioned is full of anti-life hate and it takes a long time to bring it out. The deep problem then is the home. The compulsive family, as Wilhelm Reich called it, is a dangerous thing. This applies to all classes. Summerhill gets small children from middle-class homes. Incidentally each and every one who comes to freedom drops all lessons for weeks, even for years, a proof that lessons don't touch the child emotionally and intellectually. Many of these nicely brought up children when they come to us go through a phase of behaving like little savages, bullying, destroying, hating.

The first enemy of children is the ignorance of parents. Generally speaking if a mother was spanked as a child she will spank her child. If she was shaken as a child she will do the same. Her attitude will be, 'I had to obey as a child, my child must obey.' Parents simply carry on the old tradition of authority.

I should call the second enemy the unhappiness of marriages, and how to better that I cannot even guess, for marriage means falling in love at twenty-two and being supposed to retain that love at sixty. Sexual love can be an evanescent phenomenon. I am inclined to think that nearly all the problem children I have known were the result of marriages that had lost their love, and too often marriages in which love had become hate. Chains bring hate. Oddly enough the child who is homesick in a happy place like Summerhill is nearly always from an unhappy home.

One little boy said to me: 'I want to be at home to protect Mummy when Daddy hits her.'

The causes of the wrong treatment of children are legion. A father with a mother complex may hate his son as a rival for mother's love. A nagging mother may hate her daughter, envious of her youth and good looks. There is a lot of hate in a home. In Summerhill brothers and sisters have sometimes to be kept away from each other. This hate element is less in self-regulated children, in homes where parents do not act as authorities, where there is give and take in a love atmosphere. The only children who were not a success in Summerhill were those who had no love as babies. The chip on their shoulders could not be removed, and this applied often to adopted children who must have had the unconscious feeling, not thought, 'My mother left me, and although my foster parents are kind to me, when I see other kids being visited by their parents I feel that I lost the most important thing in life.' The question really boils down to asking how a home can be made a love nest. It is platitudinous to say that parents hate their children because they hate themselves. I think it was Carl Jung who said that we hate in others what we hate in ourselves. I should like to believe the corollary that we love in others what we love in ourselves.

The problem is parental, always parental. Children are ruined by the complexes of their parents. Adults can read a score of books on child psychology without being able to derive any benefit because of their own repressions. Parents who are all wrong sexually will give their offspring sex guilt complexes for life. How many children are spanked for sexual play because mother cannot have an orgasm? How many children get a sex guilt from a father who shines in his local as a raconteur of water closet and sex stories? I now think that the aggressiveness and hate of so many children comes from a plethora of repressions, not all sexual—power of parents demanding obedience, duty, manners, quietness—but I still think that the parent who has an unsatisfactory sex life is the one who does the most harm. And since we live in an anti-sex society, of course sex is repressed in children. True, things have changed superficially; you can bathe now with very little on, while in my young days you could not. And you can print four-letter words nowadays.

Mini-skirts, the right of the modern girl to acknowledge her sex urges, the new laws on abortion and homosexuality, these all point to advance. But people's basic attitude is still anti-sex. The fundamental attitude remains that sex is not right, that there is something wrong with it. A certain amount of guilt is still attached to it. Most likely the children of religious parents have the least chance of growing up sexually healthy, but even people who have no definite religion are affected by the attitudes to sex that have come largely from religion. Certainly the Catholic Church has made sex one of the filthiest things in the world.

This anti-sexual attitude, inculcated in the child at the pre-verbal stage by the suppression of masturbation and the taboo on nakedness, may never be put into words. It is all in the atmosphere. It is in the voice of the mother when she talks about sexual subjects or approaches sexual objects. It is in her body tensions. It is in her attempts to offer the child distractions whenever it touches its genitals. There are still mothers of small children under two who say, 'Darling, don't sit with your legs apart' when the children are sitting on the floor playing with their toys.

In my family our parents did not speak of sex, but when I had sex play with my sister at the age of seven, the thrashing I got was enough to make me a neurotic for life. Words did not come in. I remember when I was about eight or nine some boy telling me how babies were made and I couldn't believe him. I looked at my father and mother and thought they couldn't do a filthy thing like that. So it was in the atmosphere. It had no need to be verbal; it was just in the general atmosphere of hush-hush.

It's slowly changing, but everything goes so slowly. I have seen it again and again. Kids who have come to Summerhill have felt guilt about masturbation but when they have found that masturbation does not matter at Summerhill the change in them has been amazing. They felt happier with the other children. I don't think many of them have retained any guilt about it.

But most schools confirm and reinforce the guilt that has been implanted at home. One of the results is that children grow up to accept sex as a pornographic and guilty thing. So much sex is wrong because it is guilty. It is sadistic, by which I mean that it is a form of rape—with no tenderness about it. And this is true even about promiscuous sex among the supposedly liberated, for virtually everybody is inculcated with sexual guilt in early childhood.

Much parental repression is due to anxiety, and factually all parents have grounds for anxiety—dangerous roads, electric plugs, unsafe trees, boiling kettles. What is wrong is the way they react to anxiety. Self-regulated children who have a love and trust attitude to father and mother do not need slaps and angry voices to make them aware of dangers. To a child every angry shout, every slap means: 'My mother does not love me'. Indeed the basis of bad behaviour by children is lack of love. Some might say that too much love could be a basis of bad behaviour, but this is not true. You can have too much licence, but not too much love. If a mother is giving a child too much licence she is over-compensating for the lack of love, in the same way that a lot of parents give their children expensive presents as a substitute for love.

A spoilt child is not necessarily a loved child. Often he is a kid whose parents tend to think 'my boy is wonderful . . . you see . . . he's going to be a great boy and we'll do everything we can to assist him and make him happy', and to assist him in an image they have created for him. But in my own experience, problem kids have been mostly unloved, not over-loved. The parents of a spoilt child differ from the self-regulated child's parents in that the self-regulated child's parents are not fools. They do not give their children too much money and they do not need to. The self-regulated child has self-discipline as distinct from imposed discipline. This is the discipline we have in Summerhill, but you can't achieve that unless people want it. With a heavy father and a roaring mother, the child can't be expected to develop self-discipline. And of course there must be give and take in the home. If you've got a couple of sons who want to turn on the TV to watch 'Top of the Pops' and you want to see something else of more value, then you've got to give and take and come to a compromise about it.

The middle-class child has a greater chance of normality than a poor child. The underprivileged class, that is the vast majority of citizens, have tremendous handicaps. On the whole they are kindly folks—any village or local gathering tells us that; they are honest and social. They are learned and skilled in their trades, but about fundamental things they are ignorant, for their meagre schooling dealt mostly with all that had no bearing on their lives: history, maths, geography. The great improvement in wages may lead to a conscious culture, but in the past bad housing, grinding work with the only relief the pint in the local, gave them no chance of understanding a thing about—say—child nature.

The opportunities for a creative life are almost entirely absent. There is no space; one cannot get away from one's noisy kids, so that kids become a nuisance. The middle class have culture, nice houses, good food, books, intelligent conversation. The boys do not need to form gangs at street corners. The children of the well-to-do have a thousand interests that the slum children do not have. The education of the middle class affords more awareness. A banker or a teacher can read books about psychology or philosophy. How many spectators at a cup final even heard of psychology?

Not that all middle-class parents treat their children in a good manner. Indeed it is possible that middle-class children in many cases are in a sorry plight, for their instincts have to be suppressed by outer conventional behaviour, good manners, the 'stiff upper lip', the urge to get on by passing exams. As the old school tie men phrase it: 'It isn't done'. And, as they are the people who support the Establishment that rules, their repressions are more dangerous than those who only serve humbly.

The middle classes have their own shut personalities, their emotional limitations, their traditions. Public school men usually send their sons to a Public school, sometimes when they confess that they themselves were unhappy there. The journal of the middle class, the *New Statesman*, is about the most unemotional paper I know. If it contains an article on education it is usually about learning and never about living. The middle-class teachers are in the same boat, as can be seen in the articles they write for *The Times Educational Supplement* and the *Teacher*. No one reading them would think that the writers had ever heard of Freud or Homer Lane or indeed of dynamic depth psychology. On the whole the middle class accepts the definition of education as learning.

Since the teacher is tied hand and foot, we should not look to him for reform of education. After all he gets a child who has had five or more years of parental conditioning. I used to say that if I were rich I wouldn't take a new pupil over seven. I have modified that now to seven months before birth. The problem to be tackled is the home. The question is not so much one about what parents should do; rather is it one about what parents should not do. Thousands of fathers and mothers are miserable because their children make them strangers. Children lie to their parents, not only because of fear, but also because they feel that, owing to the gulf between their ages, the parents will not understand. And so millions of parents feel that they have lost their children, and the sad truth is that they have lost them.

Why? Because of discipline, nagging, moralizing, in short trying to make the young accept the mores and beliefs of the elders. I have seen it so often in my school. A girl of sixteen said: 'Every moment I am at home I am unhappy. Mother will hardly listen to me; she wants to rule my life and justifies her discipline on the grounds that I am too young to make up my own mind. She won't even let me choose the colour of my dresses. I know I should love her but I hate her and that gives me a guilty conscience.' And it is so in many a home. The parents are unhappy too. Poor ignorant souls, they cannot realize that they brought the loss of their families on themselves, that they sacrificed their children to an out-dated code of parental behaviour.

The purpose of conditioning children is simply to extend your own personality on to your children. It is not in the child's interest. It is simply the parent's idea of what the child should be, just as the educators, including so-called progressive ones, think they know what a child should be. It's the idea of moulding people in your own image, so to speak. God making humanity in his own image, repeated again. And of course the ultimate aim is to fit them into the Establishment, to fit into the *status quo*.

The conditioning of the home environment prepares the child to accept the conditioning of the school. A boy who goes to a Public school simply accepts all that they tell him about the importance of games, of conformity, of leadership, of keeping firm control over the emotions, and all the rest of it. His home life has conditioned him to accept being moulded by others to fit into roles of their choosing. With the weapon of approval and withdrawal of approval he has been taught at a very early age to take external authority inside himself and make its attitude to life his own.

When I was at King Alfred School I saw how the children were conditioned by John Russell, the moralist. John Russell had strong feelings about kissing and four-letter words. They were conditioned to be nice, polite and moral little kids. In this case, for King Alfred School was a progressive school, the main method of doing this was his personality. He was rather like an archbishop. He was an old man by this time, and had a tremendous voice and a tremendous appearance. He was a father symbol but a kindly father symbol. It was just difficult to rebel against him. It's much more easy to rebel against a stern father than a mild one. The children 'became' John Russell, they became his attitude to life.

In Summerhill we try to avoid that as much as possible. Ask any Summerhill kid or ex-Summerhill kid what Neill's religion was, or what his attitude to drugs was, or what his politics were: they wouldn't know and they wouldn't care.

Why cannot parents and teachers stand by and allow a child to grow at its own pace and in its own way? If I believed in original sin I should define it as the god almighty complex that makes a man imagine that he can tell others how to live. One sees it in the nursery. Baby strives to climb on to a chair and smiling father kindly lifts him up destroying the delight in conquering his environment. The stupid art teacher takes a brush to improve Mary's painting. The stock joke about Willie's never being able to play with his toy train because daddy is always running it is founded on reality. Hardly any adult knows anything much about what a child is and what he wants to do and say. 'We know better; we'll tell the little devils how to behave in life.' Parents who were reared in freedom do not live their children's lives for them. Their children are not haters; they could not possibly be anti-Semitic, or racialists or moulders of character.

The first rule for parents should be: I shall not make my child in my own image. I am not good enough, wise enough to tell my child how to live. Neglect of this elementary rule accounts for I should think most of the delinquency among the youth of the world. Any young mother, whatever her social class, should look at her new-born baby and say: 'Here is something new, something wonderful, something beyond my knowledge and experience. I must let it grow in its own way and at its own pace.'

Let me try to picture a family in which the teenagers have no desire to rebel, to flout parental authority. If the parents have a religion they do not force it on their children. The kids feel free but there is no licence in the home, meaning that little Willie does not *want* to smash the furniture or tease the cat. (If he did want to, there would be something wrong. He would be hating something or somebody and he would be wanting to get his own back. Children from happy homes, with parents who get on well together, do not want to do things like that.)

Parents and children are on an equal footing in most things. There is no effort to teach—say—table manners, no prohibitions about language. The parents are seen naked by their family. In the Sunday press recently some doctor wrote against the danger of children seeing their parents naked—their sex would be too early aroused. This utter nonsense must have been read by thousands.

I am not contending that in such a family children can do everything they like. Adults have their rights. Father must say strongly that he won't have his car used as a hut for gangster games. Mother has the right to say that she won't have Mary using one of her best pans for making toffee and then leaving it unwashed. That is fair give and take, and when the relationship is a love one such little tiffs leave no hatred or resentment behind. In one of my books I wrote that in a strict home the parents have all the rights, whereas in a falsely liberal one the children have all the rights, the result being a lot of spoiled brats.

The children in this family will have been self-regulated from the word go. They will never have been forced to eat food they did not want to eat: it is a crime to compel a child to finish what is on its plate. We all know that a child's eyes can be greedier than its stomach. Robert Ollendorff shows in his chapter the misery that is caused by coercive parental attitudes about food. Given the choice of foods, self-regulated children will eat according to their individual physical needs. Nor will they have been forced into a potting routine: babies will come to use the pot without so-called toilet-training, which too often means scolding and mild bullying. It is enough that they should know that the pot is there and what its purpose is: they will soon learn to use it and when they want it they will simply sit on it. Parents should go at the child's pace. It is one thing to ask the child, without making an issue of it, to use the pot when he needs it, but quite another to make the child sit on the pot at regular times. One should never do this. Toilet training as it is called should never be associated with tut tuts, with looks and words of disapproval, or approval. And this applies to masturbation. Countless millions of children have carried a sex guilt because they were lectured or punished for a natural act. Indeed much anti-life feeling must spring from toilet training. The mother gives the baby a sexual sensation when she washes and dries its genitals. Later on when the masturbation Verbot comes along the child must be shocked: mother started it and now she spanks me for it.

Few parents say to themselves, 'I shall never give my child a hate of its body.' A million lads and lasses who have taken their 'A' levels are plagued with guilt over masturbation, and all the school subjects in the world can do nothing to abolish their guilt.

Recently some unknown person sent me a pamphlet issued by some Catholic organization. It was appalling. Masturbation was a sin and the after effects were dreadful physically and psychologically. I have never had an RC pamphlet pointing out the dangers of beating children in RC schools. Some months ago an RC Inspector of Schools told a Catholic audience of teachers that beating was more prevalent in Catholic schools than in Protestant ones.

I am really assuming that the imaginary family I am writing about has not a body-hating religion, indeed I am assuming it is a Humanist one. And I hasten to say that a Humanist can be as dangerous to children as an anti-life Christian, can be as moralistic about youthful sex.

For it isn't what you believe that matters; it is what you are, what you do. I wish I could see millions of people reading

Wilhelm Reich, the sanest man on early ruination of children that I ever knew. I have said before that I am not sure that he is right in attributing all the ills to the suppression of genitality, but he is possibly 90 per cent right, for children who have not been lectured to or punished for masturbation seem to be much more balanced than other children. The sergeant-major type of father who beats his boy for some minor fault has most likely never mentioned sex in his home, but the military type with its puffed out chest and its retracted abdomen is a good illustration of what Reich means—the symbol of repressed sex.

In the main Reich is right. The suppression of genitality is the suppression of noise and activity in all spheres. It was Reich who said that the ruling classes encouraged infant sex repression on the grounds that if you psychologically castrate the young they will grow up to be emasculated men who have not the guts to challenge anything. Organized religion, by always being on the side of the Establishment, helps the rulers and capitalists in this killing of life in the cradle. Capitalist is not the right word. From all I hear, Communist States have the same suppression of the young, the same indoctrination, the same moulding as the West has. Politics do not cure sick men.

Malinowski's study of the Trobriand Islands in *The Sexual Life of Savages*, mentioned by Robert Ollendorff in his chapter, makes an excellent parable. In a matriarchal society sex was free from the beginning, young children had sex play, adolescents had a sex life with the approval of the parents. Malinowski failed to find any evidence of sex crime, nor of homosexuality until the missionaries came and segregated the sexes. This means that our anti-sex society is primarily responsible for our sex crimes and many another crime.

It was Reich who coined the phrase 'self-regulation', which means, roughly speaking, going at the child's pace, not imposing your expectations on him, letting the baby have freedom in his own feeding, toileting and sexuality, not forcing him to sit on the pot or saying 'tut tut' or 'naughty', or 'good', never giving him a conscience about things but letting him choose, as far as he can, what he wants to do. The child is allowed to do exactly what he likes so long as he does not interfere with someone else. That is the difference between freedom and licence.

It would be marvellous to have a school of children who have been self-regulated from birth. Alas, most of the children at Summerhill have not been self-regulated. But Summerhill is run on the principles of self-regulation and it works. That's what our self-government is. If you don't want to do maths it's nobody's business, but if you want to bully somebody or make a noise at midnight it's everybody's business. The children are free to do exactly as they like as long as they don't interfere with the freedom of others. I have had my school in East Suffolk for forty-three years, and for at least twenty of these years I had many problem children, thieves, destroyers, aggressors, but not once was any pupil brought up before a juvenile court for delinquency. Freedom plus approval won over the wish to be antisocial.

Self-regulated children, and this includes children who have been at Summerhill for a while, have a different sort of relationship to adults from other children. It is a fearless relationship; they just take them for granted. They aren't respectful, I'm glad to say, but treat adults as equals and friends.

Reich believed that the child, unconditioned, was a naturally social and loving being, and I think we have proved this at Summerhill. William Golding's tendentious novel, *Lord of the Flies*, is frequently cited by those who believe that human nature is inherently evil and that children must be made good by discipline, but to me the book is an excellent unintentional thesis on the wrong education. Make children afraid and make them follow what H. G. Wells called 'God, the great absentee' and beat them up, and then put them on a desert island, and of course they will be full of hate and start killing each other. But if a planeload of Summerhill children were stranded on a desert island it would be very different. First there would be girls among them, which is an important difference. They would all have a council meeting to decide what to do. There would be no question of leadership, no forming of gangs. They would simply try to find food and other necessities together.

This chapter is not a treatise on how to bring up children in the family. If I have a definite aim it is to persuade parents and teachers that education does not mean learning at school. That is incidental. What the schools do not touch is the emotional side of children, the vital side. In their subtle way they do deal with character, forming it from outside with their discipline,

their idiotic gulf between teacher and taught, their school
uniforms to condition children to being uniform in mind and
soul. They have no trust in a child's natural wisdom.

I once asked a boy of eight what he spent his pocket money
on. He said he didn't spend it, he saved it to buy history books.
He is now a professor of history and has written some brilliant
books. Another boy in the same class would never miss a maths
lesson. He is now a professor of mathematics. In the next lower
class a boy was interested in animals. He is now a zoologist.
I quote these cases, not to boast, but to show that the teachers
who hold that children have to be driven are talking nonsense.

Instead of teaching history and maths that will be forgotten
for ever we should teach children so that they can use their
feelings before they use their heads. Parents should realize that
a child is a bundle of energy; it cannot sit still, it must speak in
a loud voice, it must experiment because its curiosity is bound-
less. It is of a world different from that of adults, and this fact
is at the bottom of much family irritation and anger and hate.
The ages cannot mix. As I write now a dozen small ones are
making a hell of a row outside my office. I am not disturbed
because it is my life, but I acknowledge how difficult it would be
for a father or mother cooped up in a small house. The teacher
always has it much easier than the parent, mainly because his
love-hate emotions are not involved. Balanced parents can
stand the racket, but how many parents are balanced? Much
trouble arises from the age gulf, and the sad truth is that the
gulf cannot be abolished; there has to be a compromise so that
junior can have his 'Top of the Pops' and senior his 'Twenty-
four Hours' on TV.

What can teachers do about the present educational system
that is geared to head learning, and in many ways is militating
against child nature? Consider the instinct to play. The usual
school periods run from about nine a.m. to four p.m. with maybe two short breaks for play plus a lunch hour. I hold that it is
much more important for a child to live through its play
instinct than to sit at a desk, but in all educational systems play
is of minor importance, even under the Montessori system
where play is used as a means for learning. Our million football
fans never had enough play as children.

It may be that play is a means that has come about in the

course of evolution, to bring about all the sensory control, the co-ordination and the happiness in movement that the body needs. Puppies play all day with each other. I don't know for certain what play means, any more than anyone else does, but I know that it's there and should be left as it is and not bastardized into a means of making a child learn something. We have certainly never done that at Summerhill.

Alas, the teacher is muzzled. He does not make the curriculum. He has to follow the State plan of learning, and Summerhill cannot escape that either. The school inspectors who come round seem to be primarily interested in methods of teaching and, of course, the number of lavatories. Most of them show no sign of appreciating that our criterion isn't learning but living, that our concern is the psychology of each child. But to be fair to them they cannot easily inspect happiness, balance, sincerity, community spirit. I have more than once said that no one can teach anything of real importance and I think that applies to school inspections—no one can inspect what is of importance.

I cannot imagine any Minister for Education ever ordering schools to be primarily play places. No minister has so far had the charity or guts to ban caning: he would have the church schools, RC and Protestant, at his throat. The pundits have cleverly combined the loving Jesus with that old fool Solomon.

Many young teachers tell me that they hate the whole set-up but can do nothing about it. That is true. All a teacher who believes in freedom can do is to be, in Homer Lane's phrase, on the side of the child. But that in a disciplined school can lead to disaster, as it did at King Alfred School when I was given self-government for my classes alone.

At Summerhill we do believe that the child's emotional development is of primary importance. We have children who live through a phase of hate, bullying other children, precisely because they have been conditioned all their lives, and come from broken homes, many of them. We simply have to tolerate it, knowing that in a year or two they will be all right. And it isn't any sort of therapy that makes it all right: it's self-government, the community, the council meetings. It's being judged by their peers and not by fathers and mothers and teachers. Freedom is the cure, not therapy.

For this reason I am all in favour of boarding schools. In the days of large families the children in a family formed a sort of community, but nowadays, when you get one child or two children in a home with no one to measure themselves against except the adults, I think a boarding school is excellent for them.

Some people might think a child would feel rejected by his parents if they sent him away to school. This might happen if it were a strict school. If he went to a prep school and was beaten up, perhaps he would. He would feel 'my parents hate me to send me to a school like this'. At Summerhill the unconscious feeling is more likely 'my parents love me to send me to a school where I am happy'. I think that's the real unconscious reason why they all love to come back. When they come back at the beginning of term they're all delighted. I see other boarding schools at Liverpool Street station and they look terribly unhappy.

It's remarkable how Summerhill children are so open and frank and free with you, while small children who have been brought up with authority are quite different and react in a bewildered way, or become cheeky, when you make a joke with them or come down to their level so to speak. When our kids have to leave and go on to another school they are never afraid of the teachers. Several teachers have told me that old Summerhill children have got an independence and are unafraid. They're very well behaved and law abiding too. They don't go out of their way to be rebellious against stupid laws. They lack the component of hatred needed to make a real rebel.

Hatred is caused by trying to fit children into a mould, which is attempted in most schools. We get introverted children sometimes, who don't want other people. They sit and read quite a lot. You can't do anything about that; you don't want to change them. Theodore Faithful, when he ran his school, used to get an introverted child and try to make him an extravert, which I think is all wrong. You've no right to do a thing like that, to try to change a person's nature. We don't expect to succeed in that sort of thing: we've had children here for years who have never spoken in a meeting, and we've had children who have spoken too much.

Occasionally we have had a kid from a very difficult background who has been a really persistent bully. One was adopted and never accepted his loss of his original mother. One was from a family who spoiled him and let him do as he liked, making him a sort of king of the home. But very often the bully is one who has a younger brother, and every kid is a younger brother to him. We had a little American boy who was always bullying a little girl, and I said to him 'why are you always bullying Teresa?' and he said 'Because she's so like my baby sister'. So he was conscious of the fact that he was a bully. Not that that stopped him: the Freudians err by thinking that if you make the causes of a complex conscious it cures it.

I've made a mistake sometimes. I've had a boy from seven to fifteen or sixteen who was a bully all the way and I should have chucked him out but I didn't because there was nowhere to send him. If there had been a school where they would have dealt with the kid's psychological problems I would have chucked him out, but I didn't and I think, looking back, that it was a mistake. I have chucked out two or three in my time because the little kids were coming to me and complaining that they were being terrorized. I've said 'You're not coming back next term because you're frightening the kids', or something of the kind. I couldn't sacrifice everyone so I've had to sacrifice them.

It says a great deal for the lack of a system of authority based on fear and punishment that a bunch of little kids felt they could come to me and complain that they were being bullied. In an ordinary English school in which the teacher represents punishing authority this would have been unthinkable. They would have known that nobody would be on their side because they would have been 'sneaking'—breaking a code of ethics based on fear. They would have simply had to suffer until they in their turn were big enough to bully others.

Our kids even come and tell me what's wrong with the teachers, including me. Once they came and told me I was an awful teacher, which wasn't true. They were children who didn't want to go to lessons, but went 'because my parents expect me to go', and then blamed the teacher.

One boy, who came far too late to Summerhill, and whom we could not help much, was a sort of Fascist who wore jack-boots and a black leather jacket. Some of the younger kids paraded with him just for fun, but he did not have any influence on the kids at all. I never feared that he would: I trusted the sanity of the kids. We had a Norwegian Fascist once too, who used to go and visit Mosley and then come back and stick fascist bills on the walls. The kids didn't tear them down; they just wrote things like 'to Hell with Fascism' on them.

This non-interference with our children presupposes a genuine trust in them, in their innate goodness and natural wisdom. And because of this non-authoritarian attitude to them they are able to accept limitations on their freedom that make sense. Of course the bigger girls at Summerhill would like a sex life, but I have to tell them I cannot allow it because even if their parents agreed, it would be a terrible risk to my school, because if it became known, the school could be shut down. I think it's because of that non-moral attitude that we've been saved from pregnancies. We have not had a single pregnancy, that I know of, all the years I've had at Summerhill.

It is a platitude to say that education aims at preserving the *status quo*, at raising a new generation that will have the mores and the manners of the older one. Like all platitudes there is truth in this one. In my youth it was the aim of society to give children enough schooling to enable them to work for their masters. A labourer earned fourteen shillings a week but at that time whisky was 2s 6d a bottle and Swedish matches 1½d for a dozen boxes, meat 8d a pound. But the wages were often starvation level ones. In my father's village school children learned some Latin before they left at fourteen to work on farms.

The purpose of a school in those days was to bring up people who could read enough to be wage slaves, and nowadays it is modified slightly to give them the skills required by a technological society. There is no fundamental difference. It is still intended to fit people to the station in life to which God has called them, still, as Michael Duane's analysis in his chapter on State education shows, a class education. There are some good primary schools. I went to see one recently. I liked it: the kids were chattering away, in fact happy, and were playing different things. But I was told that some of the mothers were protesting to headquarters that the children were not learning to read soon enough. This fetish about learning to read early is almost universal and is a quite unnecessary area of anxiety between parents and children, which only exists because parents accept the supposition that education should be geared to the needs of society, not to those of children.

This should not be so. Society is a fixed thing whose whole unconscious aim is to perpetuate its own existence in its own way, hence Russian education and hence American education and British education are all establishment education.

You cannot go in advance of the parents and you cannot go in advance of the teachers. Education does nothing to teach prospective parents how to deal with children. It would be a step forward to teach girls of sixteen or seventeen about bringing up children. Just the ordinary, commonsense things: don't spank a child, don't make it afraid, don't force it to do things or eat things it doesn't want to, don't make it completely obedient to your voice. This might possibly help the girls not to repeat the neurotic patterns of their own upbringing.

I am quite sure that if the cane were to be abolished by law in Britain there would be a tremendous rebellion among teachers. Both parents and teachers think that character moulding is necessary. The headmaster thinks it is necessary to use the cane to give him a quiet life. Teachers are afraid of the young, they don't know what the young will do so they keep them down anyhow. 'Give us a peaceful life, don't bother us. This is wrong, this is right, so you've got to obey.' That's their attitude. They want to keep the system ticking as it is. I think a lot of teachers really hate their kids. One can tell by the way they bully them, the way they shout at them, and the way they beat them. It isn't really surprising when teachers are cooped up in a classroom with so many kids who don't want to be there.

Not only would I abolish the cane, but I would abolish all big schools including comprehensives and erect a lot of one-storey buildings all round the outskirts of London and other towns. I'd take the kids out every day by buses. It could be done. I would have small schools with self-government. You would need a lot more teachers to do it of course, but the real question would be to decide whether it was worth it. At the moment society doesn't want it. A few months ago in *The Times Educational Supplement*, I advocated the return to the pupil-teacher system where you went in as a pupil-teacher and served four years teaching all different elementary subjects and you sat an exam to go to a training college after you had had the experience. Of course, nobody would take that up. It's out of date. But on the other hand, people who go to the training college learn a lot of useless stuff and then they go out to teach, having no idea about children. They've never lived with children. The pupil-teacher did live with children. I was only fifteen when I became a pupil-teacher. The kids in the school were fourteen and so I was one of them, so to speak. I played with them for the first year or so. That system has gone for ever, I think, but nevertheless it would be much more satisfactory than the present system of teacher training, which is totally irrelevant to the needs of children.

It is a question of choosing what sort of education we want. It is impossible to talk or write about education without thinking fearfully about the state of the world, the world full of hate and greed and social injustice. Teachers and parents think that three 'A' levels are important in a world of racialism, crime, exploitation, barbaric prisons, psychological castration of children. Education should mean striving to make a happier world, a more just world, a freer world, and all the school subjects and BA degrees in the world do not a single thing to help humanity to sanity and content. And the great majority cannot understand this simple truth. I have written many articles for *The Times Educational Supplement* about the emotions of children, about freedom from moulding, and there was little or no reaction. Recently I had an article about the stupidity of school subject teaching, saying that what we learn in school had little to do with our life afterwards. I instanced History in which I got a high mark as a degree subject. I said that today I don't know who won the Wars of the Roses or what the Long Parliament did. The result? Ooh, the subject teachers rose in arms when their sacred cow was attacked. History is of great importance, but the nature of the child is a minor matter. And outside the school too that is the wide-spread philosophy of education and life. 'But, sir, our aim is to train children to think, to reason. Mathematics teach a child to reason.' But I have never seen a staffroom in which teachers ran to the Maths master for advice.

My fear is that all this disciplining of children could lead to a Fascist world, all this paternalism against which the students are rightly rising. In Germany I saw a system of education that was all head work, all discipline. Obedience was a great virtue. The emotions of children never had any outlet, so that when a hater came along, the nation, against all its own interests, followed like sheep. And it could happen in any country given the economic circumstances. In the USA Wallace got over ten million votes. McCarthyism had much success. I am rather surprised that other countries do not follow Spain and Portugal and Greece and set up their own Fascism. Yet I am pleased to know that, in spite of our national suppression of the young, life seems, so far, to have kept anti-life from getting too much power. On the other hand it is depressing to see on TV police bludgeoning crowds, working-class folk being beaten up by working-class soldiers and policemen. Millions of workers in the USSR stand idly by while the workers of Czechoslovakia are robbed of their freedom.

Fascism can't live with freedom. And disciplined children are not free from the word go. You see that in any armed force or any police force. As Reich points out, when he saw the soldiers and policemen shooting down the workers in Vienna it struck him that they were being shot down by their own class, by the proletariat. It wasn't capitalism that was shooting them down, just the agents of capitalism, so when you become a policeman or a soldier you automatically reject all your own class and become a member of the Establishment.

And this is the non-sexual result of a sex-negative upbringing. As Reich pointed out, repressing sex is the chief method of inducing conformism. If you are made guilty about your own sexuality, you can be made guilty about anything. Thus sex repression is a means to make the workers behave: it castrates them psychologically, makes them into eunuchs without the guts to challenge anything. As Reich shows in *The Mass Psychology of Fascism*, this is the basis of the character structure in which Fascism takes root.

If all kids were brought up in freedom as at Summerhill you wouldn't have a sick world, an aggressive world. This is how I see Summerhill: it's an island, so to speak, among all the continents, trying to say that life would be better if people were free, that hate would be less if people were free, that violence would be less if people were free. Kids brought up in freedom do not become exploiters, nor do they allow themselves to be exploited.

People would not allow their lives to be controlled so much by other people. The reason why workers in Britain never strike for workers' control is that they have been educated to be inferior, to stay in their own lower class, to take orders. It is an education for submission to the *status quo*, an education for despair. Kids who had been used to participating in a direct democracy (not a fake, representative democracy) from the word go, would not grow up to suffer from apathy, alienation and blind submission to authority with inner hatred and self-hatred as the other side of the coin. They would take direct part in the running of their own communities instead of expecting to be ruled from the top. The violence of society against its members —a criminal code as a substitute for violence—would not be allowed; prisons would become more like the Little Commonwealth. It would be terribly difficult at first: for the first generation or two the products of our slums would be coming out. But the final result would be an end to the hatred of authority— hatred for life, hatred for change, hatred for the young—and an end to the reactive hatred of the rebel. People who have been brought up as free children do not go in for violent extremism. If you go in for violent extremism you are merely letting out a lot of hate that you should have let out when you were a kid. It's irrational hate: ultimately the Oedipus complex, hate of father, hate of authority of any kind. I think it is only a minority in the student movement who really become violent. Every crowd attracts violent people, just as Summerhill very often attracts the neurotic teacher. But I am all with the students in that they are having a big scene against what they are being taught and how they are being taught. This is necessary. When I think that there is a degree course in psychology which deals with rats but never touches children at all, never touches humanity, never touches students, I think they ought to be rebelling against that sort of thing.

Here I must mention the danger of the post-Freudian psychology, stemming mainly from America, the Pavlov-Skinner-Watson Behaviourism aimed at conditioning the child. One could call it a pseudo-scientific version of the Victorianism that killed the life in millions of children. The alarming feature is that this psychology is growing in strength. The conditioning of rats naturally leads to the conditioning of children, indeed it seems to me that it is a resurrection of the old adage—father knows best. The damnable thing is that it fits in with the attitude of many teachers with their passion for discipline and moulding.

I have just been reading B. F. Skinner's *Walden Two*. Here is a utopia that must be the dream of many an industrialist: citizens moulded to obey from infancy, their lives planned by Planners, wise men who remain in the background in this frightening book. It makes me think of Fascism, of the thousands of Germans who yelled their heads off when Hitler spoke in the Templehof in Berlin. That also frightened me. This new Pavlovism, Watsonian Behaviourism alarms because it must appeal to the Establishment.

As far as I can make out Skinner dismisses the psychology of the unconscious as dream stuff, intangible energy that may not exist. It cannot be measured and it is therefore of no importance. Skinner pigeons and rats can be studied; their reactions to stimuli can be registered, so why not apply this to humans? Why not condition children so that they will not only react to the Planners' stimuli but accept it as the rule of life? In his reply to my criticism of his methods in *The Observer* (11.5.69) when I had asked him if he knew of anyone wise enough, good enough, to mould anyone's character, he wrote 'surely character is moulded, and presumably by men wise enough to mould it. Whether they are good enough, or know what they are doing, is another matter. The danger lies in supposing that the moulders are not needed . . .' But at Summerhill we have clearly demonstrated that they are not.

Skinnerism appears to me to assume that the emotional is to be ignored because it cannot be measured by any computer. Scientific methods can assess the qualities of John Brown aged seventeen, his IQ, his academic achievement, his weight and height, his hobbies, but I cannot even guess what sort of scientific investigation would tell about his daydreams, his sex repressions, his fears, his ambitions, and even if machines could do that what could the scientists do about it? Depth psychology they seem to ignore; it cannot be seen under the microscope and therefore it is either non-existent or a nuisance in the way of conditioning a healthy citizen.

So far as I can see the main difference between Skinnerism and Fascism is that Skinner does not want to leave the moulding to madmen and sadists, but wants to keep the moulding in the hands of the wise men. I wonder how they are going to find those wise men. I am eighty-seven but would not dare to mould a dog.

But we are asked to assume that in our science labs, our behaviour clinics we have wise and good men who know it all, know how folks ought to live. The new religion would appear to be based on the fact that God is in the lab and all's right with the world. I have an uncanny suspicion that the new mechanistic psychology is in the hands of men who are afraid of their own emotions, men who want to believe that fears and hates and loves do not exist. They must do so because they cannot control, cannot analyse emotion. Men who might describe Milan Cathedral in terms of so many stones, so much mortar. In a way the new moulders, like the Christians, believe in original sin, in their case original sin being emotion, libido, life force, call it what you like.

Chapter 5

The Child, the Law and the State

by Nan Berger

'The right of a father to the custody and control of his children is one of the most sacred rights.' So said Lord Justice James in the Chancery Court in 1878 in a case where the religious up-bringing of three children was in parental dispute and where the children themselves, aged nine, eleven and twelve, were known to be in opposition to the father's wishes. Refusing to hear the views of the children, the Court gave judgement in favour of the father, Mr Agar Ellis, confirming the judgement at an earlier hearing before Vice-Chancellor Makins who had thundered 'I intend my judgement to leave him (the father) master in his own house'.

The judgements of these courts were important because from them came a strong re-affirmation of the rights of parents—in practice fathers since mothers had few rights in law in relation to their children—and it issued two subtle warnings. One to those who were beginning to feel that the law was too heavily weighted in favour of the rights of parents and were cam-paigning for powers of intervention by the State and one to children that the law would not take heed of their desires and wishes when they were in conflict with their parents.

The spectre of the victory of Mr Agar Ellis still lingers round the law in relation to children and haunts the courts administer-ing it both on the question of State intervention and the right of children to be heard.

The Chancery Court has always had special powers in rela-tion to the rights of parents over their children and was, until the beginning of the twentieth century when the first Children Act was passed in 1908, the only court which had power to interfere with a parent who abused the rights he held in a manner which stopped short of criminality. But it was a court which was concerned only with children who had property expectations. It would not assume responsibility for guardianship for a child without means. No child could be made a ward of court unless a fund were settled for its maintenance. 'The Court,' said Lord Chancellor Eldon at the beginning of the nineteenth century, 'cannot take on itself the maintenance of all children in the kingdom.'

As a court protecting children of the poor the Chancery Court had no relevance and has little today even though cases involving property are no longer the only cases considered by this court. It is frequently used, in its jurisdiction concerning guardianship, by parents who seek to reinforce their disapproval of their children's mode of life and choice of friends by making them wards of court—a costly procedure. Chancery judges, in any case, tend to be remote from the ordinary realities of life and on the whole 'protection' by this court is one of the 'rights' which children can do without.

1. *Protection of Working Children*

DURING the nineteenth century there was a spate of legislation relating to children but none of it challenged the idea so firmly held in common law that children were the possessions of parents. None of it contained even a hint of giving status to the child as a person. The child was the property of its parents who had complete control over its being and life and the new laws buttressed this idea.

The emphasis of these laws was protection and the intention of those who campaigned for them was to save children from the worst results of the industrial revolution. The reformers were, for the most part, do-gooders with the sentimental attitude to 'little children' so beloved of the religionists, whose Christian conscience was outraged at the thought of defenceless children working in the appalling conditions of the new machine age, which resulted in ill-health, disablement and often death.

Few of the reformers had any idea about the needs of children as persons and if they did none of it was reflected in the legislation they pushed through a reluctant parliament. Some of the more far-sighted saw the need to give children education which would enable them to man more efficiently the machines of the developing industries of the future. Some also saw the need for protecting property against destitute children who were forced into crime in order to exist at all. The employing classes—the owners of the new mills who were also the property owning classes—saw only one aspect of children's lives: their ability to work in the mills and make profits for the masters.

The early part of the century saw a series of Acts passed which regulated the employment of children in the textile mills. The first, the Health and Morals of Apprentices Act of 1802, limited working hours to twelve and made the masters responsible for teaching children to read and write. It was sponsored in parliament by Sir Robert Peel, a Lancashire millowner who died in 1830 leaving £1½ million. The apprentices were pauper children sent off in job lots from parish workhouses, who were only too pleased to get rid of them, to millowners who undertook to house and feed them. That it was pauper children who were first helped by the law was an indication of public opinion at the time. No question of interfering with parental control arose since the children were orphans either through death or desertion. No question of the State taking on the responsibilities of parents was at stake as the State, through the poor law, was already partially involved in the lives of these children.

'Free' children, those who were not pauper apprentices, had to wait until 1819 for their crumb and it came through Robert Owen, the Socialist manager of a cotton mill in Scotland where conditions of employment were infinitely better than the average for the time. He bullied a now reluctant Robert Peel into getting a committee set up to enquire into the conditions of children in cotton factories, which resulted in the 1819 Act forbidding children under nine to work in these factories at all and limiting the hours of those under sixteen to thirteen and a half a day.

The opposition of the employers to this Act was mainly on the ground that it was wrong for the government to interfere in the freely made arrangements between master and worker. They hated government interference even more than they hated the reduction of hours and the age limitations. It was natural for the children not to be involved in any ·protest since they were in the position of slaves, put to work by their parents to whom their wages were paid. They were property, not people. The opposition of the employers to the principle of inspection was equally strong though in practice such inspection was quite ineffective. If the children saw inspectors in the factories, they argued, they would assume that these inspectors had power over the masters and all subordination would be at an end.

In any case the age limit was almost impossible to enforce without registration of births (which was not compulsory until 1837). Parents of the under-nines who desperately needed their wages were only too willing to sign false declarations.

Ineffective though this legislation was, it pushed in a wafer-thin wedge to support those reformers who wanted the government to take increased responsibility for the protection of children at work and it made the passing of the 1833 Act, sponsored by Michael Sadler, Tory MP for Newark until he lost his seat, and later by Lord Ashley (who later became Lord Shaftesbury and founded many institutions for homeless boys), a little easier.

Sadler's Bill originally sought to limit the working hours of children below eighteen to ten a day but this was more than the employers would stand for. They realized that if they agreed to this the hours of adult workers would be reduced since the work of children was essential to that of adults. They painted pictures of profits diminishing to the point of ruin for them and persuaded Parliament, instead of passing the bill, to set up a commission to visit factories and see conditions for themselves. The millowners did their best to show their factories in a good light but the commissioners were swayed by the evidence of the foremen and overseers who spoke of how they had to chastise the children to keep them alert at their work and by the conditions they could see for themselves of child ill-health and injury. In their report the commissioners spoke of the 'permanent deterioration of physical condition, product of disease, wholly irremediable, and the exclusion from education' adding: 'That at the age when children suffer these injuries from the labour they undergo they are not free agents but are on let out hire, the wages they earn being received and appropriated by their parents and guardians.' Considering that under common law the services of children were available to their fathers up to the age of fourteen, this was a surprisingly progressive comment.

The Act which was eventually passed, limiting hours, prohibiting night work for those under eighteen and strengthening inspection, was claimed as a victory for the reformers because of its school attendance clause. Those children whose working hours were limited by the Act to forty-eight a week had to attend school for two hours on each of the six working days. On Monday morning they had to turn up at the factory with a voucher showing they had made the necessary attendance in the previous week. Otherwise they were not permitted to work. That was the law.

In practice not many of them could produce a voucher. Long working hours and the absence of schools enabled the law to be flouted and the employers got away with it. But the principle was that if hours of work were reduced so must some other kind of activity be put in its place. The do-gooders firmly believed that the devil would find work for idle hands.

What education there was at the time was provided by charity, mainly religious charity and the employers who did obey the law used these schools to provide the Monday morning voucher. It relieved them of the necessity of setting up schools of their own as Robert Owen had done. No one was much interested in what the children learned at school, certainly not the employers. The voucher was the only thing that they considered their affair and they even opposed the first government grant, the princely sum of £20,000 to a charitable institution to extend its schools, on the grounds that it was wrong of the government to spend public money on the children of the poor.

Legislation concerning education and concerning factory work was now embodied in the same Acts, and the same inspectorate was concerned both in trying to enforce the voucher system and in trying to protect the children from over-greedy employers. For the next thirty-odd years this situation continued. Labour legislation was extended to factories other than textiles and to other fields of employment: chimney sweeping; mining; lace manufacture; bleaching and dyeing; banking; shopkeeping; and agriculture. In most Acts there was a clause making school attendance a condition of work—a sort of work permit. The 1844 Factory Act introduced an extended scheme—the half-time system—under which children from eight to thirteen were to work either ten hours a day on three days or six hours every day and were compelled to attend school on alternate days for three hours a day.

The Education Acts of 1870–1891 made it compulsory for all children under twelve to attend school and forbade them to work during school hours. At this stage began the swing from a position where factory legislation dictated when a child should go to school to a situation where educational legislation dictated when a child should be permitted to work.

Not until the Act of 1918 was the half-time system finally abolished and very stringent regulations about child work enforced.

The pattern of a child's life in relation to education and work was now set. Education was one thing; work another. As educational provision increased through the twentieth century and the academic demands on children became greater, in order to produce a sufficiently skilled labour force and literate recruits for the forces, the break between school and work became more sharp. Children were taken further and further out of the adult world and remained until a much later age dependent on their parents. In recent years further extension of education into the age groups where the majority are at work has not given these children any greater means of being either independent or being regarded as full human beings. Educational grants for the very poor are insignificant and a very small percentage of children are grant-aided students. Such grants are in any case dependent not only on parental income but also on parental permission.

The present law which makes it compulsory for a child to attend school between the ages of five and fifteen does little to enhance the status of children or lead them to a self-regulating life. Compulsion of this kind would be totally unacceptable for adults in the so-called free world. Why should it be acceptable in relation to children? Can there be one code of civil liberty for adults and another for children? It can be argued that compulsory education is for a child's own good; that education is a privilege bestowed on all; that schools are enlightened and that the welfare of the child is the paramount consideration. In fact compulsory education is the beginning of the conditioning of the individual to the unquestioning obedience on which an authoritarian State depends. No conscientious objection is allowed; no pay award made for work done; submission to the school hierarchy is demanded; infringement of school discipline and absenteeism are punished.

Compulsory education, added to the legal concept of *in loco parentis*, puts teachers in an authoritarian position from which it is impossible to escape. The submission of children to conformity is an integral part of the system.

To put teachers *in loco parentis* means that they must assume the authority of parents when children are in their care and it buttresses the inability of society to accept that children must be *given* responsibility in order to learn how to take it for themselves. To deny a child responsibility reduces its ability to be self-regulating. Much of the authoritarian attitude to children on the part of teachers derives from their position *in loco parentis* which incidentally gives the teacher the right to punish the child in any way in which a parent is permitted to do in law. The concept is spelt out in detail in the Children's and Young Persons' Act, 1933, which reads, following the section prohibiting cruelty to children, 'Nothing in this section shall be construed as affecting the right of any parent, teacher or other person having the lawful control or charge of a child or young person to administer punishment to him.'

When a parent voluntarily puts children in control of nurses and school teachers it could be said that he has appointed such a person as his agent. But when a parent is compelled to send a child to school, so that it is impossible to say he has voluntarily made such an appointment, the law still holds, the argument being that the power of punishment is inherent in the position of a school master, possibly, in legal phraseology, as an 'easement of necessity'. In more common terms because it suits the Establishment to have it that way.

So far as the primary school child is concerned compulsion has no validity. Small children are naturally curious and gregarious and there is no need to compel them to attend school. Those who have to be compelled by law are those in special need and their difficulties are aggravated by the enforcement of the law demanding that they should attend school.

Adolescence brings a different situation. Preoccupied with growing up, the child looks to its school to give some relevance to its learning. If the law of compulsion were removed schools would have to provide for these needs—a trend which is already marked at the primary stage, especially in such schools as the Eveline Lowe Primary School in South-East London—to attract children to education.

An alternative to compulsion is for the right to a number of years of secondary education to be given to everyone through a voucher system. These vouchers would guarantee education to all those who wanted it at times of their own choice. The question of what adolescents do if they are not at school would present no greater problems than the enforced idleness in a schoolroom which now characterizes much secondary education. Idleness is not a natural way of life except for a few determined characters who will pursue it in spite of attempted compulsion to make them do otherwise.

Freed from legal compulsion education could alter from a law to be obeyed to a privilege to be enjoyed.*

If the law which makes education compulsory were to be abolished it would follow that laws concerning work for children would have to be altered. Those who chose to work rather than to attend an educational course would be protected from the worst exploitation in the same way as adults are protected—by trade union action and State intervention. For some young people a combination of current work and education would be the answer. For others longer spells of education interspersed with spells of work would be more acceptable. Many would choose to take their education all in one period, as they do now, and others might delay the use of their vouchers until they had completed a longer period of work. The Youth Employment Service which now has a statutory obligation to help the school leaver find work would also have it for the worker-student or for the young person who wished to defer the use of his educational vouchers.

None of the factory or educational legislation of the nineteenth century affected the relationship between the child and it-parents. The only law which protected the child at home was the Poor Law Amendment Act of 1868 which provided punishs ment for the parent if the child's health could be shown to be seriously impaired by failure to provide shelter and main-

---

* For some of the points in the paragraphs on education I am indebted to Brian Richardson.

160

tenance. This law was poor protection. Magistrates were not easily convinced that they should punish parents except for the most outrageous situations and in any case it was very difficult to decide what was neglect and what was inability through poverty. Nor was it easy to decide what was reasonable punishment for a child and what was cruelty. This Act was not, in any case, passed for the benefit of children but to keep children 'off the rates'.

Sixty years after an Act was passed making cruelty to animals a punishable offence, an Act was passed to make cruelty to children an offence. It was passed mainly as a result of the campaigning of the National Society for the Prevention of Cruelty to Children which had been formed in 1884.

The Act of 1889, sometimes referred to as a Children's Charter, was more concerned about wrongs done to children than it was about rights but it did make a tiny inroad into the all-powerful rights of parents and was the first glimmering of the idea that children had any rights at all. A child could now give evidence against his oppressing parents, even when too young to understand the nature of the oath to speak the truth, and husband or wife could give evidence against the other. Those in charge of children could be punished for ill-treatment, neglect, abandonment and exposure, and the magistrates were given power to remove a child from the custody of its parents to a place of safety. Powers were given to the police or other authorized persons to enter a house, by force if necessary, if it was suspected that a child inside was being subjected to cruelty.

The Cruelty Act was the forerunner of the many Children's Acts passed in the twentieth century beginning with the Act of 1908, an Act which still forms the basic pattern of all subsequent Acts. It made considerable changes in the law as to the punishment of persons under sixteen, its aim being to keep children out of prison, and it formally created a special court for dealing with children and young persons, the juvenile court.

It abandoned the situation where children were treated according to the common law principle of equality before the law under which they were liable to trial before an ordinary court and to receive punishment in the same way as adults did. Children under seven escaped such treatment because they were deemed 'incapable of a guilty mind' and those under fourteen if the prosecution failed to prove that the child knew it was doing wrong. Age could therefore gain an acquittal for a child but not any different treatment from that which would be given to an adult if guilt were established.

By the end of the nineteenth century this principle had been slightly modified. Children under sixteen were no longer hauled off to Assizes but were tried summarily by a Magistrate's Court which had power to commit them to reformatory schools and industrial schools. After 1902 Borstal detention became an alternative to normal imprisonment for some young offenders and five years later magistrates were given powers to put children on probation.

The 1908 Act extended considerably the action which could be taken on behalf of children who were being deprived of a family life and those who had come before the court for an offence.

Those who took on the boarding of children under seven for reward had to notify the local authority who had the power to inspect the premises where children were kept and remove them in certain circumstances. No one who kept children for reward could take out life insurance on them, previously a favourite trick of the baby farmers looking for a quick cash return on boarding sickly infants. Local authorities were given power to remove children from parents (or guardians) to a place of safety pending legal proceedings for cruelty. Courts were given the power to order long-term separation of children from cruel parents and keep control over them until they were sixteen, committing them to the care of a relative or other fit person.

Parents whose children were thus removed could be made to pay for the maintenance of the children.

Thus the 1908 Act evolved the principle that a child could be brought before the Court when in need of care and protection as well as when it had committed an offence and the State assumed the right to interfere in the relationships between parents and children.

But this principle did not in any way enhance the rights of children, though it gave them some protection and established that the State had a responsibility to look after those whose parents would not or could not do the job themselves. The

State, when it took children away from parents, assumed the same rights over them as their parents had.

Little if anything in subsequent Children's Acts has altered this situation and you can search through existing legislation as it affects children and not find a single sentence which enhances the dignity of childhood or recognizes that children are people in their own right and not just appendages of adults. Where parental authority has been restricted as being unreasonably oppressive through cruelty and neglect, the State has taken over and given the child some protection. It has not added to the child's freedom or status.

The trend of legislation has followed the basis laid down in the nineteenth century with emphasis on protection against physical maltreatment, on 'putting away' the deviant child in a place where by corrective training it would learn to obey the rules of an adult-orientated society and in providing institutional care or foster parent care for those children who are orphans, abandoned or whose parents are temporarily or permanently prevented by one reason or another (or are unable or unfit) to provide accommodation, maintenance and upbringing.

The Children Act, 1948, which resulted from the recommendations (for the half million children then in institutions and in foster care) of the Curtis Committee, laid the responsibility on local authorities to set up Children's Departments with the duty to look after the welfare of all children deprived of home life and the duty to administer the various Acts in relation to children, especially the Children and Young Persons Act, 1933. The 1948 Act made it the duty of a local authority to *receive* into care children up to the age of eighteen, and in some circumstances older children, who were deprived of a proper home life. Children cannot, under this Act, be taken into care against the wishes of their parents nor can the local authority, having taken a child into care with parental agreement keep the child in care if the parents wish to reclaim. To do so the local authority must obtain an order from the juvenile court.

The Act, in defining the duties of the local authorities to children in care, states that they shall exercise their powers in the best interests of the child and 'afford him proper development of his character and abilities'.

The Children and Young Persons Act, 1963, stated that it

was the duty of local authorities 'to make available such advice, guidance and assistance as may promote the welfare of children by diminishing the need to receive them into care . . . or bring them before a juvenile court; and any provisions . . . may include giving assistance in kind or in exceptional cases in cash'.

Neither Act makes any reference to the duty of local authorities to seek the views of the children involved, to give guidance directly to them, to give them support in their efforts to develop as self-regulated human beings. Nothing in the Acts indicates that independence and self-regulation among children is an idea to be pursued. The whole wording of the Acts is in terms of acting on behalf of the child and not in supporting a child in its efforts to grow up. Legislation which had respect for children as full human beings would do all of these things and would have written into it the right of children to be consulted directly about their situations by whomever had overall responsibility for their wellbeing and by those who were in some temporary custodial capacity (school teachers, staff of residential establishments, staff of 'corrective' institutions, for example). It would also make it obligatory on local authorities so to construct their Children's Departments that children themselves would regard them as *their* departments, as places where they could go to get help, advice and support. Nowhere in the legislation which set up these departments is there even a hint that it was envisaged that this should be so. Very few, if any, of the existing Children's Departments have a set-up which is remotely likely to encourage children to make an approach.

The Children and Young Persons Act, 1969, framed after at least four years of inter-professional discussion on two White Papers—*The Child, the Family and the Young Offender, 1965* and *Children in Trouble, 1969*, deals with the legal proceedings involving children and young persons and the powers of the Court, and with children 'in care'. It also strengthens the law on private fostering of children.

It is a basic Act, repealing much of the Act of 1933, and now it is on the statute book it can be expected that no other Act of a similar nature will be passed for at least as long as the period that has elapsed between the Act of 1933 and that of 1969. It is therefore setting the pattern for the treatment of children in need of help, either because of their circumstances or because they have broken the law, for the next forty or so years.

It might have been expected that this Act would make a break-through, even a minor one, in recognizing the need for giving children opportunities for self-determination and for choice; their need for an identity within their own families even though they might be removed from that family into residential or other care. That it might have given a specific knock on the head to the salvationist attitude of protecting children from 'bad' families or associates, and have given support to the idea that a child has a right to keep contact with its family and friends even though it is in care and that to remove it spiritually as well as physically to a 'nice' home or foster home far removed from its own cultural and local background is detrimental to its development in meeting the challenges which confront it.

The Act does have some good aspects, notably that it will mean that fewer children will come before a Court as in need of care and protection and that no one who has not attained his fourteenth birthday can be charged with any offence except homicide. But a child between fourteen and seventeen can now be brought before a juvenile court for *any* offence whereas formerly offences were restricted to those punishable in an adult with imprisonment. In any event the Court cannot find a case proved unless the child is deemed in need of the 'care and control' which he is unlikely to receive without a Court order.

Orders for a child to be removed from home are no longer divided between Fit Persons Orders and Approved School Orders but limited to a 'care order' lasting until eighteen, thus allowing the local authority to make the 'best available provision', including care in a 'community home' which will take the place of approved schools. This measure will give greater flexibility in dealing with children in trouble, but this flexibility will be useless unless residential care for children and the attitude to it is radically altered. Nor does the abolition of the previous possibility of committing a child to the care of a private person, such as a relative, strengthen the concept that wherever possible a child should remain within its own environment.

The Act permits Courts to commit a child to the care of the local authority until it is eighteen, which is in any case far too long, since the majority at this age are at work and can have other adult responsibilities: for example, marriage is permitted at sixteen with parental consent; national assistance can be claimed at sixteen since this is the age when parents are no longer legally responsible for the maintenance of their children. But there is a dangerous sub-clause in the Act which permits committal until the age of nineteen if an order is made in respect of a child in its sixteenth year.

An even more objectionable clause expressly denies a principle of child care which was spelled out in the Children and Young Persons Act, 1948. This Act made it the prime duty of a local authority to use its powers to further the best interests of children in its care and to afford them opportunities for proper development of character and abilities. [Section 12 (1)]

The 1969 Act expressly denies this principle when it says:

'If it appears to the local authority that it is necessary, for the purpose of protecting members of the public, to exercise their powers in relation to a particular child in their care in a manner which may not be consistent with their general duty under Section 12 (1) of the Act of 1948 to further his best interests and afford him opportunity for proper development, the authority may, notwithstanding that duty, act in that manner.'

The local authority can, under this clause, put public interest before that of the child and is to be judge as well as guardian. A child may be deprived of his liberty by the local authority which is under no obligation to give the child an opportunity to be protected by a Court hearing and does not have to undertake the burden of proving its case. Such a power is contrary to the conception of the Children's Departments being bodies which will act in the best interests of the child and of being an agency *of* the child and one to which those in trouble with their children could turn. The deprivation of the liberty of a child had, until this Act was passed, been seen as a matter serious enough for the powers of 'putting away' a deviant child to be reserved only for the Court which had to weigh up the consequences to the public of leaving him at liberty. A decision was reached only after the child had had an opportunity to defend himself. This right is now taken away and with it the basis of trust of the child 'in care' in those looking after it.

That juvenile Courts as they are run at the moment are not

places where it is easy for a child to speak and stand up for himself is acknowledged by those who have the wellbeing of children, including deviant children, at heart. But the proper remedy is not to give these wide powers to a local authority but to make the juvenile Courts places where children feel they can be heard; to reduce the ordeal of appearing before a Court by modifying the procedure even further towards an atmosphere of informality. Courts could be *made* to show a real concern about how to create opportunities for children before them to be *heard*, in an atmosphere of respect for them as human beings.

For the deviant child who posed problems of public safety there were already methods of dealing with the situation before the 1969 Act was passed. The insertion of a 'public protection' clause can only mean that local authorities are to be pressed to be more punitive towards the child in trouble and to deprive even more children of their liberty. As matters stood before the Act there were already more children in custodial care than is essential for society's wellbeing and they are certainly more cut off and isolated than is necessary for public safety.

Even children in non-custodial care are deprived of the liberty to which they are entitled. Those in residential homes are subject to a very low tolerance of risk and over-protectiveness which has more to do with the protection of the staff than of the child; there are too few opportunities for choice of activity and self-determination; too few possibilities of building up a variety of relationships because of the restrictions on visits by families and friends; and too little skilled therapeutic help available for the child to regain lost and repressed parts of its personality which are always at risk when a child is separated from family and friends; too little opportunity for a child to have 'life space' with its own belongings.

To regulate these deficiences by law, except in a general statement of intent, may be difficult but they could be embodied as rights for the child in Regulations issued by the Home Office which exercises general control over residential establishments for children 'in care'.

The emphasis on the physical and material wellbeing in legal enactments governing children, whether 'in care' or in their own families, is very marked and is an essential part of the State's responsibility to assist in maintaining a high standard of health in children. But this emphasis crowds out the need to make provision for the emotional and social needs of children and is often used as an excuse to deny children an atmosphere of freedom for development. For example, in residential homes for small children the spit-and-polish-keep-it-all-clean-and-hygienic-or-we-may-be-accused-of-neglecting-the-children attitude clearly interferes with the important need for staff to *talk* to the children, play with them, allow them to make an enjoyable mess so essential to development. Similarly in residential homes for older children the emphasis on avoiding any public or official criticism if there are physical mishaps, severely restricts such normal activities such as tree climbing, rough and tumbles among the kids, exploratory outside trips near rivers, mountains or even where there is traffic. It leads to an 'over-protectiveness' (for want of a better expression: it has nothing to do with protectiveness in fact) which denies the child its right to develop, a denial which is just as important as the denial of food and shelter; yet the latter is deemed legally and morally indefensible.

2. *Breaking the Law*

THE new Children and Young Persons' Act, 1969, may alter the manner in which a child who breaks the law—or rather the child who is detected in breaking the law—gets to one or other of the closed institutions maintained for his incarceration, but it will not alter the nature of these institutions whatever name-changes may take place. Nor will the treatment the delinquent receives in these places alter except in minor details. Renaming of attendance centres, detention centres, approved schools and borstals will not alter their régimes.

Attendance centres, where a child may be required to present himself at specified times in his leisure hours for a specified number of hours each week—evenings or Saturdays—are intended for those who are, to quote from the official description, 'open to the effects of punishment and the influence of attendance centre staff in teaching them to respect the law and the property of others'. The staff may be policemen (off duty) or prison warders and the main punitive element in such centres is the deprivation of leisure time or in other words getting children out of the way for specified periods. The régime is one of physical training and disciplinary tasks or lectures on such subjects as first aid or 'citizenship'. Few if any children who suffer this type of punishment get anything more out of it than a determination not to be caught again. Its effect is deterrent rather than remedial.

But at least attendance centres do not take delinquent children away from their own environment except for a short time. Detention centres do. This form of punishment is at present the standard means of dealing with young offenders for whom a long period of residential training is not justified or necessary but who cannot 'be taught respect for the law by such non-custodial punishment as probation or fines'.

The régime in detention centres is repressive, based on harsh physical conditions, a military-type discipline with work chosen for its unpleasantness, a complete subservience to authority with no possible chance for the inmates to make anything resembling friendly relationships with officials in charge who are for the most part ordinary prison officers with no special training in the care of young people but with a good deal of army experience.

Physical violence against inmates is considered to be part of detention centre life. Thumping, kicking, punching and rough handling are accepted as part of the system though caning is not a permitted punishment.

The official view of this régime is that it is designed to deter offenders from committing further crimes by administering the short sharp shock of punishment. That this conflicts with Home Office statements that punitive methods of control have no place in the treatment and care of children and statements from the same source that punishment alone can never rehabilitate is obvious. That it is not even effective is shown by the figures for those who are reconvicted. For the under seventeens the reconviction rate within five years is 75 per cent.

In terms of a child's right to be helped and not merely punished committal to a detention centre is a flagrant denial of every principle of rehabilitation.

The approved school is for the child who is deemed by authority to need a long period of training removed from his home. Removal from home is a keynote of this type of 'corrective training' and it frequently means being removed a very long way from his home, into a strange environment where visits from friends or family are almost a physical impossibility. Most of those sent to approved schools have been found to have committed an offence, mainly thieving, but some hundreds (720 in 1966) are there for other reasons, e.g. because they were 'refractory' while in the care of the local authority; because they were 'unsatisfactory' while on probation; because they were truants from normal schools.

The enquiries into the savage beatings at the Court Lees School in Surrey in 1967 have tended to obscure the inadequacies of the whole system of approved schools which include the lack of qualification of the majority of staff employed, in even the most basic elements of looking after children, let alone disturbed children; the lack of understanding by the managers of the sort of family background from which the children come; the negative methods of discipline in nearly all schools, based on the final sanction of the cane; the lack of any real attempt to compensate the children for the want of home background, which they lack through being in a closed boarding school; the lack of any attempts to bring families into closer association with the school and the almost total absence of facilities for visiting parents. Add to all this the disregard for children as individuals and their treatment as 'naughty' people who have to be debased and shown their place by a rigid system of punishment and reward designed to reduce their dignity and make them resentful and you have an environment which is at least as likely to turn out disgruntled, inadequate people as it is to turn out 'law abiding' citizens, and is extremely unlikely to turn out well adjusted human beings.

The government promised, after the Court Lees scandal, to overhaul the whole system of the régime at approved schools but it is unlikely that any government will have the courage to make basic changes in the treatment of juvenile offenders which would change the present policy of committing them to closed institutions with punitive overtones. Isolation from society is one of the main ingredients of care for children, whether offenders or non-offenders. They are pushed out of sight so that society will not have to take responsibility for them. Society's anxiety about delinquency is reflected in its need to push delinquents out of sight in closed institutions. It may be necessary to accept that society has to be protected against its most deviant members but there are far more children in custodial care today than is essential for society's wellbeing. The child has a right to expect that society will deal with its deviancy with understanding and not with insensitive repression.

The idea of an open community for deviant children is not a new one. Leila Berg and A. S. Neill have already mentioned in this book the experiment carried out more than fifty years ago by the American-born Homer Lane in Dorset. He established a community of children who were in trouble, who lived in cottages in family groups in what was called Little Commonwealth. The community was quite open. Each child shared 'family' responsibilities, the older taking responsibility for the younger. Those who could worked. Those who were unable to work or would not had to be supported by a form of taxation on the others. Each had a hand in making—and enforcing—the rules of the community. There were adult leaders but the children lived with them and not under them. The keynote of the enterprise was the promotion of self-determination. The atmosphere was one of love and kindness and self-imposed discipline. The inmates could act out their feelings of rejection and hate without fear of repressive punishment.

Little Commonwealth was closed down not because the creation of a therapeutic community for deviants had failed but because Lane was accused of improper behaviour with two young girls who were inmates of the community. Had the community not been closed because of these allegations it would probably have been closed for some other reason. Authority then, as now, cannot accept tolerance toward deviants. Society itself demands that repression shall be used against anti-social, difficult unhappy children and it demands that such repression shall be administered behind closed doors. Unless society's attitude can be changed such children will continue to be isolated in closed institutions from which they emerge even more damaged than when they entered.

As we have said, not every child in an approved school is there because of some offence against the law. Some find themselves committed to an approved school because they are behaving in a way which society cannot accept. For example, in 1969 a girl in the care of a London local authority was brought before a Court as being 'refractory' because she was associating with a young married man and the magistrates committed her to an approved school. Had the girl not been in care and her parents rich they might have tried to break the relationship by making her a Ward of Court. In a normal family the affair would no doubt have been allowed to take its course—and its consequences.

As the girl had already suffered the deprivations associated with being 'in care' yet another was heaped on her for committing an offence against the mores of a prudish and intolerant society.

3.   *Rights in School*

CHILDREN in school have very few rights and teachers standing *in loco parentis* have very extensive rights including the right to administer corporal punishment to children. It is assumed that since the law permits parents to assault their children physically, teachers should also have this right. The powers of a head teacher in terms of controlling the lives of children within the school mean that in such matters as discipline, uniform, personal appearance generally, freedom of speech and freedom of association, the word of the head is law against which there is no right of appeal either for the children or for their parents.

Beating of children—which is really an assault upon them— should be abolished by law. Those who defy the law should be treated in the same way as any other lawbreakers.

Children have a right, which should be written into the basic Education Act, to form school councils or unions over which they have control, which can provide opportunities for pupils to express their views on how schools should be run. They also have a right to some means of appeal from decisions affecting them made by the teachers and parents.

They have a right to expect that their parents will have free access to their school and are involved in decisions about discipline and there is no reason why this cannot be written into Acts concerning education. Similarly, the law could determine the position in relation to uniform which at the moment is in the hands of the local authority and the head teacher. The procedure in most schools is that parents sign an undertaking to provide uniform (for which inadequate grants are given to those below a certain income level) and children can be punished for not wearing correct clothing even though they have not signed, nor been consulted about signing, undertakings. Uniform in schools has little to do with education, although a great deal to do with subjugation to mass conformity, and should be legally freed from compulsion.

4. *Religion*
THE law in Britain takes a special interest in forcing religious teaching and conformity on children. Religious instruction (RI) is the only subject which the law requires to be taught in schools. This requirement was written into the Education Act of 1944. Prior to this Act 'scripture' was not a compulsory subject although it was widely taught.

There are two questions at issue in relation to the rights of children in connection with religious teaching. First, children should not be indoctrinated with a religious faith (especially in schools which are paid for out of public money) at an age when they have no intellectual equipment to understand the implications of such indoctrination and therefore can exercise no judgement. Secondly, if the State insists on such indoctrination there should be more adequate safeguards for those who do not wish such indoctrination.

As things stand at the moment it is not at all easy for a child to opt out of RI. The parents may inform the school of their wishes but when it comes to the point of the child having to actually walk out of a classroom where this subject is being taught it may fail to do so because of a dislike of drawing attention to itself. This certainly applies to small children. In secondary schools this problem may not be so acute but there is another difficulty. Children of secondary school age may have strong feelings about religion not shared by their parents. As things stand they cannot opt out of RI on their own account. It is their parents who must give notice to the school. Children should have the right to take action on their own behalf in this as in many other things, a right which we now deny them.

5. *Adoption and Fostering*
NOWHERE do the attitudes of possession towards children show themselves more starkly than in questions of adoption and fostering. When people adopt it is basically with the idea of

either starting or adding to their family. The whole adoption procedure is geared to making the child the property of the adopting parents and cutting whatever ties it has to its natural parent or parents. There is no question of trusteeship. Adoption is for keeps. The fostering procedure is quite different. Here the foster parents are looking after a child on a temporary basis, sometimes for the length of its non-adult life, sometimes for a short period whilst its mother is in hospital. But in long-term fostering the attitudes of society towards children—attitudes of possession—frequently become uppermost. Foster parents get attached to children because they love them and to satisfy a loving attachment in a society based on property, it is necessary to own the object of one's love—to have and to hold. Sharing a child with its natural parents under such circumstances becomes increasingly difficult although the very basis of foster care is to keep the child in touch with its natural parents wherever possible so that one day the family may be re-united.

So arise the tussles between the foster parent and the natural parent at the point where either the foster parents feel they want to adopt and the natural parents refuse their consent, or where the natural parents for one reason or another, some good some bad, decide they can have the child back with them.

The law relating to both adoption and to fostering is heavily weighted in favour of the natural parents. Foster parents are required to sign an undertaking to allow a foster child to be withdrawn by the placing agency (local authority or voluntary organization). Placing agencies are bound to return a fostered child to natural parents when requested to do so. Consequently foster children are not protected from unreasonable demand by a natural parent to remove them even when they are well established in foster families.

For all children in the care of the local authority, including those who are in foster families, the law needs to be altered in order to give them more security by inserting specific clauses into the relevant acts that the welfare of the child shall be paramount. In addition the law should be altered so that where a child has been in the care of the local authority for three years, whether fostered or not, and where it appears to the local authority that the natural parents are not making efforts to enable the child to be re-united with them, parental rights shall vest in the local authority without any formal act. The natural parent would have the right to apply to the court for the restoration of rights but in considering the case the court would have the duty to put the welfare of the child first.

These alterations to the law would limit the rights of parents but if justice is to be done to children in care this limitation must be accepted.

Children who are in foster care as the result of some private arrangement are in an even more precarious position than those fostered under local authority arrangements. Under existing law they must be returned to the natural parent on request. The rights of the natural parent could, if necessary, be enforced by issue of a writ of habeas corpus. Foster parents do have one method of preventing the immediate removal of a child from their care—they can make the child a ward of court and legal aid is available for this purpose. On the lodging of an application the child becomes forthwith a ward for a period of twenty-eight days and the custody of the child is vested in the Court. The foster parent asks for the care and control of the child, and, so long as an appointment is made for a hearing within this period of twenty-eight days, the wardship continues until determination of this issue between the foster parent, local authority, and natural parents as the case may be.

But this is a clumsy, expensive instrument in a delicate situation and cannot be regarded as a remedy which serves the rights of children since it can mean protracted delays until the issue is finally decided.

A better protection for the child would be to amend the law by putting a private foster parent in the category of persons who may be granted custody of a child under the Guardianship of Infants Acts, at present confined to the lawful parents and putative fathers of illegitimate children. Proceedings under this Act could then be taken when the child had been in the care of foster parents for a period of years, say three, in order to restrain the natural parent from precipitate or unwise removal of the child from the foster parents. This would not provide a complete solution for the future of the child since the question of custody is never closed and can always be re-opened by application to a court.

In some cases the only satisfactory solution, from the child's point of view, is the finality of the adoption order. At the moment the law is not strong enough to enable a Court to dispense with the consent of the natural parent (except in a number of statutorily defined situations unlikely to be fulfilled in such cases) where such action would infringe the rights of the natural parent, even if it can be shown that adoption is in the best interests of the child.

Adoption procedure has been regulated by law since 1926 and subsequent legislation has placed the adopted child, so far as the law is concerned, in almost the same position as the non-adopted child, once the adoption order is made. True he cannot inherit title or honour but for the vast majority this is no privation. Nor does he become legitimate by adoption. If he is illegitimate to start with adoption procedures do not alter his status. But this disability is more social than legal and could largely be removed by a regulation making the normal birth certificate issued to all children the 'short' certificate which bears no identification of parenthood. On this certificate should be added a note to say that the person named on it has the right to apply to the Registrar of Births for information about his parentage.

The law of adoption, unlike some of the other laws relating to children, does not require the court which considers the application for adoption to regard the welfare of the child concerned as paramount. It is one of the 'welfares' which have to be considered but it is not the paramount one. Here again the rights of children should be put in front of parents and adopters and a paramount welfare clause written into adoption law.

When a mother offers a child for adoption she must sign a form of consent but she cannot do so until the child is six weeks old. She can, however, withdraw her consent at any time up to the moment the Court Order is made and she will be asked several times between the first consent and the Court proceedings to re-affirm or withdraw her consent. This provision can have devastating results for the child as well as for the adoptive parents; it can cause great anxiety in the adoptive parents who may have difficulty in becoming completely involved with their adopted child while the uncertainty lasts and this can have a bad effect on the child. For the child who will have been with the adoptive parents for at least three months, which is the statutory time which must elapse between the notification by the adoptive parents of an intention to adopt and the making of the court order, and may very well be much longer in cases where enquiries are extensive or where formalities take time to complete, it may mean an uprooting from an established relationship if the mother withdraws her consent.

In the interests of the child the law should be altered so that the mother gives a once only consent. She should be given as much time as she wishes to make this decision but once having made it she should not be constantly required to re-affirm it. Placements of children should not be made until the mother has made her decision.

Adopted children, however well they are integrated into their new family, are different from natural children and while every effort must be made to minimize the differences, the rights of the child are not increased by a pretence that this difference does not exist. It follows that a child has a right, first, to know that it is adopted and, second, to have means of knowing, should it so desire, who its natural parents were. Adolescents frequently wish for this information and at present there is no way in which they can find out if the adoptive parents withhold the facts. It should be written into the law that children who are adopted should be told and should be a condition on the adopting parents that they will do this. Like sex education it is not a question of choosing a time when the 'facts of life' shall be told to a child, but bringing the child up from an age when it cannot even understand the concept, in the knowledge that it is adopted so that it gradually learns the meaning in an atmosphere of love and security and is never faced with the traumatic shock of the telling.

The law should also make it clear that children who are the subject of adoption proceedings at an age where they are aware of what is being decided for them should be consulted unless it can be shown that very strong grounds exist to indicate that consultation would not be in the interests of the child.

A Home Office Departmental Committee, reporting in November 1970, proposed that adoption should be only one of a range of legal provisions available for children not being brought up by their natural parents. Such provisions could include various types of guardianship which put in suspense rather than sever parental links. For some children such guardianship would be a better alternative than the finality of adoption and would bring us one small step nearer the conception that parents whether natural or acquired stand as trustees for children rather than as possessors.

6. *Illegitimacy*

THE disabilities from which children suffer because they are illegitimate are partly social—especially in late school and work situations—and partly legal.

In the middle ages the illegitimate child was *filius nullius*—the child of no one. Neither the putative father nor the mother had any rights or duties in respect of him and the child had no rights of succession in respect of either parent. Modern legislation has removed many of the disabilities and those which remain are not of great consequence, legally speaking, for the majority of children, except in one respect: relationships with their fathers.

There is no way in English law in which a father may legally recognize his illegitimate child. The nearest thing to recognition, in England and Wales, is that the father may have his name on the birth certificate (but this will not be very helpful to the child in any situation except application for affiliation orders) and, in Scotland, the possibility for the father to make a statutory declaration of paternity. But neither of these actions gives the father any rights or duties in respect of his child.

In Europe generally, other than in Great Britain, there is the possibility for fathers to recognize their illegitimate children in a way which will provide a legally valid child-father relationship. The significance of the relationship varies from country to country—from giving no more than a financial basis for the maintenance of the child (Germany) to the situation where an illegitimate child is indistinguishable from that of one born in wedlock (Poland).

The whole conception of illegitimacy could be dispensed with if it were not for the notion that the child can only have an entity in relation to someone else, that a child must be the possession of someone. If the socially conceived notion that a child must carry on the family tradition were thrown overboard and the concept that the child is a person in its own right fully accepted, the distinction between legitimate and illegitimate children would disappear. There is nothing intrinsically different between a child born in wedlock and one born out of it; only social attitudes make illegitimate children inferior citizens.

7. *General*

WHILE much could be done through alteration and modification of the law to bring freedom to children, children could not, like Negroes and women, be liberated entirely by the actions of others. Freedom, if it is gained at all meaningfully, is self-gained and the most helpful thing which could be done toward this end would be to make children involved in the decisions in their own life from a very early age. Children are persons. Childhood is a stage of life itself, not just an apprenticeship. Until society can recognize this and actively give it expression, children will remain appendages of others, unable to develop in their own image rather than in the image of someone else.

Our laws are a reflection of our attitudes to children; attitudes which basically regard children as possessions (*my* children, often not even *our* children). Laws will only be changed when attitudes change and attitudes will change only when there are enough children who have been given their freedom to make an impact on public opinion. This is, of course, already happening but not quickly enough and with too much compromise. It needs a William Morris with a twentieth-century version of the thought 'Children have as much need for a revolution as the proletariat have'.*

* Thomas, Edward, *The Communism of William Morris*. The William Morris Society, 1965.

Chapter 6

Freedom and the State System of Education

by Michael Duane

1. *Education Today: The System*

'*Almost all (the 88 working-class men and women who survived the grammar school) are professional class people. Over half (30 out of 39 with the girls) became teachers themselves. . . . Up to a third report themselves dissatisfied with their work and position in society . . .*

'*On working-class life in general many expressed harsh opinions. With their own education they were pleased, and most wished to see no changes in the present system, unless it be that grammar schools should become more selective still, and penalties be imposed to prevent lower working-class children from entering them in any numbers . . .*

'*Today most of these 88 children have developed into stable, often rigidly orthodox citizens, who wish to preserve a hierarchical society and all its institutions as they now stand.*'

Brian Jackson and Dennis Marsden,
Education and the Working Class, *1962.*

'*Teachers are not going to change their middle-class status. . . . And even if more teachers are recruited from lower socio-economic groups . . . they are likely to acquire a middle-class outlook along with their new occupational status.*'

Frank Riessman, The Culturally Deprived Child, *1962*

'*Our schools will not be what they should until we give them the teachers they need.*'

The Newsom Report, Half Our Future, *1963.*

'*The very conditions of the classroom situation often make effective education impossible. Large classes reduce the possibility of individual teaching, maximize impersonal authoritarian methods of class control, and increase the passivity of the lower working-class pupil. A general rule should hold for the primary stage of education. The lower the status of the pupil, the smaller the number in class. This is the basic condition for a* psychological *relationship (interpersonal rather than intergroup) between teacher and child. The social organization must enable the* person *as well as the function of the teacher to be felt and perceived. The teaching situation for the lower working-class child is often persecutory and exposes him to persistent attack on his language and so his normal mode of orientation.'*

Professor Basil Bernstein,
Social Class and Linguistic Development, *1961*.

'*. . . the most highly skilled and highly paid teachers should teach the lower classes, which should be smaller than those at the top of the school.*'

Richard Mulcaster, *1530–1611*.

'*British sociologists have sometimes been accused of being obsessed with the underprivileged. But I regard the 80% of children in secondary modern schools as underprivileged; and in the circumstances I am prepared to be viewed as obsessed.*'

Professor David Glass, *1964*.

Any education system is the growing point of its parent society. It is here that the future shape of the society is being formed. It is here that society reveals its true nature by the means it uses to shape its future. Therefore, in order to understand how far it is possible to bring more freedom for children into the State education system, we must see how that system works in relation to the parent society; what objectives it sets before itself; what methods it uses to reach them; what results, intended or unintended, follow; what forces or influences outside or ancillary to the system it draws on, such as the family, religion or other social organizations; and how it uses, or rejects, the previous experience of the child himself.

Of course, we talk like politicians when we talk about systems, influences, objectives or organizations as though we were talking about education. Education takes place in concrete situations with particular people and things. A school filled to the roof with educational materials and equipment and staffed with highly trained and qualified teachers will be an educational monstrosity if the staff are not loving, sexually mature and healthy adults, convinced from their own experience that children are born with all the impulses necessary for their full growth as human beings, and prepared, as teachers, to exercise their professional skills in the service of the children rather than for their personal advancement.

Nevertheless, schools and colleges exert pressures on their teachers of which the teachers are often unaware, because the historical and evolving purposes of those schools and colleges are too subtle and wide-ranging to be easily grasped in the minutiae of daily business, and because no one can work for long in any institution without identifying with some, at least, of its standards and objectives—even in a concentration camp, as Bruno Bettelheim's *The Informed Heart* so painfully shows.

Further, in using the word 'society' when we talk about education we are likely to convey the illusion that in this country the whole population works together in a coherent and integrated manner. The complexity of the education system in Britain would expose this illusion if nothing else did. Within that system, as within the country as a whole, there are contradictory movements, reactionary and progressive. The *Black Papers* on education, published in 1969, were widely quoted by the right wing as a stirring manifesto of traditional values, and derided as reactionary, élitist and irresponsible by the left wing. They revealed much anxiety in the minds of their authors about how far 'progressive' or 'permissive' (both undefined) methods had 'invaded' education at all levels and 'threatened' traditional standards of scholarship and social function. Above all they revealed how readily supposedly thoughtful men fly to slogans rather than to evidence in order to defend what they hold dear.

The diversity of forms seen within the British education system springs not from creative experiment but from historical accident and attachment to outdated assumptions. Within the system there are two main subdivisions, the private sector, made up of private schools and colleges, including all the well-known progressive schools and the Public schools (whose headmasters are members of the HMC or Head Masters Conference), and the public sector, made up of the schools, colleges, universities and other institutions wholly paid for out of public funds.

Purists will object to the use of the word 'State' in describing schools in the public sector since, in law, education is administered by local authorities. Local control is, however, a political fiction since the central government contributes more than 50 per cent of the cost of building, staffing and maintaining schools; exercises control through Her Majesty's Inspectors (another fiction implying that they function directly under the Queen and are, therefore, 'outside' politics), the 'watchdogs' over public expenditure, disseminators of educational ideas and arbiters of educational 'efficiency'. A school can be closed or a teacher dismissed as a result of the recommendation of HMI, whose word with the local authority—since he is so close to the purse-strings—carries great weight. The degree to which standards of building, staffing and maintenance in different types of school have become national is a direct denial of the 'local control' thesis, as the forcing, by Tory Ministers, of local authorities to abandon plans for comprehensive schools or, by Labour Ministers, to formulate such plans, shows that power over the purse-strings gives the last say on important issues.

On the other hand, the central government in Britain, should it wish to implement progressive policies, can move only as far as 'public opinion', manipulated or interpreted by the press in the interests of business and industry, will tolerate. 'Government' and 'control' under a system of parliamentary democracy in a capitalist economy is a matter of estimating how far it is possible to pursue certain policies in the face of powerful pressure groups and vested interests and still remain in office.

Private education starts at the age of three in Nursery Schools which have a teacher/pupil ratio of 1 to 13. In these schools there is an emphasis on play and on associating the beginning of formal education with enjoyment, so there is much freedom for the children to choose their own activities, plenty of toys and sensory apparatus, paints, water, sand, climbing frames, Wendy houses, clothes for dressing up, plants growing, animals such as rabbits or hamsters for the children to feed and observe —everything, in fact, that a good home would want to provide for its children. In particular, stress is placed on having trained and well educated staff who can see that the children use their verbal powers to the full and, by means of stories, conversation about their various activities, songs, nursery rhymes and puzzles, develop the awareness of the importance and flexibility of language that is the central characteristic of middle-class education. Emphasis is also placed on internalizing values by discussion or explanation so as to lower the threshold of guilt and create control from within.

Increasingly the middle class are sending their children to the State schools for infants (aged five to six) and juniors (aged seven to ten) because they have begun to realize that the system of 'streaming', or allocation to forms by academic ability, places their own children at an advantage.

The fact of streaming in junior schools, as Professor J. W. B. Douglas has so clearly shown in *The Home and the School* gives middle-class children the best qualified and most experienced teachers and the most interesting books and equipment in the top streams. It leaves the lower working-class children in the bottom streams with the least well qualified, the temporary, the part-time, the supply teachers and the unqualified. This occurs because in training colleges students are led to develop greater interest in subject matter, without a corresponding understanding of suitable methods of teaching it to children; because the academic tradition in this country gives high prestige to the specialist teaching of a subject, and because higher rates of pay are used as an inducement to bring about such specialization. Thus the initial advantages enjoyed by middle-class children are perpetuated and increased in the junior schools, so that when the time comes for the children to sit for the '11 plus', or, more correctly, the '10 plus' (and the various techniques that have come to replace it), it is the middle-class children who are allocated to the grammar schools. Professor Douglas' study showed that, even if children with the same measured intelligence quotient at the age of seven are taken, those from middle-class backgrounds have several times the chance of working-class children in gaining grammar school places. This comes about because both the systems of selection —devised by middle-class psychologists—and the academic syllabus of the junior school are concentrated on those skills that the middle classes find essential for their tasks of organizing, controlling and communicating—i.e. mathematics, language and the power to form concepts. Middle-class children are brought up from infancy to develop these skills to a high degree.

In addition to these advantages in State schools for the middle-class child, the growth of organizations such as Parent-Teacher Associations or the Confederation for the Advancement of State Education—both essentially middle-class organizations—is ensuring that the middle classes are more and more able to bring pressure to bear on the local authority and the Department of Education and Science. The Nursery School Association has so far had little effect because the provision of nursery schools and classes is at the discretion of the local authority. Very few nursery schools or classes are, therefore, provided by local authorities. Even where they are provided the ratio of teachers to pupils is 1 to 26 as against 1 to 13 in private nursery schools, and the range and variety of equipment compares very unfavourably with that in the private schools.

Since the war there have been notable advances in methods of teaching in *some* infant schools and in *some* junior schools. To judge from the press publicity given to these more enlightened methods the ordinary layman could easily be persuaded that there had occurred a widespread revolution in teaching methods. Unfortunately this is true of only a small minority of these schools, and the changes have been brought about mainly in middle-class areas, where parents are active in securing the best education possible for their children, through direct contact with the heads of schools, education officers or members of Education Committees, or through the pressures that can be exercised by CASE or PTAs.

In the vast majority of infant and junior schools, and especially in lower working-class areas, the methods used tend to be more old-fashioned and repressive because the average quality of the teachers is lower, their turn-over is higher and the cultural gap between the teachers and the children greater than in other areas. Corporal punishment is almost universal, slapping with the hands being the common method of punishment in infant schools and the cane being more often used in the later stages of the junior schools. Corporal punishment is much less frequent in middle-class areas because the parents do not tolerate it so easily and because the children have been more thoroughly prepared by their parents' expectations to work well at school. Discipline can more often be exerted through verbal means, since the 'threshold of guilt' is lower with middle-class children than with working-class children. This point will be dealt with more fully later.

While infant schools in middle-class areas more often concentrate on play, sensory experience and language in the form of nursery rhymes, stories and conversation, infants in working-class areas are more often compelled to spend long hours learning their 'tables', weighing, measuring and calculating from oral instructions or, as soon as they have learned to read, from books or cards.

Learning to read is held to be of the utmost importance, but while much lip-service is paid to the necessity of creating 'reading readiness' by a wide range of experiences, pictures and talk of particular interest to the children, the unhappy fact is that books are thrust straight at the children and repetitive reading aloud after teacher alternates with ill-digested 'phonic', 'look and say' or other methods, so that most children from working-class homes find the process of reading at school boring, irrelevant to their lives or interests and without point. Books of the *Janet and John* type proliferate in such schools. In these books the background is middle-class. Parents are referred to as 'Mummy' and 'Daddy'; the family has a detached house and a car; there are visits to relatives and holidays by the sea; there are games in the garden with the dog Spot and a ball—the whole paraphernalia of what a majority of teachers, as seen in their style of life and expectations, envisage as a desirable life.

The method of teaching reading in these books concentrates on repetition of words and phrases, combined in various ways *ad nauseam*. 'Here is Spot', 'Spot plays with the ball', 'Spot brings the ball', 'I throw the ball for Spot', 'Spot runs for the ball', etc. There is never a natural or normal situation. Children must never be grubby, greedy or late for school. Parents never speak crossly, lose their tempers or swear. The language of both adults and children is textbook English. All sentences are spoken in full, without the normal short-circuiting of natural speech. The whole effect is dreary in the extreme even for middle-class children, who manage to learn to read in spite of such books and teaching because the foundations have been laid in their nursery schools and in their homes where reading is seen by them to be a normal and necessary part of life. The effect on working-class children is to give them such a distaste for books and reading that only the fortunate few survive the process and retain a desire to read because, again, in their homes books are used with pleasure.

It is, of course, desirable that all children should learn to read. Reading is the means by which the individual communicates with those outside his immediate group in space and time; the means by which the individual is, or can be, brought into contact with the whole of human culture. But the solution —to make literacy universal—lies not in better techniques for teaching reading or in the improvement of training methods for teachers, but in social changes that will have the effect of making reading as essential to the normal lives of all people as it is, at the present time, for the middle classes. This, of course, presupposes a social revolution that will spread the burden and the excitement of making decisions about their own destinies to *all* men and women, not just to those who form the present ruling classes. Where there is a need to read, men will read.

In the junior school, and particularly during the last two years, the '11 plus' overshadows everything else except for those children in the very lowest streams who have already been deemed incapable of attempting it, and so will not even be allowed to sit for the standardized tests of intelligence, arithmetic and English that form the core of the 'selection procedure'. It is on the results of this *test*—correctly named by popular usage in spite of the attempts by administrators to persuade the public that there is no question of 'passing' or 'failing'—that pupils either gain a place in the grammar school or fail to do so. Only in borderline cases does the recommendation of the head of the junior school carry weight.

It was at one time hoped that the establishment of comprehensive schools would remove the necessity for the use of tests to 'allocate' children to different type of secondary schools, and that junior schools would thus be relieved of the pressures imposed on them by the '11 plus'. This hope has proved false for two main reasons. The first is that teachers in the mass are unable to do without outside incentives to make their children work. In the junior schools only a very small minority of the teachers have rejoiced at the abolition of the '11 plus' and used the added freedom to work from the starting point of their children's interests. The second, more obvious reason is that the so-called comprehensive schools are not, in fact, comprehensive at all. Since they retain the organization and purposes of the separate grammar schools and secondary modern schools, they retain streaming and competition in work and games (as well as punishment, religious instruction, uniforms and prefects) as the cornerstones of their thinking. Hence the junior schools see it as their function to get as many children as possible into the top stream of the comprehensive along with the other middle-class children and they concentrate, therefore, on academic subjects during the last two years because they know that success in these subjects will be the main criterion for selection by the head of a secondary school.

The Secondary Stage

Private secondary schools exist for about 5 per cent of all secondary school pupils because parents in the middle- and upper-class strata of society want, and can pay for, a better education than the State provides. They know that education plays a more and more important part in securing wealth and leisure, and that in a technical society experiencing change in materials, methods and organization at an unprecedented rate, only the best education will do. In general, therefore, private schools have smaller classes, better educated and better paid teachers coming from the same social background as that of their pupils. A much higher proportion of their pupils remain at school until after the age of seventeen (in the last twelve years the number doing so has actually risen within these schools by 50 per cent) and a much higher proportion find places in universities or in colleges of further education. Public schools have a teacher/pupil ratio of 1 to 11 as against the ratio of 1 to 21 for the State system as a whole; 84 per cent of Public school teachers are graduates, mainly of Oxford or Cambridge, and they come from professional, managerial and propertied families. Within the country as a whole 80 per cent of the most highly paid positions of authority and decision—the Cabinet, the judiciary, the upper echelons of the Civil Service and the Services, the most lucrative directorships in both private and nationalized corporations, industries and services—are held by people who have been educated in Public schools.

It was thought at one time that as the State spent more and more on education the Public schools would not be able to keep up, especially in the provision of the costly buildings and equipment required in the teaching of science or such things as language laboratories for modern language teaching. There is, on the contrary, no sign of failure to compete with, and excel, the level of provision in the State system. The number of wealthy parents wanting Public school education for their sons has, if anything, increased in spite of rising costs, as a knowledge of modern techniques has become more important than nepotism. The buildings and equipment stand comparison with the best in the State system, financed as they often are by large grants of money from industry and commerce.

Within the State system as a whole the picture is quite different. Barely one teacher in five is a graduate, mainly from universities other than Oxford or Cambridge, and those who are graduates are clustered into grammar schools which educate only 20 per cent of the secondary age group. Grammar schools have a teacher/pupil ratio of 1 to 15; their children, selected by the '11 plus' for high academic ability, come—at least 90 per cent of them—from middle- and lower middle-class families, because the tests, claimed for many years to be objective in selecting innate ability irrespective of social class or previous education, have now been clearly shown to be heavily biased in favour of middle-class children and to test achievement and not innate ability.

Grammar school teachers, 74 per cent of them graduates, are themselves from the same kind of background as their pupils, the middle and lower middle class. The few who come from a skilled or semi-skilled working-class background tend to be the non-graduates teaching woodwork, metalwork, needlework, housecraft or physical education.

Secondary modern schools are filled by nearly three-quarters of the nation's children. They have a teacher/pupil ratio of 1 to 22; their pupils, with few exceptions, leave school between fifteen and sixteen—i.e. at the first possible opportunity; their staffs come from lower middle-class and working-class families and barely one in ten are graduates.

I omit consideration of comprehensive schools as a separate type, because they are, as I have mentioned, almost without exception, organized on traditional lines and are little more than grammar and secondary modern schools under one roof.

It is certainly true to say that within the comprehensives as a whole there is more fundamental thinking and experiment than in any other type of school,* but the results of that thought and experiment have not yet affected the majority of these schools. If anything they have, as at present organized, introduced a new and even more psychologically destructive element into our education system. Under the old dispensation of separate grammar and secondary modern schools it was possible for those parents whose children had failed to reach the grammar school to blame the injustices of the selection procedure and the 'system'. Now, however, with an apparently democratic system where 'all have equal opportunity' in the same school, those who are relegated to the bottom streams and the same poor quality of teaching that they would have had in the secondary modern school can only blame themselves or their parents for their failure. Since they do not understand that their failure to succeed academically lies in the injustices perpetrated by a socially divided society, they presume that it is their own or their parents' inadequacy that causes them to fail. So, to the dehumanizing effects on the working class of mass-production techniques is added the internalizing of failure and the even more intensive destruction of the child's confidence in himself and his parents.

Public schools and grammar schools (including the upper academic forms of comprehensive schools) supply over 90 per cent of all students in universities and colleges of further education. Barely 6 per cent of university students come from the manual working class. The lower levels of the working class— the semi-skilled and the unskilled workers' children (some 35 to 40 per cent of the total population) are virtually unrepresented in higher education.

The question so often found puzzling by those who believe that this country provides equal educational opportunity for all, irrespective of social background, is how there continues to exist such disparity between the quality of education in grammar schools and that in secondary modern schools (for, if entry to higher education and to secure and well-paid work is a criterion, grammar school pupils fare better than those from secondary modern schools). The answer lies in the terms of an

* See B. Simon and C. Benn. *Half Way There.*

'agreement' reached between the teachers and their employers —the notorious Burnham Agreement, swallowed by the teachers' representatives because they could command neither the unity nor the strength to resist it. Although the consequences that would follow on the adoption of this agreement were clearly pointed out at the time and have been reiterated ever since, with a growing body of evidence to support the critics, it remains in force as perhaps the most powerful socially divisive instrument within the State education system. The terms relating to pay and conditions of teachers have created such disunity among teachers that it has so far proved impossible to form a united profession and to acquire thereby a unique power to speak as both parents and teachers.

The Burnham Agreement governs the pay of teachers and the scale of staffing in State schools. Pay is calculated on three levels: a basic salary paid to all qualified teachers; an additional allowance for the possession of a university degree or its equivalent in, e.g. art or engineering, with a somewhat higher allowance for a 'good' degree, usually defined as a second-class honours degree or higher; and, finally, an allowance paid for the exercise of some special responsibility concerned with the running of the school. Historically, this latter category has been closely associated with the teaching of academic subjects to more advanced levels. Since grammar schools are staffed by graduates to the extent of 74 per cent as compared with less than 15 per cent in secondary modern schools, and since more than 50 per cent of grammar school teachers are paid the special allowances for academic subjects as against under 20 per cent in secondary modern schools, the average pay of a grammar school teacher is about 25 per cent higher than that of the average secondary modern school teacher. Different local authorities award different 'densities' of special allowances.

The difference in average salaries for grammar and secondary modern school teachers has another important effect. Grammar school staffs are more stable than secondary modern school staffs. This is particularly noticeable in the poorer quarters of large towns and cities where the social class backgrounds of teachers and pupils are most dissimilar and where, therefore, there are the most frequent and bitter disciplinary conflicts. The nature of this conflict will be looked at somewhat more closely later. Suffice it to say at this point that it increases the instability of secondary modern school staffs, who are ever in search of jobs in middle-class areas or of jobs carrying higher special allowances. In some schools that I have known in lower working-class areas the *annual* turnover of staff was as high as 42 per cent, which means, in effect, that in three years, or less than the average stay of a child at a secondary modern school, all the staff, except perhaps the head teacher and those who hold the largest allowances, will have come and gone. A comparison of advertisements for posts in secondary modern schools as against those in grammar schools in, e.g., *The Times Educational Supplement*, will quickly show that, even allowing for the fact that there are four secondary modern schools for every grammar school, the number of posts advertised for secondary modern schools far exceeds those for grammar schools.

The second important provision in the Burnham Agreement is responsible for the radical differences in the teacher/pupil ratios between grammar and modern schools (1 to 15 in the former and 1 to 22 in the latter). In fixing the method by which the staffing of schools and, in particular, the salaries of head teachers are calculated, the Burnham Agreement allocates all children of thirteen and fourteen two Burnham Units, those of fifteen four, pupils of sixteen six and those of seventeen and eighteen ten. The staffing and the head's salary are based, not on the number of pupils in the school but on the number of Burnham Units accumulated. But since it is a well-known fact that working-class children leave school as soon as possible, whereas middle-class children stay on until at least the age of seventeen to get the 'O' and 'A' levels which are necessary for entry to the university or to colleges of further education, it follows that grammar schools accumulate a much higher number of Burnham Units than secondary schools *of exactly the same size*. I found, in a comparison of secondary modern and grammar schools with five hundred pupils in each, that the grammar schools accumulated twice the number of Burnham Units as the secondary modern schools, with the result that not only did the grammar school heads receive a much higher salary than the secondary modern heads, but, for exactly the same number of pupils with considerably higher academic ability, the grammar schools had 50 per cent *more staff* (35 as against 22).

Hence the national staff average of 1 to 15 in grammar schools as against 1 to 22 pupils in secondary modern schools—a drastic differentiation in favour of middle-class children who are already better provided with more comfortable circumstances and better educated parents.

Thus, in the education and qualifications of their teachers; in the salary structures to attract the best qualified teachers to schools for the middle class; in the smaller size of their classes; in the fact that their pupils get more individual attention; in the selection of their pupils by academic ability and from the cultural background of the middle class; on all counts the social-class bias is made to work in favour of the middle-class and against the working-class child. It becomes clear, therefore, how the State system of education and the private system of education together reflect the basic structures of our mass-production society. Together they provide for three levels:

1.   The wealthy owners of property and power who form the power élite in our 'democratic' society, educated in Public schools.

2.   The professional middle class whose social function is to be the communicators, planners and executives, educated in grammar schools.

3.   The manual workers equipped with sufficient literacy to read or understand instructions, oral, verbal or diagrammatic, and conditioned through linguistic and psychological means into attitudes towards authority that make them unable to challenge the positions of those higher in the social scale, or to question and take effective action about their own place in the system. They are 'educated' in the secondary modern and the comprehensive schools.

The system is, in effect, the élitist structure first formulated by Plato and modified to suit the conditions of mass-production. It achieves its effects by means that are more subtle than those envisaged in Aldous Huxley's *Brave New World*.

At this point it is possible to see the close link between the future social functions of their pupils and the actual curricula of the schools. The main difference between the grammar schools and the secondary modern schools lies in the attention they devote to communication, the central activity of the middle class. The middle class exists to produce, develop, exploit and communicate ideas which, when turned into material goods, processes and services, will increase and protect the wealth of those who already own the land, the property and the equipment of this society. The main school subjects—mathematics, science, geography, history and, above all, language—are the modes in which past experience is preserved for the further development of technical expertize in producing more goods at relatively lower costs. Hence the overriding emphasis in grammar schools on amassing factual knowledge, on acquiring dexterity in manipulating symbols and in grasping and expressing complex relationships of all kinds, but especially mathematical and scientific relationships—the groundwork of technology.

The rapidity of the rise in importance of mathematics and science in the curriculum of the Public schools, the grammar schools and the universities can be seen to parallel very closely the later stages of the industrial revolution, when improvement in technical efficiency switched from the pragmatic, day-to-day improvements possible to the man on the spot—the pump man who maintained the engine that pumped water from the mine workings—to the drawing-board engineer preoccupied with materials, stresses, life expectancy, production costs and optimal working rates before he even sets pencil to paper to sketch out the tentative shapes that will take final forms determined by precise calculations. The day of the craftsman who aimed to make a railway engine that would last 'for ever' is over because the modern engineer knows that new discoveries in fuel, in propulsion systems and in materials are being made at such a rate that his machine is often out of date before it leaves the drawing board. So the grammar school emphasizes theory as being the more fundamental part of experience—the Platonic 'reality' behind the transient perceptible forms.

The secondary modern school, at least in the 'A' forms, approaches the grammar school as closely as its more limiting conditions of larger classes, lower quality teachers, shorter school life of pupils and poorer provision of books and equipment will allow, since the later stages of industrial development have created a demand for technologists—a relatively new class of experts who link the office and the shop floor and consider themselves to be part of the lower middle class. For these

pupils the secondary modern school strives to get as many 'O'
levels as possible. For the rest it aims at a basic literacy sufficient to follow instructions, to calculate amounts and costs of
materials and work, and to acquire manual dexterity; if they
are boys, to become as skilful as time permits in the use of hand
tools and the control of some woodworking and metalworking
machines; if they are girls, to cook, sew, and learn something of
the other skills needed to run a home and perhaps such skills as
typing which will equip them for the lower grade jobs for
women in commerce and industry. They will become shop
assistants, typists, factory workers, and office cleaners.

Both types of school pay much attention to games even
though nine-tenths of the population live in towns and cities
that cannot provide the space for them to play. The theory
behind the obsession with games derives from the Public school
need to occupy the energies of their pupils in remote country
sites and, by exhausting them physically, to keep their thoughts
away from sex—*mens sana in corpore sano*. On the other hand it
derives from the need to keep the working population, often
crowded into dense slums, fit for work. Absenteeism through
unfitness is wasteful in an economy based on three eight-hour
shifts per day in order to keep machines operating for maximum
production.

Both types of school claim to devote intense care to the
formation of character. The grammar school (modelling itself
on the Public school) puts service and loyalty to authority first.
This includes respect for religion (with a preference for the
Established Church), the rule of law and the preservation of
traditional values. The notion of 'character' includes that of
'grit'—the ability to persevere against difficulties and in spite of
opposition, in the limited field of academic achievement, but
not when such perseverance is harnessed to the promulgation
of unorthodox views in religion or politics. It includes the
acceptance of personal ambition and fierce competition as the
driving force and the mode of 'getting on'; the unquestioned
right of those who have acquired property to keep it; a strong
aversion to collective action by lower social classes; an aversion
to 'extremes' in dress, manners and opinions—hence the
acceptance of school uniform—and, if at all possible, no powerful
interest in the other sex.

From it all emerges the image of a man who will spend a lifetime behind the counter of a bank or in a laboratory as a research chemist or a works chemist; of a dark suit travelling from the suburbs to the office and back, or of a slightly rumpled, chalk-dusted Mr Chips figure in a permanent state of slight abstraction in the 'higher thoughts' of his subject; of an army or air force officer (the Navy until very recently was the prerogative of the Public school). Only very rarely does it include the possibility of careers in the higher ranks—membership of the Cabinet, a professorship, a major directorship, the taking of silk or a seat on the bench in the Law Courts—these are tacitly agreed to belong, as of right, to the Public schools or, possibly, the better known Direct Grant grammar schools.

In the Public school there emerges a contempt for democracy —except such forms of democracy as are confined to the upper middle class. There also emerges the notion that the upper middle class has the *right* to rule and to own more than three-quarters of the land and other forms of wealth. Such a result becomes inevitable when you isolate staff and pupils belonging to a very narrow band of the most privileged section of society in the 'hothouse' conditions of a boarding school (to use Royston Lambert's description).

The secondary modern school, too, inculcates 'respect' for authority, law and religion (but it does so by a greater stress on the penalties attaching to disrespect for these things, whereas the Public and grammar schools stress the 'reasons' behind them), since they are held to be conducive to social stability, however conformity is achieved. The secondary modern school is less optimistic about inculcating respect for learning. Many of its exercises in 'character formation' are a watered-down version of what takes place in grammar schools because the staff have all themselves been educated in grammar schools and try to repeat what they experienced. But because they have to control larger classes and because there is a wide discrepancy between the middle-class culture of the staff and the lower working-class culture of more than half of their pupils, the schools more often resort to corporal punishment, especially in the lower streams, and to other forms of brusque conditioning to achieve the outward appearance of discipline. Corporal punishment in these schools, as in other schools with a high proportion of lower working-class children, is held to be justified by a majority of the teachers *because the children are accustomed to it at home.* These teachers then find themselves with the dilemma that they either use the methods of a culture they despise to control their pupils or they try the 'rational' modes of the middle-class parent (reasoning and talking-through the problems) only to find chaos in their classrooms because to the children such techniques are alien and simply indicative of 'softness' on the part of the teacher.

Young teachers who try to use more rational methods in schools run on authoritarian lines find themselves in trouble not only with their pupils but with the staff. The staff will use every device against them, from friendly advice, through ridicule and sarcasm, to pressure on the head teacher to have such young teachers removed. They see more liberal methods as a threat to the system they have built up against the dangers of chaos, the lowering of standards, and indiscipline—in other words the dreadful prospect of their own loss of control. Most young teachers, finding themselves in this situation, rapidly give way to pressure from their colleagues and the head because their own conditioning in grammar schools has destroyed their ability to stand out against authority.

The secondary modern school tends to project a diffused image of what it hopes to achieve in the education of its pupils. The clearest is the image of the highly skilled worker, the craftsman who will leave school and go to a technical college to become a craft apprentice, technically intelligent, reliable and cheerful; not bothered overmuch with literature or art; intending to own a car and a caravan in which he can take his wife and children on holiday with an outboard motorboat strapped on the roof of the car for a fortnight on the Costa Brava. Below the 'A' form the image blurs rapidly and the teacher-oriented culture of the school finds it difficult to meet, in terms that teachers would fully accept, the practical requirements of society for bus conductors, milk roundsmen, caretakers, office cleaners, lavatory attendants, betting-shop assistants, waitresses, barmaids and door-to-door salesmen. Before the actual life in front of them the teacher simply feels helpless.

It is now necessary to examine how an élitist and socially divided system not only maintains social class differences but, more radically, differences of intellectual and perceptual capacity. We have to understand how personal and social ambition and motivation vary from one social class to another so as to *perpetuate* the class differences and secure for the wealthy and well educated power and knowledge to maintain their place in society and to educate their children to do the same. It is when we see the subtlety and the depth of influences of this kind that we will realize something of the real nature of the struggle to make children more free, because it is here that we see how the barriers to freedom are built into the individual at both conscious and unconscious levels.

2. *Confrontation in the Classroom: New Light on Non-Communication*

DISCIPLINARY conflicts in the classroom are more numerous and more intense in working-class secondary modern schools than they are in schools for the middle and upper middle classes. They point to a serious breakdown in communication between teachers and working-class parents and children. Many, not least Professor Alison Davis of the USA, have seen here a clash of cultures rather than an outburst of natural wickedness on the part of the students, the clash deriving from the fact that teachers and working-class pupils come from different cultures which ultimately spring from different types of work.

Work occupies people's thoughts and energies during the greater part of their adult life and strongly influences our thinking about education. I was reminded of this recently when examining the practical teaching of students training for infant teaching. In every class I entered the children were being made to count, measure, weigh and calculate. Not a single student doubted that the greater part of the school day should be spent in such activities and spoke of climbing, painting, listening to stories and talking as if they were 'mere' leisure pursuits of much less importance than preparation for work as adults. I was reminded of this too, when one of my students was rebuked by the headmistress of the infant school in Hoxton where she was doing her teaching practice. She had introduced play with water to a class of five-year olds whose 'Creative Activity' periods had been limited to jig-saw puzzles. The children entered eagerly into this play, had spilt water in carrying it to the classroom from the cloakroom and were, at the student's request, carefully mopping up the water when the headmistress arrived. She rebuked the student in front of the children for wasting time on such activities. 'These children' (it was a school in a lower working-class area) 'will have to spend their lives in *work*, not in play, and the sooner they are helped to realize this the better.' Among inspectors, and the staff of at least one teachers' training college, this woman is regarded as a 'good' headmistress.

In the eighteenth and nineteenth centuries towns grew for machines. Machines needed fuel, materials, railways, offices—the whole array of business, industry, commerce and communications—and, therefore, schools to train men and women for working in these complexes. Therefore from the 1870 Education Act and the beginning of compulsory education for all, school was seen as a place in which to prepare boys and girls for work in mills, factories and offices. The purpose of education, as embodied in the 1870 Education Act, was to teach the 'three R's', since Reading, Writing and Reckoning were essential to industry and commerce.

Since that time, although machines have grown more complicated and the knowledge required to make our society function has become vastly more detailed and extensive, basically the same relation has been maintained between school and work. My Chairman of Governors at Howe Dell School in Hertfordshire—himself a manufacturer and distributor of 'wine-gums', Chairman of the local bench of magistrates and later Lord-Lieutenant of the County—endorsed the view of a fellow governor of the school who had given it as her opinion that 'for these children (local working-class village children) music was one of the frills' and added, for good measure, that she was an LRAM, and must, therefore, know what she was talking about.

The Labour Party members of Bob Mackenzie's school governors, in a depressed mining village in Fifeshire, disapproved of the pupils 'wasting' their time building sailing boats, making guitars and learning to ski in the Scottish Highlands because 'it was more important for boys and girls to get "O" levels than to be enjoying themselves'—even when the rate of unemployment in that part of Scotland at that time was so high that the possession of 'O' levels made not a ha'porth of difference to their getting a job.

The teaching profession is notorious for the multiplicity of gadgets, gimmicks, tricks, systems, tools and machines that it has invented to 'lighten the load' of learning. The shelves of university Departments of Education are crammed with research on the process of learning. If only one per cent of all this had been applied by teachers it might seem, even to the casual observer, that the tasks set for the children might have been better done and more thoroughly learnt. But the whole paraphernalia of education, from infant school to university, still rests on the assumption that education is a kind of force-feeding of knowledge that is useful, i.e. that can be applied in commerce and industry.

'Tricks of the trade' have long been a real, if unacknowledged, part of the training of teachers, often in conflict, as many students know to their cost, with the principles enunciated from the platform by their tutors and lecturers. These same tutors and lecturers, the students find, in the privacy of the study, urge them to yield to reality in their teaching practice schools and to postpone the application of their theoretical 'principles' to more propitious times. I shall return to this topic later. It is enough to say at this moment that the teaching profession has always had to accept that the theory of education, based on the psychology of the child and on the assumption of a civilized and humane parent society, must give way to the powerful pressures from industry, administration and politicians of all parties, to the conditioning of children for their work as adults, however grim, distasteful and inhuman that work may be. Hence the rapid rise over recent years of the 'behaviourist' school of psychologists such as H. Eysenck and B. F. Skinner, against which A. S. Neill warns us in his chapter. The degree to which this school and its doctrines is replacing the individual study of children, as represented by the work of, for example, Susan Isaacs, is a measure of how far the universities and 'objective research' are at the mercy of commercial, industrial and political interests.

Now we are discovering, through the brilliant work of Professor Basil Bernstein and his colleagues in London University, that the subdivision of labour that is the very foundation of a mass-production society is accomplishing the task of taming, emasculating and limiting the vision and the intelligence of children to what will be required solely to operate machines and manipulate tools, and confining them to deal with words and ideas in the modes laid down by the existing structure of society, without asking any disruptive questions about the purposes of such activities. The way this is being done—in a context of ever-increasing specialization of work, of a growing gap between the social rewards of those at the top and those at the bottom, between the quality of life for those who 'think' and those who 'do'—is by the moulding and reinforcement of social values, attitudes and modes of perception through the use of the various codes of language that grow in different social groups and occupations.

In what follows I have, without committing them to endorse every variation that has been added from my own experience and thinking, to acknowledge a very great debt to Basil Bernstein and to Denis Lawton for disentangling the multiple relationships between the social class background of the speaker and the forms of language that he uses; for teasing out the complexity of systems of value and relationships in a particular social group; for indicating the range of options open to the speaker under different circumstances, and for elaborating the possibilities and expectations of function that have been 'inducted' in the speaker (in the sense used by Robert Ollendorff) as the accepted way in which he relates to his world.

There is too little space in this chapter to do full justice to the range and subtlety of Bernstein's thesis and to the various modifications that further research has provided. I can only indicate the general lines of thinking that have been confirmed and reinforced in subsequent studies, in order to show how powerfully his work is assisting our thinking about discipline in school, about the breakdown of negotiations in labour disputes and about the limitations of psychotherapy based solely on psychoanalysis—in fact about all personal or group conflicts where unspoken, unrealized or unconscious differences of previous experience and valuation are likely to exist.

He points out that lower working-class children are brought up to speak codes of language closely restricted to their material circumstances, whereas middle-class children acquire not only such restricted codes but the elaborated code, a form of language use *not* tied to particular forms of environment of work and relationships. Groups of men working closely together on a job for a long time develop a vocabulary and a grammar of reference for that job and for all the details associated with it, the techniques, processes and relationships as well as the personal functions and interrelationships that arise in the course of the work. The special feature of such a code of language is, like the purpose of all codes, a concise, accurate and comprehensive system of reference for all those who know the code and the circumstances to which it is appropriate. It is a code of language that is understood fully only in the context of the work situation (Bernstein later describes it as a 'context-dominated' code—*New Society*, February 1970). For communication among the members of the special group the code is totally satisfactory. To those who are outside the work and the situation the code will be, to a greater or lesser degree, incomprehensible. They, on the other hand, to the extent that they participate in other groups engaged in familiar work—or leisure pursuits—over long periods of time, will similarly develop other codes of reference suitable for their purposes. In every case the code will be restricted to the situation, the task and the people engaged in it and will, therefore, be a 'restricted code'. Obviously there will be as many restricted codes as there are particular work situations fulfilling the requirements outlined above. The increasing subdivision of labour over the last 200 years has produced a wide spectrum of labour extending from the highest stratum of professional workers to the lowest stratum of unskilled workers, and each concerned with a particular range of activities, processes and relationships; with the manipulation of tools, machines, materials and ideas appropriate to it.

Further, to the extent that particular work situations have elements in common—to the extent, for example, that many specific jobs require the expenditure of heavy muscular effort without the need for delicate precision of control, and to the extent that such effort can be started, guided and stopped by non-verbal signals or minimal use of words, shouts or grunts in conditions of loud noise—to that extent a number of restricted codes will have elements in common, especially elements that

refer to the personal relationships within those various situations and to the expectations about what language can do in
those situations. Codes arising from unskilled manual work will
not include complicated cause-effect relationships because such
relationships will have been worked out at administrative levels
much above the point at which the human physical energy is
applied.

Restricted codes will operate at any level of occupation. The
architect and the astronomer will speak in restricted codes
provided they are talking to colleagues in the same field of
work about that work. Such codes will be used whenever the
speaker can be confident that close familiarity with the subject
under discussion and the values held about that subject will
be held by those with whom he is speaking. 'Familiarity with our
common experiences and our common attitudes towards them
makes it unnecessary for me to spell out everything in full',
would be the underlying feeling in such a conversation, and the
speaker would be likely very often to use such phrases as 'You
know', 'You see' or similiar indications that his hearer did not
need to have the statement set out in full.

We can expect restricted codes to appear whenever groups of
people work or play together over a period. So families, work
teams, jazz fans, bowling clubs, mountaineers, engine-drivers
and psychotherapists will each develop codes relevant to their
situations. They will each evolve an 'in' language.

Further, and this can be seen to be important when we are
considering the effects of such restricted codes on children
brought up without access to other codes, each code accen-
tuates the values and attitudes that it finds important and
'plays down' those that are irrelevant. This means that children
brought up in certain codes will have their attention, at both
conscious and unconscious levels, directed to certain elements in
their experience and diverted from others.

Now, to the extent that codes overlap because the experiences
and values of different groups overlap, to that extent will common features develop. Clearly many occupations that can be
classified as professional or middle class will develop linguistic
features that extend beyond the characteristic features of any
single restricted code, because their members—lawyers, teachers, doctors, scientists, entertainers—have, as part of their

normal work, to communicate with people who use widely different codes. More particularly, because, in speaking to people with whose personal experiences and valuations they are not closely familiar, they cannot assume that their hearers are already in close accord with them, they have to make fully explicit a vast amount of what they could, with colleagues, take completely for granted. They have, in other words, to elaborate in detail the precise meaning they wish to convey; to spell out their meaning with no possibility of misunderstanding. The cost of a building, the result of a lawsuit or the functioning of a machine on sale to the public may depend on precise expression when instructions are being conveyed. They cannot depend, as they may between fellow-workers, on an intonation or the lift of an eyebrow.

People whose work demands such explicit communication develop an 'elaborated' code, a code of language which puts into specific verbal form all the complexities, subtleties and nuances that restricted codes convey by shrugs, frowns, pauses, by tone, volume and silence, as well as by words. As the developers, exploiters and communicators of ideas they have to construct a language capable of carrying every shade of meaning (external and internal, as in psychiatry) that any of their members find to be important. For this reason such an 'elaborated code' will have to have a range of such delicacy and flexibility of expression that it can embrace all the other codes. The speaker of such a code will, normally, in his work situation, use the restricted code appropriate to that work, but he has the ability, outside that situation, to express and understand this wider code. The speaker of an elaborated code will *tend* to use a richer vocabulary and a more extensive range of grammatical structures when speaking to those outside his own work or social group.

One consequence of a code of language that is expressed more completely in verbal form and relies less on non-verbal 'gesture'—i.e. the elaborated code—is that its hearers will be able to respond with particular accuracy to a precise request, whereas a hearer accustomed only to a restricted code will have to 'translate' into the nearest equivalent form. So, two children, brought up in radically different codes will perceive the same statement in different ways and behave differently. An instance of this occurred when I spoke to a group of boys who were working well but rather noisily. I said, 'Do you mind making rather less noise. We can't hear ourselves think.' Those boys with good verbal capacities continued what they had been doing but more quietly. George, the son of an unskilled labourer, looked up puzzled. Bill, a friend of his, seeing him look puzzled, said, 'Sir says, "Shut up!" so belt up, George! get it?'. I then had to explain to Bill that I did *not* mean George to stop talking altogether and abandon what he had been doing, but merely to do it more quietly.

As the planners and regulators of society, for whom language is the central mode of operation and control, the middle class build up a high respect for rationality, foresight and control and extend this into the modes used in socializing their children. Violence and impulse are played down and the verbalizing of feelings, and, especially, of the consequences of action explored and encouraged, it being held by them (as witness the rapid growth of Freudian concepts among the middle class) that what is verbalized can be controlled.

Parents first, through language, make the child aware of the future consequence of present action. The parent, whose relationship with the child is embodied in language to a high degree, expresses his disapproval of actions that lead to bad consequences, reinforcing his disapproval with reason. The child remembers the parental words of disapproval when similar situations occur again. The child's fear of or anxiety about parental disapproval causes him to inhibit his impulse to action. Thus the child begins to feel guilt at an earlier point in the contemplation of action. In other words his 'threshold of guilt' is lowered. In this way the group, through the parent, internalizes its values in the child and thereby induces 'self-control'. Such control from the 'internalized' pattern of values not only enables middle-class children to avoid violence and other unpredictable behaviour but has the important result of preparing them for the long and frequently dull process of academic education which increasingly demands the memorizing of masses of factual and technical information. To this process they are also held by their own increasing capacity for looking ahead to the rewards that perseverance will bring.

The middle-class child is encouraged to verbalize as soon as possible (middle-class babies of four months make a greater range of vocal noises than lower working-class babies) because his parents have acquired a high sensitivity to the importance of language. He is encouraged to ask questions and to seek for reasons in everything he does. His parents and teachers make a point of giving him full and accurate answers within his comprehension and thus establish for him the feeling that everything he encounters can be understood. Further, the whole process of formal schooling (which starts for most middle-class children at the age of three in nursery school, but not until five for most working-class children) is felt as a continuation of this process on the same basis of middle-class assumptions in the teacher as in the parent. Hence for the middle-class child school is merely an extension of certain aspects of home life, making familiar demands on him and enlarging his range of interesting experiences. As he grows older he is helped to see the direct connections between success at school and success in a career through the examples of his parents and the parents of his friends. School and home, therefore, reinforce each other in preparing the child for the middle-class pattern of behaviour and expectation from life.

The lower working-class child, on the other hand, is brought up by parents not equipped with a high regard for verbalization, not speaking an elaborated code, but relying to a greater extent on non-verbal means of communication (gesture, tone, volume and posture) to convey meaning, emphasis, attitudes and values. Education is seen by the parents, and therefore by their children, to have little relevance to the performance of their work. The lower working-class child may see his father switch from one job to another several times in the course of a few years with nothing more required than a few brief instructions from the foreman. Inevitably he will tend to view school, especially as the time approaches when he will be legally entitled to leave, as an obstacle between him and the freedom of being able to earn a wage. Social mobility being what it is in Britain, over 90 out of every 100 of his friends will continue to do the types of work being done by their fathers, so there is little incentive for him to work harder at school in order to lift himself out of his social class. Such an act would go against the grain of his social group, which encourages a feeling of solidarity and of hostility towards non-conformists to its social code, since, as the exploited group throughout the period since the start of the industrial revolution, it has depended on group solidarity for survival.

Further, the pattern of earnings for the lower working class is such that, at about the time when the older children are reaching school-leaving age, their father's income is dropping because he no longer has the strength, the stamina and the resistance to illness that enabled him to earn at his maximum rate during the first fifteen years of his working life. When his child is encouraged by his teachers to stay at school the parents want him to go out to work because they now need him to begin to be self-supporting.

Since, in the matter of the socialization of their children, the lower working-class have had neither the wealth nor the expectation of wealth, stability of work or control over their own destiny that the middle class take for granted, they have not built up the patterns of social valuation that middle-class people would find acceptable. In particular they have not been able to acquire the attitudes towards planning, foresight and consequences of action that would enable them, if they so desired, to develop the techniques of 'talking through' behaviour problems with their children. Their children do not, therefore, have the 'low threshold of guilt' that the middle class strives to create. Reasons for conformity to parental demands are more often based on status—'Because I tell you' or 'Because she's your mother'—than on logic. For this reason schools like Risinghill which attempted to bring about the internalization of values through discussion and the example of well-loved and respected teachers, will continue to be regarded as 'undisciplined' and to be closed or forced to change their procedures to brusquer and more repressive forms.

From Bernstein's analysis of the effects of the restricted and the elaborated codes on the outlook and capabilities of their speakers it is clear that a large proportion of the disciplinary conflicts that arise in schools, and particularly in schools with a large number of lower working-class children, arise from the clash between the teacher's middle-class cultural expectations and those of his lower working-class pupils, each failing to understand the point of view of the other and each disvaluing what the other holds dear. The teacher frequently sees himself as a missionary whose task is to reject the child's culture, language and modes of perception and replace them with his own.

It is also clear that children brought up in the context of an elaborated code have the capacity to understand restricted codes and have, therefore, in the school situation, a considerable advantage over those who have been limited to restricted codes, since the school and the teachers make elaborated code-type demands on their pupils. For this reason those who as children entered school speaking the elaborated code—mainly middle-class people—fill the universities, the professions and the seats of power, while those who were confined to restricted codes cease their education at fifteen and do the most menial and poorly paid jobs.

The astonishing dichotomy that exists between the high level of the philosophy, the pyschology and the practice of education as preached in colleges and departments of education, and the near-barbarity of what passes for education in schools for the lower working class is only partly explained by the clash of cultures outlined above and by the social conditioning of intending teachers at home and in the school. If we are more fully to understand just how there can develop such a contrast between theory and practice it will be necessary to look at what happens in the training of teachers for their work. To this I shall now turn.

3. *The Training of Teachers*

WITH very few exceptions teachers in State schools have all passed through grammar schools. The rare exceptions are the occasional artist, craftsman or musician who at some point has found himself teaching children and enjoys it. A substantial minority enter teaching because they have failed to secure a university place and take the next best step towards a professional or, at least, a semi-professional career. Some of these are lucky enough to find a college that inspires them with a vision of education as the core of the process through which the infant human animal can be brought to be a creative, loving, thinking human being. Many of the girls in this group who do not find such inspirations take the first chance to escape through marriage.

Within my own experience—confirmed by a recent survey— nearly 40 per cent of all the secondary teachers with whom I have worked fail to find reasonable satisfaction in their work and have resigned themselves to a life of, at best, tedium and, at worst, active frustration.

After reading through many thousands of reports written by head teachers recommending their pupils for acceptance by colleges of education, one begins to realize that the great majority of teachers have become what they are because they were regarded as amenable, conforming and inoffensive pupils, imbued with a deep and abiding respect for 'authority' in whatever form, better than average at their school work, though not often the 'high flyers' of the academic world, and likely to become highly respectable citizens and models for their future pupils. In their turn they will recommend their own pupils in similar terms. Such reports show that, culturally and characterologically, teachers propagate their own kind.

Outstanding university students who are inclined towards teaching are advised, as I was told by a Cambridge don, to go straight into the higher levels of educational administration within the Department of Education and Science and 'not waste time in teaching'.

To say that all teachers are middle class is to say that those few whose parents may have been working class have been effectively educated out of that class and have taken over the values, language and behaviour of the middle class. This can be seen in the greater relaxation more commonly displayed by upper middle-class teachers in dealing with children of the lower working class, as against the greater anxiety or insecurity displayed by teachers in transition from a working-class background. From my own observation it is these latter teachers who more often reveal a kind of fanaticism in their attempts to impose middle-class standards or what they imagine to be middle-class standards, on working-class children. A working-class friend of mine recently had cause to complain to her daughter's headmaster that the girl was being made to sit with her blazer on in a temperature of 80 degrees Fahrenheit. The head replied, 'We set our standards here by the Public schools. Pupils will wear blazers at all times.' The school was a mixed secondary modern school in Fulham.

As there are differences in the salaries, qualifications and social backgrounds of teachers in Public, grammar and secondary modern schools, so there are differences in whether or how they have been trained. Few teachers in Public schools have been trained in the normal three-year colleges. On the other hand fewer than one in six are non-graduates and training has not yet begun to be obligatory for graduates.

In State grammar schools the non-graduates—a quarter of the total staff—are normally those who teach cookery, needlework, metalwork or games. They have usually been trained in the three-year colleges and hold a lower rank in the academic hierarchy of the school. Since the war there has been a growing recognition that some training—the one-year postgraduate course in a university department or school of education—is important, and this is reflected in the growing proportion of trained graduates in grammar schools, at present about 60 per cent.

In secondary modern schools the majority, nearly 90 per cent, of the qualified full-time teachers were trained in colleges of education, the graduates having been trained in university departments. The older teachers were trained under the two-year system; the younger teachers under the three-year system. Many of the part-time and temporary staff (representing a third or even more of the total staff in lower working-class areas) are completely untrained and pressure from whatever source, teachers' unions or Ministry, to make training compulsory must remain ineffective so long as the general shortage of teachers (which is ultimately determined by the Government's unwillingness to recruit more through better salaries) continues to result in so many classes of fifty in infant schools, forty in junior schools and over thirty in secondary schools.

The urgent need for teachers at all costs means that the suitability of candidates for training is measured almost solely by academic rating—five 'O' levels and, if possible, one or more 'A' levels—with little regard to the character and personality of the intending teacher. Further, it means that, in spite of an elaborate system of practical and theoretical examinations, along with a continuous assessment of the student's progress by means of essays, 'special studies', material prepared for the classroom and so on, something less than 3 per cent of all students fail to qualify. For this reason teaching is regarded, by those in search of 'professional' status in a career, as a 'soft option'.

The postgraduate year's training is simply a course of lectures and seminars on the history, sociology and psychology (with or without emphasis on child psychology) of education and on the principles of education, or what the great educators from Plato onwards have said about education. Out of the nine months available for the course, up to a third may be spent on teaching practice in school, during which the student is unlikely to receive more than six visits from his tutor and will have to conform to whatever pattern the school thinks suitable for relationships between staff and pupils. He will be lucky if he is able to see his tutor once a week for half an hour to discuss essays, teaching practice or other work.

The three-year course should provide a framework for something better. More of the staff than in the one-year course have usually had recent experience of teaching in schools, though it is not impossible to find lecturers who have moved to colleges of education without ever having taught children. One young man taking his teaching practice in a school noted for the high level of delinquency and for disciplinary problems was being supervised and examined by a tutor whose only experience of teaching had been in a girls' finishing school in Switzerland.

The academic quality of the work in colleges of education is lower than that in university departments. This becomes a problem simply because the colleges feel themselves to be academically inferior and strive by, for example, cramming as many students as they dare into B.Ed courses, to gain academic status. Many universities regard their Departments of Education as not academically respectable, and it is common to find a similar distance maintained between the departments and the colleges in spite of efforts to give the colleges 'parity of esteem' by shared resources, staffs, curricula, and some degree of integration in the system of examinations. A move from a college to a department is regarded by most college staffs as a 'promotion', with the result that the colleges have more than their fair share of ineffective teaching. Psychology is too often concerned with the behaviour of rats and pigeons and with abstract concepts of 'learning', 'attention', 'memory' or 'will' than with the dynamic aspects or the social aspects of behaviour or with the study of actual children in real situations.

Out of the twenty-seven months of the the three-year course about four months are spent on teaching practice in schools. Of the remaining twenty-three at least half is spent on the student's own studies, designed to raise his own academic standing but not being required to have any direct relevance to his teaching. Some imaginative lecturers use their teaching in this area as a practical demonstration of good pedagogy; the majority still rely on 'chalk and talk'. In effect, therefore, the three-year course resolves itself, so far as training for teaching is concerned, into a four-month stretch of practical work in schools—the value of which depends on the quality of the school and the attitude of the staff to students in training—and barely twelve months of lectures and seminars on theoretical aspects, and with little or no connection between the practical work and the theoretical exposition. An instance of how present forms of organization militate against coherence is illustrated by the common experience of students who may be observed teaching a lesson in one term but may not meet the tutor to discuss that lesson until the following term.

The central failure of teacher training as a whole is a failure of imagination and a failure to practise what it preaches. From the rostrum of all colleges students are urged to make the child's interests the foundation of what they will do in the classroom as teachers. 'Child-centred education' is an almost universal slogan. Yet those same students are impressed by those same lecturers, when they come to do their practical teaching, to fit in with the habits and the wishes of the staffs of the schools in which they will practise, however inefficient or insensitive to children those schools may be. Above all, those colleges that preach 'child-centred education' conspicuously fail to make themselves 'student-centred'. In a number of colleges Staff-Student Consultative Committees have sprung up, but these committees have only trivial powers, limited to making minor recommendations about meals or leisure activities. The students have no power materially to affect the structure of the syllabus, the mode of assessment of student results, the appointment of staff or the dismissal of inefficient or idle staff or, in general, the government of the college.

I have before me an account of what happened in a College of Education in Yorkshire during the summer of 1969, with copies of the letters and statements issued by the principal, the academic board and the governors of that college when a substantial number of students openly questioned the authoritarian and political implications of the training received at the college. The pattern of reaction revealed by these documents is familiar and is almost identical with what has happened in other colleges where such questioning of authority has been expressed. Individual students and members of staff thought to be sympathetic to students' views are interviewed, often during vacations when there is no opportunity for consultation with other students or staff. One girl who had criticized the running of her college was interviewed by the principal and the dean of the college, was refused legal representation at that interview and was threatened that if she criticized the principal again she would be refused her Teacher's Certificate. At another college, known to me personally, several students active in the Students' Union were alleged to have smoked 'hash' and were compelled to leave the college on the grounds that their work was 'unsatisfactory', although their individual tutors had made no complaint about their work. These three tutors, however, did not have the courage to oppose the principal's decision or to make public the facts of the case, for fear that they might then put themselves in jeopardy with the principal.

It must be remembered that, until less than a generation ago, the majority of training colleges were founded and maintained by the Church or by bodies with a religious orientation, and were single-sex institutions. Compulsory attendance at morning worship was the rule and is still common. Where it is not actually compulsory (and compulsion is found less often in colleges founded by local authorities) students complain that a variety of pressures are applied which suggest that non-conformity in this matter might prejudice the award of a 'good' report at the end of the training period. Some colleges still have a chaplain on the staff. His duties very often include the 'pastoral care' of the students. He is the person to whom they are supposed to take their private problems. However enlightened he may be in refusing to pressurize students with religious propaganda, it is inescapable that the religious life of the college will be seen by the students as simply another way by which authority, in the person of the principal and the staff, seeks to enter their private lives and to control them from within.

The total effect of the system of training teachers is, therefore, to perpetuate in the students the same relationship to authority that the authoritarian family initiated and the academic system of schooling continued and strengthened. It has given rise to the old jibe that teachers go from school to college and back to school again. The system makes it almost impossible for the teacher with a middle-class background to have any first-hand experience of working-class parents or children before being confronted with a class of from thirty to fifty children from such a background. Only those students who venture on a building site, behind the bar of a pub, into a factory or a café for temporary work are likely to get some understanding of the conditions under which nearly half our people work and live, though even this can give no more than an inkling of what such work means since it is one thing to undertake a gruelling or boring job 'for the experience' but quite another to know that for the rest of your life you are tied to this or to something similar with no hope of relief.

But to propose other methods of training teachers or other forms of relationship between students and staffs of colleges of education is to attack the central core of values of this society. The schools could not carry out their main function of con-ditioning children for pre-determined adult roles in a mass-production society unless the teachers had been thoroughly imbued with the values of that society. A democratic society would not have to be told that the period of childhood is of vital importance to the creation of intelligent and loving adults; that intending teachers should be selected primarily for their capacity to respond with sensitivity to the needs of children; that personal attention to a child cannot be given in classes of thirty or more; that the separation of intellect, feeling and action characteristic of schools and colleges is destructive of humanity. It is for the reason that our society is *not* democratic that industrial and commercial criteria of efficiency, of personal relationships, are eroding the older concept that the teacher stood to the child *in loco parentis*. So we now have the current campaign to persuade the teaching profession that it is unrealistic to think in terms of reducing the size of classes in State schools because in a competitive economy we will just not get the numbers of teachers that the profession wants. Similarly, arguments for the raising of teachers' salaries are countered by figures to 'prove' that it is impossible. 'Teachers, of course, *deserve* much higher salaries but, unfortunately, we just are unable to give them the salaries they deserve.' It is interesting to note that those who give voice to such arguments against the increase of the numbers of teachers in State schools or against demands for the increase of salaries are themselves people who send their children to private schools. The quality of the education given to their own children will not be affected, but any proposal to increase the tax burden on the community—a burden that will have risen from the current £2,200 million or 6 per cent of the gross national product to over £5,000 million by 1980 merely to *maintain* present policies—is blocked by those whose wealth would be affected, the upper middle class, i.e. the teachers' employers. It is these people who are prepared to keep the tax bill down at any cost, and since the cost of State education for the first time has exceeded the cost of defence, education becomes the first target for measures of economy.

Nor does the 'training' of the teacher end with the conclusion of the training period. For a minimum of one year after appointment to a teaching post the young teacher is 'on proba- tion'. He will only become a qualified teacher when he has satisfied the Department of Education and Science, through the HMI, that he is a competent teacher. In practice this means that the head of the school is asked to sign a chit to the effect that the new teacher is proving satisfactory. If the head, for whatever reason, is unwilling to make such a declaration a formal visit will probably be made by the HMI or by an inspec- tor of the local authority, each of whom may actually see the young teacher in the classroom, but will place much more importance on what the head reports about him.

The purpose of the probationary year is, nominally, to test competence to teach. In fact, although this is not readily ad- mitted by either inspectors or head teachers, it is intended to discover whether the young teacher holds unorthodox views in the areas of politics, religion or sex. Many conversations that I have had with inspectors about young, recently appointed teachers on my staff have clearly been designed by the inspectors to discover this information. It is also a widespread practice, when a teacher applies for a post at another school, for the head of that school to telephone the head of his present school to enquire about his politics, and about whether the teacher is 'trustworthy' or 'reliable'—and this phrase does *not* mean trustworthy with money or a good timekeeper (though this question, too, may be asked). It means, 'Are his views sound, middle-of-the-road and, basically, conservative? Is he a practising Christian? Can he be trusted to "keep his distance" with the pupils, i.e. to maintain a formal correctness with them? Can he be trusted not to have any relations with older pupils of the other sex that are not strictly professional'—even when the girls may be eighteen and the teacher himself under twenty-four? It also means, 'Can you assure me that he has no extremist views about such things as corporal punishment or sex education? Is he anything of a "barrack-room lawyer" type? Has he ever had any serious difference of opinion with you, with the governors of the school or with the local education authority?'

More specific questions asked in such telephone conversations or in requests for 'confidential reports' (which are never shown to the person reported on, so that he has no possibility of defence against libellous statements) are: 'Can he maintain good classroom discipline?' meaning, 'Can he keep the pupils quiet so as not to disturb other members of staff or me?' Rarely is the further question asked, '*How* does he maintain good discipline, by fear or by interest?'. In such conversations I have often been asked by other heads, 'Is he a communist?' or occasionally, 'Is he an active Union member?' meaning, 'Is he likely to waste the time and energy of the staff in meetings about salaries or in agitating for a change to comprehensive education?'

The result of this 'old boy' network between heads, administrators and inspectors, and between the officials of one local education authority and another, is a tightly-knit freemasonry of which the central purpose is to exclude at any cost—even, in some well-authenticated examples within my own experience, by character assassination—those whose views, character or behaviour are likely to cause a questioning attitude towards authority among their pupils or their colleagues.

It was, of course, a pious hope of the 1944 Education Act that the establishment of democratic managing and governing bodies of schools would check any tendency towards bureaucratization by heads and officials. Such bodies, being made up of local councillors, would ensure grass-roots democracy at the level of school policy making. Unfortunately the system does not work in the way intended. Nominations to governing and managing bodies are made by the political parties; the real business of these committees is decided by the chairman and the education officer before the committee meets; only those who are wealthy or retired can spare the time to act as chairmen, which in practice means Conservative business people or retired and relatively poorly educated Labour councillors in the chair (retired Labour councillors are easy meat for most officials). So, the combined effect of chairman and official is enough to sway the decisions of most governing and managing bodies, the vast majority of whom are babes in arms when it comes to technicalities of finance or the detailed organization of schools. Troublesome managers or governors are easily removed since one-third of these bodies are elected every year. My own chairman of governors was removed from the chair simply because the chairman of the Education Committee had decided that my chairman was too sympathetic to my policy for the school—and yet the procedure at the meeting when she was so removed looked and sounded meticulously democratic!

In such ways power is caused to remain firmly in the hands of the officials and educational policy continues to be, basically, deeply conservative.

4. *Religious Instruction and Moral Education*
SINCE 1944 the giving of religious instruction and the holding of an act of 'corporate worship' have been compulsory in British schools. The Education Act laid it down in Section 7 that:

'it shall be the duty of the local education authority for every area, so far as their powers extend, to contribute towards the spiritual, moral, mental and physical development of the community by securing that efficient education . . . shall be available to meet the needs of the population of their area.'

but made no mention of the word 'religion' or 'religious' in the original draft of the Bill. The religious clauses in the Act were inserted on the insistence of the Conservative party who threatened, if they were not inserted, to fight the Bill on every clause. Had it not been possible to uncover this notorious piece of horse-trading from those who took part in the negotiations, the insertion of the religious clauses would have been evident from a study of the style. Whereas the language and tone of the rest of the Act reveals a broadly-based and quite liberal (for those times) view of education to which many outstanding people had contributed their views, the religious clauses are narrow and specific, leaving little room for interpretation, and embodying the dogmatic assertions of a small but powerful group—the property owning group that controls the finance, industry and, in the long run, as can be seen from the tribulations of the last Labour government, the political direction of this country.

It has often been wondered how it was possible to 'swing' the religious clauses into an otherwise democratic Bill. I believe that one of the factors that made this possible was that the majority of members of parliament, on both sides of the House, and of the senior officials in the then Board of Education and in the Education Offices of local authorities were themselves the products of the Public schools or of grammar schools modelling themselves closely on the Public schools. Since, among much else, the Public schools have always given great prominence to school chapel and to daily prayers, and since, being single-sex schools, they so often pervert into pseudo-religious feelings the adolescent sex drives that should find normal outlets in heterosexual love, these schools have succeeded both in accentuating the burden of guilt associated with sex for boys in a patriarchal society and at the same time in providing an emotionally charged 'outlet' in the self-abasing or machosistic sentiments so freely expressed in Christian forms of worship. It is not surprising, therefore, in a society with a powerful 'taboo on tenderness', to use Suttie's phrase, that any legitimate occasion for the expression of pent-up adolescent emotions should be recalled with pleasure by those who had experienced it. Nor is it surprising—since such occasions were confined, apart from the whipped-up enthusiasm generated by competitive games, to religious practices—that those who had been educated in Public schools naturally came to regard religious practices and religious instruction, as well as games, as very important for the formation of character.

The grammar schools which multiplied after the Act of 1902 modelled themselves on the system created by Thomas Arnold. The staff of these new schools had been largely drawn from the products of the Public schools so, even in the absence of a school chapel, daily prayers, the 'house' system and the curricula and organization of the Public schools were taken for granted. In time the act of daily worship and religious instruction became universal since all schools—elementary and junior—were staffed by those who had undergone the religious conditioning of the grammar schools. Because these teachers had experienced the corporate emotions, the sense of ritual, the heightened 'spiritual' atmosphere so often evident when a dominant and, possibly, appealing personality is in charge of a large group discoursing about love and brotherhood, they assumed that morning assembly was an important factor in bringing a sense of unity in the school.

The widespread conviction that morning assembly has a special value is indicated by the following extract from a pamphlet on comprehensive schools published by the London County Council:

'We [a group of LCC inspectors] should not leave this section on the school community without some reference to the great importance which heads attach to the school assembly. The whole school does not necessarily assemble together every day, nor indeed is this possible on any occasion in some of the schools. In many there is a varied pattern of assemblies of parts of the school and of the house assemblies. In nearly all cases great importance is attached to the school assembly as an occasion of corporate worship when the school or the part of the school concerned *become a unity in a particular way* [my italics]. On a number of occasions the school assembly has seemed to the visitor a moving and impressive occasion, making a special contribution to the development of the school as a community as well as to the religious education of the pupils.'

And again:

'All the heads regard taking prayers at the full assembly as one of the most important things they do.'

Many heads—and not only of comprehensive schools—do indeed attach great importance to school prayers and school assembly. Whether the assembly, in fact, has the importance they assume is perhaps more open to doubt. In what way, for example, does the school become a 'unity'? The children may all be singing a hymn or reciting a prayer or listening to a piece of music or a peroration from the head, and, to that extent, be doing something at the same time, but this does not constitute unity any more than the act of watching a football match and shouting 'England!' in unison constitutes unity, except at the most trivial level, for members of the football crowd. In fact, since the members of the football crowd are attending the match of their own volition and with the same purpose in mind, viz. to enjoy the game, it is likely that they are more united in feeling than the children in assembly who have to be present whether they wish to be or not. Similarly, the members of an audience listening to a concert are united to the extent that they are in sympathy with the works being played and are attending freely.

An act of 'corporate worship'—required by the 1944 Act—must imply that the 'corpus', the group, has already come to the point of being something more than a collection of individuals. It implies, also, that the individuals have come together freely, believing that there is some object or being to excite their feeling of reverence, and agreeing on the method of worship, whether it be the silent contemplation of a group of Friends or the full ritual of a missa cantata. But even in those State schools that boast a highly developed discipline and sense of community among their pupils, attendance at the corporate act of worship is not voluntary. Parents who do not wish their children to attend assembly have to 'opt out' by notifying the school, realizing that thereby they are forcing their children to behave and feel differently from their classmates. Where schools have some children whose families have no explicit religious faith; some whose parents are humanists; some whose parents are agnostics or atheists; some whose parents are Muslim, Buddhist, Jewish, Catholic or Protestant, but not to the extent of wishing their children to be excluded from general school activities, one wonders what form of religious activity will bring unity to boys and girls from eleven to eighteen years of age and from educationally subnormal to very highly intelligent.

Understandably, many heads feel school assembly to be important. Normal children are polite and amenable to suggestions made by otherwise reasonable adults. So, when the head conveys by voice and bearing his own, possibly quite genuine, feelings of awe, reverence or elation, the children are quick to respond, especially if they like him. They may, of course, not understand a word of what he is saying—I have tested this often enough to be satisfied of its truth. Where the assembly is a 'good' one it may be because the children sing well and enjoy singing, because an interesting story has been well told and their silent absorption springs from the enjoyment of the story or their interest in what the head is saying about themselves or about the world outside the school. It may be, on the other hand, that the observer of such a 'good' assembly is reading into it recollections from his own past that may have no connection whatever with the actual emotions or experiences of the children. This again I have tested often enough to realize that such outside observers may totally misinterpret such a situation.

In these circumstances—with a captive, if docile and polite audience; with little possibility of disagreement from the floor; with a programme drawn up by himself and as much time as he likes to elaborate it—it is not surprising that most heads conclude that what is happening must be important. It would be a body blow to their *amour propre* to face the possibility that so much time, thought and energy was wasted every day because irrelevant to the real problems of educating children or to the creation of a climate in which moral development can take place.

There is the further point that the sight and sound of an assembly of children singing or speaking together, or taken out of themselves with absorption is, for most adults, a very moving experience, but the emotion arises in the adults not so much from what is being done to, or by, the children as from our instinctive response to children, particularly where, as with teachers or inspectors, our instincts are reinforced by our professional solicitude for the children's welfare.

A sense of unity and purpose in a school—and heads who are not themselves fanatically 'religious' have readily agreed with me about this—comes from the work of a happy and united staff having good relations with the children, teaching them well, knowing them as individuals, spending some of their time with them in out-of-school activities and, above all, working closely with the parents of the children. A 'good' assembly is the coming together of staff and children who enjoy being together for a purpose they all recognize to be important or interesting. It may reflect the condition of the school; it does not create it.

The public meeting is as old as man, but the school assembly, which is a compulsory gathering for purposes determined and organized by adults without reference to the wishes of the children, and has, except on very rare occasions, absolutely nothing to do with the normal interests or activities of children, is a totally different experience—in terms of the development of group solidarity—from a meeting held by Stone Age villagers to deal with a pack of marauding wolves; by the ratepayers of a borough angry at a proposed increase in the rates; or by a gang of boys anxious to play football against other gangs—meetings which are all held for purposes clearly discernible to, and held to be important by, those taking part. Those who make the most intelligent and relevant contributions are listened to with care and their proposals adopted. Whoever is neither relevant nor interesting is told so, and the more urgent the nature of the meeting the more sharply will irrelevance be cut off. It is, in fact, on the democratic right of the group as a whole to determine what and how discussion shall proceed that the whole body of techniques for orderly discussion have grown. The chairman of a meeting may appear to hold authority, but his authority derives from the group as a whole. If it is necessary to depart from traditional procedure he must ask for the approval of the group to do so.

Though a meeting may, as in the case of the football crowd, the concert audience or the meeting of shareholders, be for very specific purposes impacting only on very small areas of the total lives of the participants, meetings assume more importance to the extent that the members are associated with one another in other areas of their lives. One has only to attend meetings such as those in Summerhill or Kilquhanity schools to realize how such meetings, held against a background of community life, promote a greater range of intelligence, toleration, benevolence, sensitivity and morality than that possessed by any single member of the group. It is as if any contribution that raises the level or tone of the discussion enables the other members to lift their own standards. Again, since every member is well known to all the others, any insincerity or false motive, however unconscious, will be revealed and the speaker made aware of himself as he appears to the others. There is, therefore, a kind of natural group-therapy at work with a powerful socializing effect on the individual that not only helps him to understand others more fully, but leads him to an even deeper awareness of himself. It is for this reason that small communities living closely together are more moral than towns and cities. It is for this reason that communities in the western islands of Ireland and Scotland and communities of Eskimos rarely used or even considered punishment. The therapeutic effects of living in community are now more fully realized and are used in the Henderson Hospital at Sutton, a hospital for schizophrenic patients. Here the treatment consists in living life as a community as fully as possible, eschewing drugs and individual therapy and relying on the open discussion by all members of the community, doctors, patients, nurses, administrative staff and social workers of the general and personal problems that arise in the course of normal work. To this end the patients take as much part as possible in the full running of the hospital, in helping to decide when patients shall be admitted or discharged and in the organization and administration of both work and leisure activities.

Within the last few years there has been much questioning of the value of the school assembly. In *The Times Educational Supplement* of 24 January 1969, a grammar school headmaster wrote:

'To believers, compulsory religious worship may not be harmful. . . . For the remainder, daily attendance at a ceremonial which is meaningless for them can only be regarded as a serious matter. The assumption that such attendance does some good is positively alarming to those who have tried to think the question through to a logical conclusion . . .

'It is wrong to ask teachers (or boys) to indulge in what, for the majority of those present, is a pretence. It runs counter to all the efforts we make to encourage our pupils to think honestly. It is foreign to what most parents believe and practise . . .'

In those clauses of the 1944 Act referring to religious activities other than the act of corporate worship, the word 'instruction' and not 'education' is used. But 'instruction', as distinct from 'education' is bound up with ideas of orders from a superior to an inferior, or with the manipulation of machinery or inert material. It implies that the one instructed has no say in the matter; that the instructor has ends in view beyond the understanding or the desires of the child himself. These clauses are not of a piece with the rational and democratic tone of other sections in the Act.

Following the passing of the Act many Local Education Authorities set up committees representative of different religious bodies to prepare agreed syllabuses of religious instruction, a thing that few had done for other subjects. The results, agreed to by all but Catholics and Jews, were published as 'agreed syllabuses'. These syllabuses are at one in setting out their major aims as the acceptance by the child of

1. A belief in God.
2. A belief that Christ was the Son of God.
3. A belief that the Bible is the source of God's revelation of His purposes.

The teaching of RI (religious instruction), according to many of these syllabuses, is to make use of enlightened teaching methods common in other subjects. In nursery schools and classes, for example:

'The methods adopted in the religious lesson will not differ from those employed in teaching other subjects, and full use will be made of Montessori apparatus, large realistic toys, etc., whilst there will be free activities which arise spontaneously from the child's natural energy and curiosity . . .'

The Cumberland Syllabus, however, is somewhat more blunt about the need to condition into certain habits:

'At this earliest stage of religious experience there must *necessarily* [my italics] be some teaching through formal observances. There will be the little prayer to be said at bed-time and at rising, and the grace before meals. But there are also smaller observances which may be helpful, e.g. to place the hands together in prayer or to keep the old Puritan rule of placing nothing upon the top of the Bible.'

The Sunderland Syllabus thinks as suitable for children of ten: 'The Religious History of the People of God', and goes on to suggest that children of eleven and twelve should have to consider the 'Attributes of God' such as 'Heavenly King', 'Eternal Judge' and 'Abiding Presence'. Further they are to ponder the characters not only of Jesus but of people like Wyclif, Luther, Lincoln and Schweitzer! No wonder a writer in *The Times Educational Supplement* criticized the content of religious instruction in schools as, '. . . concerned with ideas and aspirations of which the children can have no knowledge or experience. This is true of all religious instruction'.

Our schools confuse religion and morality. Recent claims that a majority of parents want their children taught religion in schools are unreliable because the surveys failed to distinguish, in terms understood by parents, between religion and morality.

D. W. Winnicott, in *The Young Child at Home and at School*, writes:

'Religions have made much of original sin, but have not all come round to the idea of original goodness, that which by being gathered together in the idea of God is at the same time separated off from the individuals who collectively create and re-create this God concept. The saying that man made God in his own image is usually treated as an amusing example of the perverse, but the truth in this saying could be made more evident by a restatement, such as: man continues to create and re-create God as a place to put that which is good in himself, and which he might spoil if he kept it in himself along with all the hate and destructiveness which is also to be found there.

'Religion (or is it theology?) has stolen the good from the developing individual child and has then set up an artificial scheme for injecting this that has been stolen back into the child and has called it "moral education". Actually moral education does not work unless the infant or child has developed in himself or herself by natural developmental process the stuff that, when it is placed up in the sky, is given the name God. The moral educator depends for success on there being that development in the individual child that enables the child to accept this God of the moral educator as a projection of the goodness that is part of the child and of his actual experience of life.'

In other words, as society has fragmented man into separate intellectual, emotional and executive compartments, so it has denied the validity of the child's good impulses and removed them to an unattainable place—'heaven' or 'God'—and left him with only the evil—the doctrine of original sin—and with the burden of guilt and despair that such realization must place on any normal human being.

The teachings of the great religious leaders have always thrown the main weight of their message on man's relationship with others, illustrated by stories or parables, and having one theme in common—the interdependence of men, the need for love. It is too often forgotten, however, that these leaders addressed themselves to adults, people already possessed of an extensive experience of human relationships and with an ability to examine the effects of their actions on others. None of the great teachers addressed themselves directly to children.

Great educators in the twentieth century—Dewey, Homer Lane, Makarenko and A. S. Neill—have seen clearly that children become moral, social beings by growing up in the society of children and adults and by experiencing in real situations the affections, hatreds, demands and other responses that human beings evoke from one another, and by experiencing and observing the reactions in themselves and in others provoked by such relationships. They learn to evaluate short- and long-term 'good' by living with their personal choices: they learn to put themselves in other people's shoes; to imagine sympathetically what others feel and think, and to do this not only within their own private consciousness but in the fuller range of human emotions available to them in literature. They discover that some forms of conduct make them disliked and, if persisted in, avoided. This is true moral education.

Since few children or adults can bear for long to be isolated from their fellows the group inevitably achieves a basic conformity, but whether those pressures are exerted on the side of reason and logic or for irrational and inhuman purposes depends, in the long run, on our general attitude to children. If children can grow up in a free atmosphere; if they can be spontaneous in the expression of their feelings, within the bounds of harm to others; if the adults are there to provide comfort, help or advice when sought, without undue interference; if the example in the behaviour of the adults is one of toleration, gentleness and reason, then the children will grow up to be gentle, tolerant and reasonable adults. Malinowski's studies of the Trobriand Islanders and A. S. Neill's work at Summerhill show how this happens.

To the extent that these attitudes pervade the whole society, to that extent will children be educated morally, whether or not specific lessons are given to that end. In *Democracy and Education* John Dewey puts the case against moral education as normally conceived:

'Moral education in school is practically hopeless when we set up the development of character as a supreme end, and at the same time treat the acquiring of knowledge and the development of understanding which of necessity occupy the chief part of school time, as having nothing to do with character. On such a basis, moral education is inevitably reduced to some kind of catechetical instruction, or lessons about morals. Lessons "about morals" signify as matter of course lessons in what other people think about virtues and duties. It amounts to something only in the degree in which pupils happen to be already animated by a sympathetic and dignified regard for the sentiments of others. Without such a regard, it has no more influence on character than information about the mountains of Asia; with a servile regard, it increases dependence on others, and throws upon those in authority the responsibility for conduct. As a matter of fact, direct instruction in morals has been effective only in social groups where it was a part of the authoritative control of the many by the few. Not the teaching as such but the re-enforcement of it by the whole régime of which it was an incident made it effective. To attempt to get similar results from lessons about morals in a democratic society is to rely upon sentimental magic.'

5.   *Punishment in Schools*

'*As for corporal punishment, though it is a recognized practice, I am completely opposed to it, first because it is disgusting, fit only for slaves and undoubtedly an insult. In the next place because a pupil whose mind so ill befits a free man's son as not to be corrected by reproof, will remain obdurate even in the face of blows—like the vilest of slaves. . . . If you coerce the child when he is young by means of blows, what will you do when he is a young man who cannot be compelled through fear and has many more important things to learn?*'

Quintilian, A.D. *35–100.*

'*Let us see to it that the rod we use is the word of guidance or of rebuke, such as a free man may obey, that our discipline be of kindness and not of vindictiveness.*'

Erasmus, *1466–1536.*

'*The school is a sanctuary against fear.*'

Roger Ascham, The Scholemaster, *1565.*

'*We asked about corporal punishment for the age-groups of pupils with whom we are concerned. Many heads have written most thoughtfully on this, some expressing firm convictions, others doubts. We are bound to record that nearly all find it necessary to retain corporal punishment as the ultimate sanction for boys.*'

The Newsom Report, Half Our Future, *1963.*

'*It (corporal punishment) has been almost universally outlawed in other western countries. It can be associated with psychological perversion affecting both the beater and the beaten and it is ineffective in precisely those cases in which its use is most hotly defended. We think the time has come to drop it. After full consideration, we recommend that the infliction of physical pain as a recognized method of punishment in primary schools should be forbidden.*'

The Plowden Report,
Children and their Primary Schools, *1967.*
Note: The *only* member of the Committee who protested against this recommendation was herself a headmistress, Miss M. F. M. Bailey.

'*The punishing adult, whether it is a teacher in school or a parent in the "battered baby" situation, is the one who had no chance in early childhood to experience the extremes of loving and hating, to relate them both to one stable person (the mother) and so to learn how to modify and control his hate. It is he who becomes the punitive headmaster, or the vindictive senior teacher, and so we get the violence which passes down a school where the child is "the last person to get kicked".*'

Eileen Elias *in* Nursery World *reporting*
Dr Andrew Crowcroft, Child Psychiatrist.

In spite of official protestations to the contrary corporal punishment is almost universal in State schools. Its use varies in frequency according to whether the school is populated mainly by middle-class children whose parents take an active interest in the education of their children and are aware of more recent findings about the effects of such punishment, or whether the school is in a lower working-class area where the population has long been conditioned to accept physical pain as the normal means of socializing children. It is much more common in boys' schools than in mixed schools, and more common in mixed schools than in girls' schools. It is used at every level from infants' schools upwards and in all types of school from grammar, comprehensive, secondary modern, to schools for physically handicapped and mentally handicapped children. The survey made by The National Foundation for Educational Research and entitled *Rewards and Punishments*, found that only two schools, out of the many hundreds examined, had deliberately eschewed corporal punishment as a means of controlling their children. Test surveys made since that main survey in the early 1950s, confirm that about 80 per cent of all men teachers and a somewhat smaller proportion of women teachers support the retention of corporal punishment in schools. In June 1968 the National Association of Head Teachers, at their annual conference, 'adopted unanimously a resolution asking their national council to take steps to maintain their right to determine the nature of punishment appropriate to the administration of their schools' (*The Times*). *The Times*' report starts, 'Amid prolonged applause and jeers at long-haired "woollies", civil servants, councillors and parents who disagree with them, about 400 head teachers defended their "right" to use corporal punishment.'

John Partridge in *Middle School*, 'a new and splendidly equipped building in a new estate', describes in sober detail the conditions that obtain in a secondary modern school that is by no means a 'problem' school, but is, in fact, regarded by the local authority as one of its better examples of what a secondary modern school should be. This book, later republished as *Life in a Secondary Modern School*, is a shocking revelation of the amount of corporal punishment taken absolutely for granted by the staff who 'would compare favourably for qualifications and practical expertize with the staffs of most other local Secondary Moderns'. To a young teacher commenting on the apparent logical necessity to strike boys harder on each successive occasion in order to make punishment a real deterrent a senior colleague—promoted, presumably, to a position of responsibility as a result of the combined recommendations of the head, the local inspector and the governors of the school—replied, 'You want to make them feel you've knocked their arsehole up to their back teeth.'

This brutality, both of attitude and of action, is so commonplace in the teaching 'profession' that it rouses dismay and disgust only among very young teachers. The others have to live with it or get out of the service, as many do. Those who protest are treated as blacklegs by their colleagues and as cranks by inspectors and administrators. John Partridge's book caused a storm of protest when it appeared, but the storm quickly died down as soon as the general public started to confirm from their personal experience what he had had the courage to expose. Sir John Newsom, fresh from the mass of disquieting evidence that his Committee had had to examine, called the book 'faithful and illuminating'. The teachers' unions, after a first rash denial of its veracity, had to remain remarkably silent. They knew that it was only too true, but they lacked the courage or the power or the will to do anything about a scandalous situation in the system of education.

Perhaps the teaching profession attracts more than its fair share of sadists because the conditions of teaching—with a teacher in charge of children in a room separated from other teachers and, certainly, from other adults including the parents of those children, for almost the whole of two hundred days in every year—gives almost unlimited scope to those with a neurotic yen for power over people with little power to rebel. Of course not all teachers are like this. What is astonishing is that so many good teachers go on for so many years with a level of pay that is ludicrously inadequate to the quality of work they do.

When they are challenged teachers assert that corporal punishment is used 'only as a last resort and after everything else has been tried and failed'. The insincerity of such statements is seen in the fact that so many parents hear of the infliction of the cane on their children *after* the event. It is seen, further, in the triviality of the offences for which it is awarded—swearing, smoking, cheek, lateness to school or lessons, running in corridors or on stairs, sliding down banisters, walking on the wrong side of corridors or stairs, long hair on boys, jewellery or make-up on girls, failure to wear school uniform or the wearing of unorthodox shoes, socks or other articles of clothing such as coloured tights or frilly knickers. It is awarded, too, for more serious offences (in spite of the fact that it has often been pointed out that the more serious the offence the more dangerous is the use of corporal punishment) such as truancy, stealing, bullying. Whatever the staff find to be disagreeable or to interfere with their concept of what is orderly; whatever seems to offend their own dignity or to challenge their authority or authority in general is deemed to deserve the infliction of corporal punishment. So Punishment Books, where any entries have been made, abound in such comments as 'Talking in class', 'Laughing in Assembly', 'Dumb insolence', 'Lying' or 'Rudeness'—which latter category includes sexual play.

Some instances of teachers' reactions verge on the deranged. Out of over 150 pages of closely typed examples of activities resulting in caning I have picked a few at random:

'A boy in the second year (aged eight) who was very shy was sent by his teacher to the headmaster with a particularly good piece of work as she thought that a word of praise from the head might help to increase his confidence. The boy reached the head's room and when asked what he wanted became nervous and simply held out his book. The head, thinking he had been sent for bad work, caned the boy and sent him back to his classroom in tears.'

'A new boy aged seven came to the school straight from Kuwait, found it difficult to settle down at once and responded by kicking and fighting. Within the first day he had begun to talk to the other children more normally. On the second day he was caned for fighting in the playground.'

'In this school Assembly starts at 9.40 and is followed by hymn practice until 10.20. The first child who talks during this period receives one stroke of the cane, the second, two, and so on. Every day at least one child is caned for running in the corridor.'

Other examples of punishment make one wonder how such adults are appointed as teachers:

'A child of seven who had not yet learned to read was being punished for being unable to spell. The teacher drew a chalk circle on the floor in the middle of the school hall and sat the child in it on the floor with a sheet of paper and a pencil to copy out the sentence written at the top of the paper, "I must learn not to be so stupid", until he had filled the sheet. He was given neither a chair to sit on nor a desk to write on. As he could not read and found it difficult to trace out the letters it took him the whole afternoon to produce a page full of unintelligible scribbles. Not a single teacher in the school saw fit to protest either at the form of the punishment or at the fact that the child was punished at all.'

'A boy was accused by a teacher of talking in the class. The boy denied it heatedly and was sent to the head. The head, after speaking to the teacher, himself accused the boy who again denied it. The head called him a liar, struck him across the face twice then punched him so that he fell to the floor. The boy micturated in fear.'

To read through these pages, verified for their accuracy by reference to parents and to other teachers aware of the incidents, is to realize in full how effective our society has been in selecting to be teachers people so ready and apt to the task of conditioning children by fear for the dehumanizing lives that a majority of them will have to live. Many people try to decry the importance of corporal punishment and to pooh-pooh the anxieties of an increasing number of parents and teachers, but the use of corporal punishment is the focal point of a whole attitude towards children that seeks to deny their rights as human beings. It is the flash that reveals the strength of the current of hatred when it meets resistance. It reveals the depth of fear created in teachers so depersonalized by the academic process that they are unable to tolerate anything that varies one iota from the image of rectitude they have so painfully built up for themselves.

But the whole concept of punishment other than corporal punishment, as it is seen in operation in State schools, differs simply in degree from corporal punishment. It springs from the same assumptions about children and about the role of the teacher as conditioner. It has the same purpose and the same goal—the production of a mass of young people with orthodox, basically conservative and traditional habits and beliefs.

The State system today creates an air of encouraging experiment and 'freedom' in its schools, but it is the freedom to be trivial, to proliferate teaching aids—teaching machines, language laboratories—to engage in frenetic searches for new curricula suitable for this or that age or school; to promote 'interdisciplinary' thinking; to devise new levels of examinations. It fills us with propaganda about rising levels of education to persuade us that we shall have to meet rising costs (from £2,300 million in 1970 to £5,000 million by 1980). Like those manufacturers of tobacco who sell their destructive wares by accompanying them with entrancing vistas of fresh mountain streams or healthy young men riding bareback in the morning sun, the State attaches to its political eyewash engaging pictures of young children so that we may be beguiled into thinking that our politicians really care about children and their education.

6. *Education: The Future*

SINCE any education system intimately and sensitively betrays the nature of its parent society, any attempt to outline the shape of education in the future must make a number of assumptions about the parent society. I shall, therefore, mention a few points that seem to me, so far as we can project our imagination into the future, important in preserving education as the means of creating democrats of the future. Some of the more obvious are:

1.   That the society in which and for which the schools exist must itself be democratic, i.e. not divided into separate groups or classes with a relationship of exploitation.

2.   That the schools shall be small enough to enable the whole school—staff, parents and pupils—to meet face to face.

3.   That schools shall be governed by a joint council of staff, parents and pupils.

4.   That the Principal of each school shall be elected for a stated period by the joint council.

5.   That there shall be no competitive examinations.

6.   That there shall be no system of rewards or punishments.

To be democratic is to adopt a way of life so utterly different from what we know in this country that most people are simply unable to envisage not only the forms of work, leisure and sex relationships that would arise, but the valuations, the attitudes and the social relations that would follow. Competition saturates work, education, leisure and social, personal and sex relationships with materialistic criteria so that we cannot measure work except in terms of money; education except in terms of the types of work that it will lead to; leisure except in terms of escape from work; and our relationships except in terms of having to impress others with our wealth, our occupation, our status, our power over others, our 'virility' or, in male fantasy, our power to subdue more females than other men. Our personal worth is measured by salary, size and type of car, house or garden; by where we live; by where we can afford to go for our holiday; by whether we have one or two holidays a year; by what school we went to; by what newspapers we read.

To be democratic is to extend into the world of work the

feelings of concern for others, of generosity, of co-operation, of involvement that we take for granted within our own family circle. To be democratic is not so much to calculate whether proportional representation is more 'democratic' than 'one man one vote'; it is 'to do unto others as you would be done by' or 'to love your neighbour *as yourself*', no less. It is to experience a sense of joy and wellbeing in having creative power released in work with others for human purposes. Work of this kind is very rarely encountered in our society or in the similar societies of the western world. It appears usually when there is a catastrophe such as a mine disaster or an earthquake. At such times ordinary people reveal their latent powers and show qualities of physical endurance, of courage and of selflessness that are simply astonishing, but which spring from the fact that they are giving service directly for the sake of other human beings in distress and with no intervention of monetary valuation of their efforts. They rejoice in the direct appreciation that flows from the victims of the disaster and from their fellow workers. The revelation of those powers makes a mockery of the claim that the incentive of money or of other material rewards is necessary to make men work.

The democratic organization of work, of whatever kind, releases similar energies because it is based on general human need rather than on profit for the few, and because, in a democratic situation, priority for production is determined by the urgency of need, whereas in production for profit it is determined by the manipulation of artificially created 'demand' through the use of the mass media.

Where the society is democratic there can be no differentiation between schools or types of school aimed at the satisfaction of different social classes. Teaching resources, equipment, books, travel and involvement in work will be arranged according to the age of the pupils rather than according to the wealth or social position of their parents. Democracy will be learnt by participation, from the earliest years, in democratic processes. The activities in, and the organization of, the school will be determined by joint discussions between the teachers, the parents and the pupils, the pupils playing more and more part in such discussions the older they grow, as can be seen in practice at Summerhill and Kilquhanity schools.

It was the fact of beginning to involve pupils at Risinghill in this way that was one of the reasons for their change in attitude to school. A School Council, consisting of elected members of both staff, pupils and non-teaching staff, began to work with enthusiasm from the day when the Council was summoned to deal with an outburst of fighting between the 'gang'—a group of boys from one of the constituent schools—and the prefects, who mostly came from another school. Each group alleged that the other was acting unfairly; the gang was accused of laying ambushes for individual prefects; the prefects were accused of discriminating against members of the gang. For well over an hour the Council listened to statements by all the members of both groups and members of the Council contributed their own comments. Finally the Chairman for the day demanded on behalf of the Council that both groups undertake to bring any future disagreements before the Council and to refrain from fighting it out in the playground. All but one immediately agreed to this. One, David, second-in-command to Fred, the leader of the gang, refused and when asked why simply stated that he liked a 'punch-up'. After some persuasion by his friends he agreed and from that day onwards, 10 November 1960, there was never again an organized fight in the school.

For some time after that the Council was frequently summoned by small boys who alleged bullying by prefects, but it came to an end when on one occasion a complaint was made by the Head Boy on behalf of the prefects that some members of staff were failing to carry out their playground duties and were leaving the prefects to do this job alone. No mention of names was made because I pointed out that it was my function as Head to deal with the allocation of staff duties and to take any necessary steps if they were not being done. Shortly after this meeting a small group of staff objected to being criticized by pupils in the Council and, although it was pointed out to them that no names had been mentioned, from that day the teaching staff refused to participate and the Council died since it did not represent the whole school.

It was at about the time of the birth of the School Council that the prefects and some of the older boys and girls began, quite spontaneously, to undertake some staff duties as the need arose. Whenever staff were delayed by illness or fog a senior member of the Tutor Group would take the register from the office, mark it, send the group on its way to the first lesson, return the register to the office and tell the Senior Master or the Senior Mistress that a particular member of staff had not yet arrived so that they could alter the timetable. They would take new children under their wing if they seemed lost, find out where they should be and take them there; or they would deal with children who were sick or hurt until a member of staff arrived. Gradually, as the system of appointing prefects as a result of election took over from the old method of appointing by staff decision, we noticed that a gentler relationship grew between the prefects and older pupils on the one hand and the youngest kids on the other. It then turned out that the pupils being elected as prefects within the Houses were the pupils who were most active in promoting interesting activities within the House—dances, film-shows, jazz sessions, parties for old people and so on. They carried this more positive attitude towards the school as a whole into their work as School Prefects and thereby helped to create a more civilized attitude throughout the school.

Within the houses run by more democratically minded heads of house this spirit was most clearly evident. Their morning assemblies began to partake more of the nature of an informal meeting to discuss various matters of interest to particular pupils within the house as well as affairs affecting the house and the school as a whole. Since the number of pupils in the house rarely exceeded 170, this informal atmosphere was possible in a way impossible in an assembly of over 1,200. Even in the best houses it never reached the level of discussion and dialogue seen in Summerhill, but I have not the slightest doubt that it would have begun to do so—allowing, of course, for the fact that Risinghill was not a boarding school and could not, therefore, have the range of topics or the depth of emotional involvement possible in a boarding school.

The more the staff as a whole take part in the joint running of the school with the parents and the pupils, the more the position of the head of the school changes to that of acting as a chairman of committee whose function is simply to see that the committee keeps to the agenda and gets through the work at a reasonable rate. His authority will depend on the committee as a whole. He will, as heads already have to do, spend a lot of time receiving visitors; he will be there to meet parents or to see that the parents meet particular teachers if they wish to, at reasonably convenient times; he will supervise the clerical staff in keeping necessary records and in keeping track of the expenditure of money. He will, in effect, be an administrator, subject to the joint authority of the Governing Council of the school and, except as the agent of that Council, without individual power. Since the authority rests with the Council the old image of the head as the 'captain of the ship' or the 'final authority' in the school will cease and with it the long and somewhat ludicrous tradition that the 'strong man' type of head is free to wield power of a personal and idiosyncratic type.

Competitive examinations will disappear. Preparation for a career will, to the extent that that preparation requires specific technical skills, be done through training within the career allied to study in institutes of further education, during which time of training the student will be paid at rates that will enable him to marry and have children if he so desires. Since the organizations within which the specific training will be done will not be shackled by considerations of profitability, the training will not be narrowly vocational and will embrace allied disciplines. It will be possible for a student at any time to transfer to other types of training if he finds his original choice less congenial than he had hoped, since there will be no bars of age or experience other than those essential to particular types of performance. A surgeon or a navigator must obviously have good eyesight and a geologist be athletic and healthy if he is to scale mountains. The school, therefore, will not be tied to specific preparation for careers but will have the task of giving its pupils the widest possible range of experience that will provide for physical, intellectual and moral growth.

Physical growth will come from the removal of restrictions on movement and from the application of greater care in the siting of schools so that there is space for running, climbing and jumping as free activities, as well as from gymnasia staffed by teachers trained in physiotherapy to correct faults of posture that may have been induced by injury, inadequate diet or lack of physical freedom in earlier years. If understanding of the importance of play is an essential part of the training of teachers and if the environment of the school has resources for a wide variety of physical movement, the physical growth of the children will, almost certainly, take care of itself. Specific skills such as swimming, games, climbing, and so on will be taught.

Intellectual growth will start with the training of young mothers into an understanding of the importance of talking to their babies from the earliest months and in acquiring a wide repertoire of the traditional rhymes, puzzles and stories through which all cultures have pleasurably equipped their children with the basic concepts required for communication. With play groups, nursery schools and trained teachers to co-operate with the mothers in the care of the children and in the use of a rich assortment of apparatus, toys and materials to provide sensory stimulus and the source of conversation, their intellectual growth will be such as we normally expect only from children in the most favourably placed circumstances in this country. We see something of the intellectual potential open to children brought up in such circumstances in studies of people who have grown up in the kibbutzim of Israel.

Moral growth comes through the continuous interaction of a democratic community engaged in constant dialogue about the wishes of individuals, the counter-wishes of others and the resolution of contrary desires through the exploration of alternative modes of behaviour by the collective wisdom of the group. Moral growth is the extension of personal sensitivity to the feelings and desires of others through a process of identification in common tasks and the structuring of common patterns of valuation through community living. The meeting is the immediate agent of this process because it puts into verbal form the individual reactions of all who speak and thereby enables others to share in the experiences of the speakers. Where fear and greed remain unresolved because there are factors inhibiting the open expression of opinion the meeting can become an agent of violence and oppression. Where opinion is free and no individual or group has a monopoly of power, then the meeting lifts the sensitivity and the wisdom of every individual in it and is in turn so elevated by the most sensitive and percipient members. Within the school every teaching or play group has this most important function. As George Dennison points out in his book, *The Lives of Children*, free play is the most powerful way in which children become socialized. A child who transgresses the

239

rules of a game finds himself the object of sharp criticism. He *must*, if the others are to continue to play with him, conform to those rules. If not, either they will abandon the game and leave him or they will eject him, but since they all want to play and he is often as necessary to them as they are to him, argument and counter-argument follow until either the game is abandoned or the rules observed or changed by agreement.

The school of the future, while it may have certain superficial resemblances to schools that we see today, will differ in the most fundamental point that the children will be free to choose whether or not to come to school and what they shall do while they are there. Most people when presented with such a prospect immediately assume that no children will want to attend school, or that, if they do, there will be bedlam of such a kind that teachers will be unable to teach. In fact, as can be seen in the few schools where such conditions prevail, not only is there regular attendance at lessons, but the actual discipline or rather self-discipline within the class is of a higher order. The function of the teacher changes from that of stuffing knowledge into the child, whether he likes it or not, to that of being at hand as an experienced adviser in providing the technical skills and knowledge that will enable the child to achieve his aims. The teacher will, in fact, be rather more deeply occupied in assembling the most educative materials and problems to suit the individual children in his care than in simply pressing them to go through a routine of learning designed for mass teaching.

The *only* essential difference between man and animal lies in man's innate ability to communicate through language. Since it is only through communication that the individually vulnerable human being learns to identify with others and to act collectively in using the forces of nature, education must be concerned, above all, with developing and extending the powers of *all* children to relate to others; with increasing their awareness of themselves, and with enlarging their understanding of, and control over the world in which they live.

Education, as distinct from indoctrination or conditioning for the purposes of social exploitation, is, therefore, inseparable from democracy.

The Authors

LEILA BERG was born in Salford, Lancashire. She worked actively in the anti-fascist left-wing movement of the mid-thirties while still at grammar school. Under pressure, she started training as a teacher but left hastily at the end of her first term when about to be expelled for organizing an Aid-Spain group and taking students secretly (the only way to do it) to Spain meetings at the Albert Hall; she never wanted to do anything but write anyway. She is now sardonic about all political parties equally. She writes mainly for children, and about children. Her *Nippers* series of first reading books for primary schools has aroused fury from a minority and delight from many, being based on a belief that children live —and learn—happily only if they are accepted, and that reading is not primarily a technique but a physical and emotional pleasure in one's own identity which middle-class children acquire long before they start school. She is the author of numerous other children's books and for two years ran a nursery school at her house. Her book for adults, *Risinghill: Death of a Comprehensive School* (Penguin 1968) aroused widespread controversy. She is the author of two more books for adults, both scheduled for publication in 1971, has contributed to *The Guardian*, *Where*, *Anarchy*, etc., and occasionally broadcasts. She is married and has one daughter and one son.

PAUL L. ADAMS, A.B., M.A., M.D., F.A.C.P., F.A.P.A., F.A.A.C.P., an American child psychiatrist who has taught underprivileged black children in progressive schools in New York, is now Professor of Psychiatry and Pediatrics at the University of Florida. A libertarian socialist and Quaker, he has been active in the peace, civil rights, unionization of teachers, and civil liberties movements. He has contributed to numerous psychiatric and educational journals and books. His research has been concerned with parental authoritarianism, poverty and the life cycle, the fatherless family, and the obsessive child. He lives in Gainesville, Florida, with his Cuban wife and their three children.

ROBERT OLLENDORFF, M.A. (Cantab), M.D. (Bonn), L.R.C.P., M.R.C.S., D.P.M., a general practitioner in a working-class district of London and a psychiatrist to the Department of Health and Social Security, has for the last five years been Visiting Professor of Psychiatry at the University of Florida, Gainesville, U.S.A. There he has specialized in the treatment of adolescents and drug addicts. The treatment of drug addiction and alcoholism has been one of the main subjects of his research and publications. He is the author of a number of psychiatric articles and a book, *The Juvenile Homosexual Experience and its Effect on Adult Sexuality*. He is married and has three step–children, ten step–grand–children and three step-great-grandchildren.

A. S. NEILL, M.A., M.ED. (Newcastle), LL.D. (Exeter), was born in Scotland in 1883. While serving in the army during the First World War he met Homer Lane who was then running his Little Commonwealth in Dorset and was to be one of the chief influences on Neill's subsequent career. He would have joined Lane's staff, but by the time he was demobilized the Little Commonwealth had been closed, so he took a teaching post at King Alfred School in London while training under Lane as a lay analyst. In 1921 he went to Germany as joint-founder of the International School, Hellerau, Dresden, returning to England in

1924 to found what must be the world's most famous free school, Summerhill, originally at Lyme Regis, now at Leiston, Suffolk. While living in Germany he met a number of leading members of the psychoanalytic movement, and later became a close friend of Wilhelm Reich. He is the author of numerous books and articles and appears frequently on television. *Summerhill* (Penguin 1968), in which he describes his school and his educational theories is a world-wide best-seller and has had great influence on progressive education. He is married and has one daughter.

NAN BERGER, born in Lancashire, now living in Highgate, London, is a freelance journalist and former civil servant. During the war she worked on exchange control in the Bank of England and later in the reference division of the Ministry of Information. She was awarded the O.B.E. for her work at the Ministry of Fuel and Power during the fuel crisis of 1947. Widely travelled, she has spent a year in the U.S.A., another in post-war Poland and has recently visited Africa and China. Mrs Berger is the author of *The Rights of Children and Young Persons* (1967), published by the National Council for Civil Liberties, of which she is an active member, and joint author with Joan Maizels of *Woman: Fancy or Free?* (Mills & Boon 1962). She is the mother of two daughters.

MICHAEL DUANE was born in Dublin in 1915. His first memory is of gunfire in the Easter Rebellion of 1916, while being carried in his mother's shawl. At the age of ten he came to live in England, where he was educated by Jesuits and at Queen Mary College, London University. He trained as a teacher at the London Institute of Education and taught in grammar schools before the war. After leaving the army he was the head of three secondary modern schools before being appointed head of Risinghill, a large new comprehensive school in a working-class district of London, in May 1960. At Risinghill he abolished corporal punishment and ran the school on progressive lines, making it an educational experiment of international interest and of indubitable success (evidenced among other things by the drop of the number of children on probation, from ninety-eight in 1960 to nine in 1964), only to have it closed down by the Inner London Educational Authority, despite the protests of parents and children, in July 1965. The story of Risinghill is told by Leila Berg in *Risinghill: Death of a Comprehensive School* (Penguin 1968).

Michael Duane has been offered no further jobs connected with the teaching of children. At present he works in a college for training teachers of adults. Meanwhile, to the extent of over one hundred and fifty lectures each year, he has been lecturing by invitation to university and college students, teachers, parents, Parent-Teacher Associations, branches of the Confederation for the Advancement of State Education and political groups. His writings include contributions to *Education for Democracy* (Penguin 1970) and *Education for the Seventies* (University of Hull Institute of Education 1969), articles for educational journals and a book in preparation on the educational system. He is the father of four children.

Bibliography

Anarchy, 7 (Adventure playground), 11 (Paul Goodman, A. S. Neill), 15 (David Wills), 18, 21, 27, 39 (Homer Lane), 43, 53, 60 (The Peckham Experiment), 71, 73, (First Street school), 82 (Braehead school), 92 (Risinghill and Kilquhanity), 101 (Approved schools, Detention Centres), 103, 107, 115. Freedom Press 1961–70
Roger Ascham, *The Scholemaster*, 1565
Silvia Ashton-Warner, *Teacher*. Penguin 1966
Virginia Axeline, *Dibs In Search of Self*. Gollancz 1966
Basil Bernstein, 'Social Class and Linguistic Development', in *Education, Economy and Society* (ed. Halsey, Floud & Anderson) Free Press, New York 1962
E. T. Bazeley, *Homer Lane and the Little Commonwealth*. New Education Book Club 1928
Joe Benjamin, *In Search of Adventure*. National Council of Social Service, 1966
Leila Berg, *Risinghill: Death of a Comprehensive School*. Penguin 1968
Bruno Bettelheim, *Love Is Not Enough*. Collier-Macmillan 1959
Edward Blishen (ed.), *The School that I'd Like*. Penguin 1970
British Medical Journal, 'Loneliness in Infancy'. 19 Sept. 1942
John Comerford, *Health the Unknown*. Hamish Hamilton 1947
George Dennison, *The Lives of Children*. Pitman 1971
   'The First Street School', *Anarchy* 73 Freedom Press, March 1967
John Dewey, *Democracy and Education*. Macmillan 1915
   School and Society. Univ. Chicago Press 1915
   Experience and Education. Collier-Macmillan 1963
J. W. B. Douglas, *The Home and the School*. Panther 1969
Michael Duane, 'Education in Britain Today', in *Education for Democracy* (ed. C. Stoneham & D. Rubenstein). Penguin 1970
   Contributions to *Education for the Seventies* (ed. F. W. Garforth). Univ. Hull Inst. Educ. 1969
Verrier Elwin, *The Muria and Their Ghotul*. Oxford Univ. Press, 1947
   The Kingdom of the Young (abridgement of above). Oxford Univ. Press 1968
D. E. M. Gardner, *The Education of Young Children*. Methuen 1956
   Susan Isaacs. Methuen 1969
F. W. Garforth (ed.), *Education for the Seventies*. Univ. Hull Inst. Educ. 1969
Paul Goodman, *Growing Up Absurd*. Sphere 1970
W. L. Goodman, *Anton Simeonovitch Makarenko*. Routledge 1949
James Herndon, *The Way It Spozed to Be*. Pitman 1971
Gerard Holmes, *The Idiot Teacher*. Faber 1952
John Holt, *How Children Fail*. Penguin 1969
   How Children Learn. Penguin 1970
   The Underachieving School. Pitman 1969
Susan Isaacs, *Intellectual Growth in Young Children*. Routledge 1930
   The Nursery Years. Routledge 1932
   Social Development in Young Children. Routledge 1933
   Troubles of Children and Parents. Routledge 1948
   See ('Ursula Wise'), *Habit Training*. Nursery World booklet D. E. M. Gardner
B. Jackson, 'Brian Jackson writes . . .', *Where*, 51. Advisory Centre for Education, Sept. 1970
B. Jackson and D. Marsden, *Education and the Working Class*. Penguin 1969
Bruce Kemble, *Give Your Child a Chance*. W. H. Allen 1970
Mary King, *Truby King*. Allen & Unwin 1948
Jonathan Kozol, *Death at an Early Age*. Penguin 1968
Homer Lane, *Talks to Parents and Teachers*. Allen & Unwin 1928
   See E. T. Bazeley, David Wills, and *Anarchy*
D. H. Lawrence, 'The Education of the People', essay in *Phoenix* vol. 1, Heinemann 1961

D. Lawton, *Social Class, Language and Education*. Routledge 1968
G. B. Leonard, *Education and Ecstasy*. J. Murray 1970
Harold Lowenstein, *Parents and Staff in a Children's Ward* (film). Concord Films, Ipswich
R. F. Mackenzie, *A Question of Living*. Collins 1963
    Escape from the Classroom. Collins 1965
    The Sins of the Children. Collins 1967
    State School. Penguin 1970
A. Makarenko, *The Road to Life* (1 vol., trans. S. Garry). Stanley Nott 1936
    The Road to Life (3 vols, trans. I. & T. Litvinoff). Foreign Lang. Pub. House, Moscow 1955
    See W. L. Goodman
B. Malinowski, *The Sexual Life of Savages*. Routledge 1932, 1969
A. S. Neill, *Summerhill*. Penguin 1968
    Talking of Summerhill. Gollancz 1967
    See John Walmsley and *Anarchy*
J. H. Newsom, *Half Our Future*. Report, HMSO 1963
J. & E. Newson, *Infant Care in an Urban Community*. Allen & Unwin 1963
Innes Pearse and Lucy H. Crocker, *The Peckham Experiment*. Allen & Unwin 1943
Innes Pearse & G. Scott Williamson, *The Case for Action*. Faber 1931
    See 'Anarchy'
'Plowden Report', *Children and Their Primary Schools*. HMSO 1967
M. L. K. Pringle, *Deprivation and Education*. Longmans 1965
Wilhelm Reich, *The Function of the Orgasm*. Panther 1968
    Character Analysis. Vision Press 1969
    The Sexual Revolution. Vision Press 1969
    The Mass Psychology of Fascism. Farrar, Strauss & Giroux, New York
Lisa Aversa Richette, *The Throwaway Children*. Lippincott, New York 1969
Frank Riessman, *The Culturally Deprived Child*. Harper & Row 1962
James Robertson, *Young Children in Hospital*. Tavistock 1959
    A Two-Year Old Goes to Hospital (film). Concord Films, Ipswich 1952
René Spitz, 'Hospitalism', in *The Family, Its Structure and Functions* (ed. Coser). St Martin's Press, New York 1964
Benjamin Spock, *The Pocket Book of Baby and Child care*. Pocket Books, New York 1946
    Baby and Child Care. Four Square 1969
Mary Stapleton, 'On from Pulborough'. *New Era Magazine*, May 1970
C. Stoneman & D. Rubenstein (ed.), *Education for Democracy*. Penguin 1970
Leo Tolstoy, *On Education*. Univ. Chicago Press 1968
Beatrix Tudor-Hart, *Learning to Live*. Sphere 1968
H. S. Turner, *Something Extraordinary*. Michael Joseph 1961
Olive Tyson, *We Shall Go Where the Children Lead*. Booklet about Olive Kendon, reprinted from *The Friend* 17 January 1969. From Olive Kendon, Firs Cottage, Goudhurst, Kent
William Van Der Eyken, *The Pre-School Years*. Penguin 1967
W. Van Der Eyken & B. Turner, *Adventures in Education*. A. Lane 1969
John Walmsley & Leila Berg, *Neill and Summerhill: a Pictorial Study*. Penguin 1970
Colin Ward, 'A Modest Proposal for the Repeal of the Education Act', *Anarchy*, 53. Freedom Press, March 1967
D. J. West, *The Young Offender*. Pelican 1967
David Wills, *Homer Lane*. Allen & Unwin 1964
    Throw Away Thy Rod. Allen & Unwin, 1960
D. W. Winnicott, *The Child, the Family and the Outside World*. Penguin 1969
S. Yudkin, *0–5: A Report on the Care of Pre-School Children*. Allen & Unwin 1968

Index

246